The French Revolution of 1870-1871

REVOLUTIONS IN THE MODERN WORLD
General Editor: JACK P. GREENE, Johns Hopkins University

ROGER L. WILLIAMS

University of California, Santa Barbara

The French Revolution

of 1870-1871

 W W · *Norton & Company* · *Inc* · NEW YORK

To Mark and Ellen

"In my youth," said his father, "I took to the law,
  And argued each case with my wife;
  And the muscular strength, which it gave to my jaw,
Has lasted the rest of my life."
                              —LEWIS CARROLL [1865]

Contents

MAPS

Preface

ALTHOUGH this book has been specifically written to be a part of a series on revolutions under the editorship of Professor Jack P. Greene, its outline began to form in my mind when I was at work on a previous book based upon the political and journalistic career of Henri Rochefort. During the reading and research for that project, I came to echo Frank Jellinek's verdict, given in 1937, that no impartial history of the Commune of Paris yet exists. The subject, therefore, very much bears reconsideration in the hope of a fairer interpretation, and that possibility has been enhanced by a variety of monographs published since 1945.

Secondly, I came to believe that the Commune of 1871 would become more intelligible if it could be perceived as part of a larger revolutionary context. This is not to say that the Commune has generally been studied in isolation. Some have seen it as the beginning of the twentieth-century revolutionary tradition; some as a patriotic outburst in the frustration of defeat, thus as an episode in the Franco-Prussian War; and some have seen it as the culmination of the revolutionary tradition dating from 1789. All these interpretations had merits—especially the last one—but also liabilities. What was needed, in my view, was a better defined context which could account for why the Commune could be seen as both an end and a beginning.

The chapter headings of this volume should at once suggest my belief that the Commune can be best seen as an important moment in a revolutionary cycle, a cycle reminiscent in both pattern and idea to the more familiar revolutionary cycle that began in 1789. Thus, one must examine both the antecedents of 1871 and its aftermath in an attempt to see the Commune as it was: the most radical moment in a revolution that began with the government of September 4, 1870, and which ended with the constitution of the Third Republic in 1875.

A nutshell review of that distressingly complex era must begin with a recognition that the Second Empire continually faced a sizable and intransigent opposition from the Left and an increasing labor unrest as industrial development proceeded in the 1860s. On the other hand, the Empire also had its disgruntled conservatives, whose irritation only increased in the 1860s as the national military position declined and when the Emperor advocated liberal political reforms. Worse, as the Emperor was aging prematurely and suffered from ill health, his ability to confront the chores of government and the claims of the opposition was apparently reduced.

The political reforms of 1869 and 1870 that inaugurated the Liberal Empire were not only well intentioned but held high promise to modernize the regime peacefully. Yet the innovations had the momentary effect of increasing political instability and thus promoted the revolutionary climate on both Left and Right. When defeat came in the untimely Franco-Prussian War, the regime was still in its period of transition and was vulnerable, first to a *coup* by the conservatives, then to a *coup* by the moderate Republicans. Once the revolutionary machinery had been set in motion, more radical parties vied for power; and the Commune of 1871 may be seen as the most radical moment in this revolutionary cycle.

The republican form of government survived the violences of the civil strife of the Commune only because the moderate Royalists, in discovering that the hopeless divisions in the monarchical party meant the impossibility of a restoration, worked realistically for the establishment of a resolutely conservative republic. A painful constitutional task, it took until early 1875 to work out the requisite compromises. We may say in summary that the Revolution of 1870–71 was in essence the substitution of the conservative Third Republic for the Liberal Empire. In other words, the Third Republic brought into association Republicans and conservatives who had formed the old opposition to Napoleon III.

I make no claim to have taken the oath of impartiality at the outset of this work, not wishing to be encumbered by that illusion. Nor do I propose that this will be the definitive work on the subject. It is an attempt to get a fresh and fair view of a most complex period in modern French history. Because it is a work of synthesis and interpretation, I am greatly indebted to a vast number of authors whose names appear in both footnotes and bibliography. And I am also indebted to my learned colleague Professor Leonard M. Marsak, who has encouraged and criticized this project from the beginning. I have also benefited much from conscientious criticism given by Professor David H. Pinkney of the University of Washington, Professor Jack P. Greene of Johns Hopkins University, and Donald S. Lamm of W. W. Norton & Company, Inc. The book is the better thanks to their suggestions for improvement.

ROGER L. WILLIAMS

Santa Barbara, California

Principal Personages

ADAM, Edmond. Moderate Republican; mayor of the First Arrondissement during the Government of National Defense; Prefect of Police, Oct. 9–Nov. 2, 1870; elected to the National Assembly from Paris, Feb. 5, 1871.

ALLIX, Jules. Socialist; elected to the Commune from the Eighth Arrondissement; an eccentric inventor.

ARAGO, Etienne. Moderate Republican; Mayor of Paris briefly after Sept. 4, 1870.

BABICK, Jules. Member of the Central Committee of the National Guard; elected to the Commune from the Tenth Arrondissement; no real political affiliation; a chemist and a religious crank; escaped abroad.

BARODET, Désiré. Gambettist deputy who won the by-election of April 27, 1873, in Paris, precipitating the crisis that led to the fall of Thiers.

BAUDELAIRE, Charles. Poet and essayist; dandy and élitist.

BAZAINE, Marshal François-Achille. Reputation made in the Mexican campaign; disgraced by his surrender of Metz on Oct. 27, 1870.

BENEDETTI, Comte Vincent. French Ambassador to Prussia during the crises of 1866, 1867, and 1870.

BERGERET, Jules. Jacobin; typographical worker and bookstore accountant; elected to the Commune from the Twentieth

Arrondissement; member of the first Executive Committee; first commanding general of the Commune; escaped abroad.

BILLIORAY, Alfred-Edouard. Jacobin; member of the Central Committee of the National Guard; a painter; elected to the Commune from the Fourteenth Arrondissement; member of the Committee of Public Safety on May 16, 1871.

BLANC, Louis. Socialist theorist and historian; one of the "Men of '48"; elected to the National Assembly from Paris, Feb. 5, 1871.

BLANQUI, Auguste. Aged (1805–1881) revolutionary advocating communism and dictatorship; one leader of the insurrection of Oct. 31, 1870; arrested by the Versaillese, March 18, 1871; elected to the Commune from the Eighteenth Arrondissement, but unable to take his seat.

BONAPARTE, Prince Jerome-Napoleon. Son of King Jerome and cousin of Napoleon III; married to Clothilde of Savoy; held radical views; hankered for power.

BONAPARTE, Prince Pierre. Son of Lucien Bonaparte and Alexandrine de Bleschamps; cousin of Napoleon III; killed Victor Noir in 1870; acquitted.

BRISSON, Henri. Intransigent Republican in the National Assembly; briefly premier in 1885.

BROGLIE, Albert Duc de. Orleanist; vice president of the Council of Ministers in 1873; premier in 1877.

BRUNEL, Antoine-Magloire. Jacobin; notable member of Central Committee of the National Guard; elected to the Commune from the Seventh Arrondissement, but remained more sympathetic to the Central Committee; escaped abroad.

BUFFET, Louis-Joseph. Liberal Catholic; Minister of Finance in the government of January 2, 1870; resigned to protest the plebiscite of May 8, 1870.

CERNUSCHI, Henri. Republican; liberal economist and journalist for *le Siècle*.

CHAMBORD, Henri-Charles-Marie, comte de. Grandson of Charles X; Legitimist pretender as Henri V.

CHANZY, General Alfred. One of the ablest French commanders in the war of 1870; opposed to the armistice terms of 1871.

CHEVALIER, Michel. Saint-Simonian Bonapartist; negotiated the commercial treaty of 1860 for France.

CLEMENCEAU, Georges. Physician, journalist, and essayist; radical Republican elected to the National Assembly from Paris, Feb. 5, 1871; also mayor of the Eighteenth Arrondissement; Premier 1917–20.

CRÉMIEUX, Adolphe-Isaac. Republican; eldest member of the Government of National Defense; first leader of the Tours delegation.

CRESSON, Ernest. Prefect of Police, Nov. 2, 1870–March 18, 1871.

DARIMON, Alfred. Republican; one of *les Cinq* elected to the *Corps législatif* in 1857.

DARU, Comte Napoleon. Orleanist parliamentarian; Minister of Foreign Affairs Jan. 2, 1870; resigned to protest the plebiscite of May 8, 1870.

DECAZES, Louis-Charles-Elie. Orleanist; elected to the National Assembly Feb. 8, 1871; able leader of the Center Right.

DELESCLUZE, Charles. Jacobin journalist; one leader of the insurrection of Oct. 31, 1870; elected to the National Assembly from Paris, Feb. 5, 1871; elected to the Commune from the Nineteenth Arrondissement; member of the Committee of Public Safety; last military commander for the Commune; died on the barricades, May 25, 1871.

DUPANLOUP, Bishop F.-A.-P. Bishop of Orléans and a Liberal Catholic.

DURUY, Victor. Historian and educational reformer; liberal Bonapartist; Minister of Public Instruction 1863–69.

DUVAL, Emile-Victor. Ironworker or smelter; Blanquist and affiliated with the International; member of the Central Committee of the National Guard; elected to the Commune from the Thirteenth Arrondissement; member of the Executive Committee; captured and executed during the sortie of April 3, 1871.

DUVERNOIS, Clément. Journalist; first a Republican, then a liberal Bonapartist, finally a conservative Bonapartist; a thoroughgoing opportunist.

EUDES, Emile. Typographical worker; Blanquist; member of the Central Committee of the National Guard; elected to the

Commune from the Eleventh Arrondissement; on the first Executive Committee and the second Committee of Public Safety; escaped abroad.

FAVRE, Jules. Republican lawyer first elected to the *Corps législatif* from Paris in 1858; foreign minister for the Government of National Defense; elected to the National Assembly from Paris, Feb. 5, 1871; with Thiers he negotiated the treaty of Frankfurt; resigned from the foreign ministry, July 22, 1871; later a senator.

FERRÉ, Théophile. Blanquist; elected to the Commune from the Eighteenth Arrondissement; responsible for shooting hostages after Rigault's death; sentenced to death and executed.

FERRY, Jules. Republican lawyer first elected to the *Corps législatif* from Paris 1863; member of the Government of National Defense; elected to the National Assembly from Paris, Feb. 5, 1871; elected to the Commune from the Ninth Arrondissement but refused his seat; major part of his career came during the Third Republic as a minister of public instruction and as premier.

FLAUBERT, Gustave. Eminent novelist of the Realist school; best known for *Madame Bovary*.

FLOQUET, Charles. Republican; appointed Deputy Mayor of Paris, Sept. 4, 1870; elected to the National Assembly from Paris, Feb. 5, 1871; later a premier.

FLOURENS, Gustave. Jacobin; high-minded but notably naïve revolutionary; major figure in the insurrection of Oct. 31, 1870; had independent wealth; elected to the Commune from the Twentieth Arrondissement; killed during the sortie of April 3, 1871.

FREYCINET, Charles de. Brilliant engineer employed by Gambetta to mobilize national resources during the invasion of 1870; outstanding administrator; major Opportunist politician during the Third Republic; three times premier.

FUSTEL DE COULANGES, Numa-Denis. Historian of antiquity known for emphasis on class warfare as a determinant.

GAMBETTA, Léon. Firebrand young Republican lawyer elected to the *Corps législatif* in 1869 from Paris and Marseilles; Minister of the Interior in the Government of National Defense, 1870; resigned his post in 1871 to protest the peace terms; called the "traveling salesman for the Republic" after 1871; later premier for only 74 days.

GASPARIN, Agénor de. Calvinist religious writer and moralist; believed French Catholicism responsible for the modern "moral decay" that accounted for military defeat in 1870–71.

GAUTIER, Théophile. Romantic poet, critic, and essayist.

GERMAIN, Henri. Founder of the *Crédit lyonnais;* elected to the National Assembly, 1871.

GIRARDIN, Emile de. Liberal journalist; opponent of the Second Empire; vociferous pro-war publicist in 1870.

GOBINEAU, Comte Arthur de. Racial determinist and anti-democrat.

GONCOURT, Edmond de. Elder of the two brothers who collaborated on novels, plays, and a famous diary; member of the Naturalist school of literature.

GRAMONT, Antoine, Prince de Bidache, Duc de Guiche et de. Pro-Austrian diplomat; Minister of Foreign Affairs after Comte Daru in 1870.

GRÉVY, Jules. Conservative Republican lawyer from Jura; elected to the National Assembly, Feb. 8, 1871, and named its presiding officer; President of the Republic, 1879–87.

GROUSSET, Paschal. Radical journalist; Jacobin; elected to the Commune from the Eighteenth Arrondissement; member of the second Executive Committee; sent to New Caledonia.

HALÉVY, Daniel. Distinguished historian and critic of the Third Republic; Franco-Jewish lineage; son of Ludovic; his views a peculiar mixture of political antitheses.

HALÉVY, Ludovic. Librettist and writer of the Second Empire; father of Daniel.

HAUSSMANN, Baron Georges-Eugène. Directed the reconstruction of Paris as Prefect of the Seine 1853–69.

HÉNON, J.-L. Physician from Lyon; Republican elected to the *Corps législatif,* 1857; one of *les Cinq.*

LABOULAYE, E.-R.-L. Professor of Jurisprudence, Collège de France; liberal who rallied to the Empire in 1870; important member of the parliamentary committee that worked out the constitution of 1875.

LEBOEUF, Marshal Edmond. Minister of War, 1869–70; popular scapegoat for inadequate military preparations in 1870.

LE PLAY, Frédéric. Conservative critic of the French Revolution; influential sociologist during the Second Empire.

LÉVY, Armand. Publisher of *l'Espérance,* a journal devoted to the improvement of labor within the Bonapartist regime.

MACMAHON, Marshal M.–E.–P.–M., Duc de Magenta. Reputation made in the Crimean and Italian campaigns; wounded and defeated at Sedan, 1870; commander of the Versaillese forces that suppressed the Commune; President of the Republic, 1873–79 (resigned).

MÉRIMÉE, Prosper. Gifted writer best known for *Carmen;* friend of Empress Eugénie's family; conservative and pessimistic.

MICHELET, Jules. Famous Romantic and nationalist historian; emphasized the greatness of France and the significance of the French Revolution for mankind.

MILLIÈRE, J.–B. Prominent Communist under the Second Empire; elected to the National Assembly from Paris, Feb. 5, 1871.

MONTALEMBERT, Charles F.–R., comte de. Liberal Catholic writer and educational reformer; one of the framers of the Falloux Law of 1850.

MORNY, August, Duc de. Illegitimate son of Hortense Beauharnais, thus, half-brother of Napoleon III; president of the *Corps législatif,* 1854–65; liberal Bonapartist.

NIEL, Marshal Adolphe. Minister of War 1867–69; failed in attempts to develop large numbers of conscripted reserves.

OLLIVIER, Emile. Republican lawyer; favored strong executive power; elected to the *Corps législatif* 1857; one of *les Cinq;* rallied to the Liberal Empire and directed the government of Jan. 2, 1870; overthrown by a conservative *coup,* Aug. 9, 1870.

PALIKAO, General Cousin-Montauban, comte de. Commanded French expedition to Peking in 1860; headed the conservative Bonapartist regime from Aug. 9 to Sept. 4, 1870.

PRÉVOST-PARADOL, Anatole. Liberal journalist and essayist; rallied to the Liberal Empire in 1870; named French Minister to the U.S.A.; committed suicide in Washington upon news of the military disaster in 1870.

PARIEU, M.–L.–P. Félix Esquirou de. Liberal Catholic; Minister-President of the Council of State, Jan. 2–Aug. 9, 1870.

PICARD, Ernest. Well-to-do conservative Republican; one of *les Cinq* elected to the *Corps législatif* in 1858; Minister of Finance in the Government of National Defense, 1870; retained by Thiers as Minister of the Interior, Feb. 19, 1871.

PINDY, Louis-Jean. Carpenter; affiliated with the International; probably a Proudhonian; member of the Central Committee of the National Guard; elected to the Commune from the Third Arrondissement; escaped.

POUYER-QUERTIER, Auguste. Norman cotton manufacturer; conservative Bonapartist; named Minister of Finance by Thiers, Feb. 19, 1871.

PROUDHON, Pierre-Joseph. Political and social theorist; mutualist and anarchist; his disciples became part of the Minority in the Commune, i.e., radicals favoring non-violent methods.

PYAT, Félix. "Professional Revolutionary"; Jacobin journalist; elected to the National Assembly from Paris, Feb. 5, 1871, resigning to protest the peace terms; elected to the Commune from the Tenth Arrondissement; member of the first Executive Committee and the first Committee of Public Safety; escaped.

QUINET, Edgar. Liberal Republican loyal to the traditions of 1848; essayist and historian; elected to the National Assembly from Paris, Feb. 5, 1871.

RANC, Arthur. Radical Republican; briefly an arrondissement mayor after Sept. 4, 1870; elected to the National Assembly from Paris, Feb. 5, 1871; resigned in March to protest the peace terms; elected to the Commune from the Ninth Arrondissement; resigned his seat after several days; escaped; condemned to death *par contumace* by the Versaillese; a senator during the Third Republic.

RANVIER, Gabriel. Blanquist; skilled lacquer worker; member of the Central Committee of the National Guard; elected to the Commune from the Twentieth Arrondissement; member of the Committee of Public Safety; escaped.

RÉMUSAT, Charles comte de. Academician and diplomat; elected to the National Assembly, Feb. 8, 1871; replaced Jules Favre as Minister of Foreign Affairs, July 22, 1871; Orleanist; friend of Thiers and ready to rally to a Republic; beaten in the critical by-election of April 27, 1873 in Paris by Gambetta's associate Désiré Barodet.

RENAN, Ernest. Professor of Hebrew, Collège de France; dismissed in 1862 for a public lecture questioning the divinity of Jesus; racial theorist who borrowed from Gobineau.

RIGAULT, Raoul. Blanquist; journalist; at 25 the youngest member of the Commune; elected from the Eighth Arrondissement; member of the Executive Committee; Procureur-général of the Commune; fanatical anticlerical; captured and murdered during the Bloody Week.

RIVET, Baron. Friend of Thiers elected to the National Assembly, Feb. 8, 1871; Orleanist Center Left; author of the law of Aug. 12, 1871 that gave Thiers the title President of the French Republic—the first legal admission of an official Republic.

ROCHEFORT, Henri. Radical journalist whose career encompassed the radical Left and the radical Right; elected to the *Corps législatif* from Paris, 1869; member of the Government of National Defense from Sept. 4 to Nov. 2, 1870; elected to the National Assembly, Feb. 5, 1871 from Paris; resigned in March to protest the peace terms; Communard sympathizer; captured and sentenced to life imprisonment on New Caledonia; a later Boulangist leader.

ROSSEL, Louis-Nathaniel. Professional soldier from Nevers; disgusted by Bazaine's surrender of Metz; rallied to the Commune; succeeded Cluseret as military commander; resigned to protest continual civilian interference; captured and shot by the Versaillese.

ROUHER, Eugène. Provincial lawyer; Minister of State during the Second Empire; leader of the authoritarian Bonapartists before and after 1870.

SAY, Léon. Orleanist economist and politician; close associate of Thiers; ready to accept conservative Republic; later a Minister of Finance.

SIMON, Jules. Young Republican teacher who lost his teaching post in 1852 for refusal to take the oath; elected to the *Corps législatif* in 1863 and 1869; Minister of Public Instruction, Sept. 4, 1870; later premier under the Third Republic.

TAINE, Hippolyte. Conservative historian and determinist; his scholarly works reflected hostility to the French revolutionary tradition, notably after 1871.

THIERS, Adolphe. Orleanist politician and historian when young, conservative Republican when older; a minister of Louis-Philippe during the first decade of the July Monarchy; liberal opponent of the Second Empire; elected to the *Corps législatif*, 1863; Chief of State from Feb. 1871 to May 1873.

TOLAIN, Henri-Louis. One of the organizers of the International Organization of Workingmen in 1864; Proudhonist; deputy mayor of the Eleventh Arrondissement, Sept. 4, 1870; elected to the National Assembly from Paris, Feb. 5, 1871.

TRIDON, Gustave-Edme. Blanquist lawyer and journalist; elected to the National Assembly from Paris, Feb. 5, 1871; resigned in March to protest the peace terms; elected to the Commune from the Fifth Arrondissement; member of the first Executive Committee; escaped.

TROCHU, General Louis-Jules. Catholic Breton background; imperial military governor of Paris, 1870; president of the Government of National Defense, Sept. 1870–Feb. 1871.

VACHEROT, Etienne. Moderate Republican; briefly mayor of the Fifth Arrondissement after Sept. 4, 1870.

VAILLANT, Edouard. Teacher; educated in German universities; Marxian socialist; affiliated with the International; elected to the Commune from the Eighth Arrondissement; member of the Executive Committee; escaped.

VALLÈS, Jules. Journalist; socialist of sorts; battalion commander in the National Guard after Sept. 4, 1870; elected to the Commune from the Fifteenth Arrondissement; escaped.

VERMOREL, Jules. Journalist; radical opponent of the Second Empire; elected to the Commune from the Eighteenth Arrondissement, where he joined the Minority and opposed extremism; fatally wounded May 26; died June 20, 1871.

VÉSINIER, Pierre. Jacobin journalist, known for his hunchback and vicious personality; affiliated with the International; elected to the Commune from the First Arrondissement; editor-in-chief of the *Journal officiel;* escaped.

VEUILLOT, Louis. Conservative Catholic journalist and polemicist; critic of the French revolutionary tradition.

VINOY, General Joseph. Replaced Trochu as supreme commander in Paris, Jan. 20, 1871; suppressed six radical journals on March 11, increasing tensions; evacuated Paris, March 18, 1871.

WALLON, Henri. Academician, Hellenist, Catholic monarchist who rallied to the conservative Republic; presented constitutional compromise, Jan. 29, 1875, that broke the deadlock in the Assembly and made the Third Republic.

ZOLA, Emile. Journalist and novelist; Republican with socialist sympathies; belonged to the Naturalist school of literature; covered the deliberations of the National Assembly in Bordeaux and Versailles; later a famous Dreyfusard.

The French Revolution of 1870-1871

ONE *The Revolutionary Spirit*

First be atheists, then you will be revolutionaries —*Victor Jaclard* (*1868*)

REVOLUTIONARIES, NO matter how enlightened, misguided, or devious posterity may judge them, are no more single-minded creatures than other men. Human motives are indeed complex; and if we are all driven by both mean and charitable aims, the great deeds of this world have been accomplished by those few who believed that they worked for results beyond mere self-interest. It is only too easy to reveal the anger, the frustration, the hunger, the outrage, and the violence of people swept up in revolutionary frenzy, from which simplistic explanations for revolutions are derived. But, as a great historian of the Revolution of 1789 has taught us, the true revolutionary spirit is grounded in an idealism which alone can inspire sacrifice.[1]

Revolutionary situations, after all, have existed most everywhere throughout history and presumably will continue to exist until mankind regains Eden; yet, actual revolutions are unusual events compelling our attention. Alone, the revolutionary situation remains a simmering passivity. Only when a revolutionary situation is merged with the idealistic revolutionary spirit does the passivity end and the action begin.

In the past hundred years, some historians have held that

1. Georges Lefebvre, *The Coming of the French Revolution,* Princeton: Princeton University Press, 1947, p. 50.

ideology is a crass façade for private or national interest; in other words, that ideology *follows* economic development. On the other hand, men in search of greater freedom have significantly argued to the contrary: That political, social, and economic institutions ought consciously to be formed according to ideals with a clear awareness of the private or national sacrifices to be offered. The true revolutionary, therefore, is neither the downtrodden hungry man nor the cynic who exploits the miseries of the multitude in his bid for power, but rather the zealot with a vision of a better world—not merely for himself but for mankind. As a visionary, he will often lack political acumen and experience, which his enthusiasm can only partially replace. Consequently, he is considerably less apt to create the revolutionary opportunity than to take advantage of an opportunity presented by the weakness or the collapse of the order he has opposed. In 1870 the imperial regime of Napoleon III was killed by the Prussians at Sedan, after which Republican revolutionaries proclaimed their victory over the corpse.

The Second Empire had survived for eighteen years, hounded relentlessly by intelligent critics who found themselves frustrated by the Emperor's continuing popularity and by the significant, if awkward, attempts of his government to accommodate itself to the pressing claims of liberty. Definitions of liberty differed, of course, Monarchists, Republicans, and Socialists each espousing a unique brand and making a unified Opposition impossible. And many members of the Opposition opposed revolution as a political method, further dividing the Opposition. As we examine the various brands of opposition to the Second Empire, it will become clear that the opposition from the Left was more formidable than that from the Right, a situation faithfully reflecting what had changed in France after 1789. But in that examination, it is easy to lose sight of the fact that the imperial regime enjoyed widespread support and that the Emperor has generally been judged the most popular man to rule France since Waterloo.[2]

Conversely, the minority which hated him did so passionately and implacably: Some were unforgiving for the illegal act which made a revival of Empire possible, the *coup d'état* of 1851; some resented the muzzling of Parliament and censorship of the press; some could not tolerate a religious policy which was ambiguous, neither clearly clerical nor anticlerical; and some, faced with the imperial promotion of industrialization and consultation of the masses through plebiscites, were convinced that the dreadful result would be the vulgarization of French civilization and the triumph of stuffiness, prudery, and hypocrisy, their conception of the middle-class virtues.

General accounts of the Second Empire, narrating successes and failures at home and abroad, give the impression that many voters became disillusioned with the regime as it suffered humiliations abroad in the 1860s. Logically that should have been the case, but the government had good reason to believe otherwise, thanks to regular reports from the departmental procurers-general, reports which were thoroughly studied and understood in Paris. The government learned not merely where republicanism and socialism persisted, not merely where clerical-monarchical sentiments were unchanged, but that most of the significant opposition to the regime was intransigent and permanent, not a response to failure at home or abroad.[3] Could such an Opposition be placated or reconciled by political concessions? Most of the Bonapartists thought not and favored the maintenance of an authoritarian regime, a policy which had the defect of leaving France indefinitely divided. Yet Bonapartism had traditionally advanced itself as the bridge between the *ancien régime* and the Revolution, as the party to reconcile the two Frances. The dilemma was clear-cut: Lacking the two-party system for easy, peaceful change, the government faced an Opposition that could not be presumed to be loyal and which was potentially insurrectionary or revolutionary in spirit.[4]

To the end of his reign Napoleon III lived under the shadow of his *coup d'état* in 1851. The Republicans, at least,

3. Gordon Wright, "The Distribution of French Parties in 1865; an Official Survey," *Journal of Modern History,* XV (December 1943) , 295–298.
4. Charles A. Micaud, "The Third Force Today," *Modern France,* ed. Edward M. Earle, Princeton: Princeton University Press, 1951, p. 150.

could not forgive the illegal action; and the Emperor was saddled with the guilt of republicide, despite the fact that the Republic of 1848 had been fatally compromised by the electorate which returned Monarchists to Parliament long before he made his authoritarian move. After the *coup,* the regime believed its security required careful censorship of the press, for even under the Republic the government had enjoyed little press support. The repressive press law of February 17, 1852, included a few novelties, but much of it was borrowed from previous regimes dating from 1814: Each journal dealing with political or social matters was required to have a governmental license, which had to be renewed for every editorial staff change; each journal had to deposit "caution money" with the government; and a stamp tax on journals was raised from five to six centimes over what it had been under the Republic. The author of this law, probably Eugène Rouher, added several new and critical features: It became illegal to publish false news, whether in good or bad faith; news of parliamentary debates had to be copied from official bulletins; and press offenses were no longer to be heard in assize courts with a jury, but in "correctional courts," really police courts, without a jury. Any paper found guilty of one felony, or two misdemeanors, within a two-year period was automatically suppressed. The most arbitrary part of the new law lay in its provision giving governmental officials power to punish journalists for acts displeasing to the government but which could not technically be described as breaches of the law. In practice, this meant that the prefects and the Minister of the Interior could issue warnings, and after three such warnings a journal could be suppressed for two months.[5]

The press law correctly mirrored the dictatorship it was designed to serve, yet the evidence is now that the more arbitrary clauses were the least abusive aspects of the law. Raising the "caution money" and cutting through the red tape to obtain the license to publish proved to be the biggest barriers to editors. Actual censorship was far less than the law provided for, but the threat of it was there to keep publishers in a state of constant

5. Irene Collins, *The Government and the Newspaper Press in France, 1814–1881,* London: Oxford University Press, 1959, pp. 116–128.

anxiety; and certainly writers in any age will be appalled by the thought of censorship. The men of letters under the Second Empire were almost unanimously opposed to the regime right down to its end, outraged that their pearls were subject to scrutiny by "an anonymous band of semi-literates," as one critic, without too much exaggeration, has described the censors.[6] For no doubt one of the most odious aspects of censorship is that those who cannot write ride herd on those who can.

A few major literary figures did rally to the regime and received its favors: Théophile Gautier whose utter indifference to politics meant that his support of the government was not a matter of principle; Prosper Mérimée whose allegiance grew from long association with the family of the Empress Eugénie; and Charles-Augustin Sainte-Beuve who had been unfairly treated under the Republic of 1848 and whose Saint-Simonian socialist tendencies were shared by the Emperor. Otherwise, the major writers resisted governmental offers of lucrative positions, and some of them found themselves in court to answer charges that their works offended public morality. The case of Gustave Flaubert, for instance, illustrates the encroachment of politics upon art. His *Madame Bovary* first appeared in installments in the *Revue de Paris*, a journal known to be unfriendly to the government, in 1857. Flaubert's frankness and realism shocked some of the more tender-minded, including Her Majesty, and enabled the government to strike at a hostile journal while avoiding the appearance of political persecution. From the authors' point of view, however, political persecution was no worse than governmental officials posing as guardians of middle-class morality—a morality which many of them, including His Majesty, knew only second hand. The defendants in the case were acquitted and, when the novel appeared in book form, the prosecution had guaranteed it a solid sale.[7]

A few months later Charles Baudelaire had his day in court, the offensive work being his *Fleurs du mal*, which first appeared

6. Philip Spencer, "Censorship of Literature under the Second Empire," *Cambridge Journal*, III (1949) , 49–53.
7. Roger L. Williams, *Gaslight and Shadow, The World of Napoleon III 1851–1870*, New York: Macmillan, 1957, p. 131.

in the *Revue des deux mondes,* then a journal of Orleanist opinion. The prosecution proved mild, but the incident only heightened Baudelaire's hostility to the standards of his day, which were necessarily linked to the regime which upheld them in court. "All the imbeciles of the Bourgeoisie," he wrote, "who interminably use the words: 'immoral', 'immorality', 'morality in art' and other such stupid expressions remind me of Louise Villedieu, a five-franc whore who once went with me to the Louvre. She had never been there before, and began to blush and cover her face with her hands, repeatedly plucking at my sleeve and asking me, as we stood before deathless statues and pictures, how such indecencies could be flaunted in public." [8]

The intelligentsia under the Second Empire thought that they sensed a degree of cultural decay around them that previous generations had not experienced, a decadence of mind and spirit for which the pharmacist Homais in Flaubert's *Madame Bovary* became the trademark, pompous and platitudinous, ambitious and humorless. A world peopled by his kind seemed insupportable, and it is said that Flaubert experienced a physical revulsion at the presence of a bourgeois, so great was his disgust with people who were satisfied to know everything second-hand.[9] What was the cause of this apparent coarsening where sensibility seemed to give way to sensuality, and where "comfort subtly usurped the place of pleasure—a passive for an active thing?" [10] Evidently the Industrial Revolution with its promise of higher living standards for all, with its heightened opportunities for profits, was whetting the commercial spirit and extending the lower middle class at a pace which the aristocratic ideal with its standard of excellence could not match. Would the advances of industrialism and democracy culminate in the vulgarization of French civilization, or could political leadership devise ways to raise cultural standards along with those of daily subsistence? The emphasis which the regime put on economic expansion far

8. Charles Baudelaire, *My Heart Laid Bare,* ed. Peter Quennell, New York: Vanguard Press, 1951, pp. 203–204.
9. Kenneth Douglas, "The French Intellectuals," *Modern France,* ed. Edward M. Earle, Princeton: University Press, 1951, p. 71.
10. Jacques Barzun, *Berlioz and the Romantic Century,* Boston: Little, Brown, 1950, II, 229–230.

outstripped imperial interest in the arts, giving the intelligentsia little cause for optimism. France seemed to be on the brink of utilitarianism, something Baudelaire and the Goncourt brothers called Americanization.

Disdainful of governmental position or sinecure, writers and intellectuals withdrew into the shelter of salons from which issued quips and witticisms that irritated the powerful and consoled the impotent. The French Academy became a principal source of opposition from 1852 to the beginning of 1870, an arena of opposition from which criticism could be leveled without serious fear of official retaliation. Of the thirty-two elections to the Academy in that period, only seven candidates were elected strictly on literary grounds. This is not to say that the remaining twenty-five elected were hacks; but quite clearly to be a Legitimist, an Orleanist, or a Liberal Catholic was a literary qualification as never before, and the political implication of the elections was widely understood.[11]

Napoleon III aspired to election to the Academy in 1863 following the death of Duc Pasquier the previous year, not in order to tame the literary lions in their den, but to satisfy a long ambition and to see his *L'Histoire de Jules César* recognized. The Academy parried official hints, and the Emperor was too shy to batter at the doors. One of the Emperor's research assistants on his project, the archeologist Louis Maury, already a member of the Académie des Inscriptions et Belles-lettres and librarian of the Tuileries, urged His Majesty to delay his candidacy until the second volume of the history should be completed, assuring him of an acceptance which, in fact, never came.[12] The Academy did, however, begin its reconciliation with the regime early in 1870 with the election of Emile Ollivier to register approval of the Liberal Empire, though the regime did not survive many months to enjoy the favor.

Some of the earliest public manifestations of opposition to

11. Robert W. Reichert, "Anti-Bonapartist Elections to the Académie Française during the Second Empire," *Journal of Modern History*, XXXV (March 1963) , 33–36.
12. Hortense Cornu to Nassau William Senior, "Louis-Napoleon Painted by a Contemporary," *Cornhill Magazine*, XXVII (Jan.–June 1873) , 613–614.

the Empire took place in the theaters, particularly the Odéon, where presumably the audience was largely university students. Works by writers known to be on good terms with the imperial family were hissed, whether good, bad, or indifferent. A relentless student hostility could close a play in a few days. Such was the fate of Charles-Edmond Kojecki in 1855, a protégé of Prince Napoleon; of Edmond About in 1862, then on good terms with the imperial court; and of the Goncourt brothers, in the circle of Princess Mathilde, when their play *Henriette Maréchal* opened in 1865. Admittedly these plays were not good, but the plays were not what was being hissed.

The most celebrated of such incidents at the Odéon occurred on May 17, 1866, at the opening of Emile Augier's *La Contagion,* the imperial couple having announced their intention to attend. Perhaps the Emperor, known to be more amused than scandalized by student pranks, was curious to see if this opposition would burst forth in his presence. During an intermission a student emitted a sharp howl and loudly identified it as the cry of the dying eagle—which got everyone to laughing, including the Emperor. At the end of the performance, which was a success, the house emptied in a flash, everyone gathering around to watch the departure of the court carriages. Just as Napoleon was seated in his carriage, five or six sewage-disposal vehicles rolled into the square, and they were immediately surrounded by about one hundred cheering students, waving their hats and shouting long life to the Emperor, a demonstration carried out with complete solemnity. Whether the incident was planned or not has never been clear,[13] but one is tempted to think so since the incident resembled the well-organized bedlam which greeted Viollet-le-Duc, the medievalist and restorer, when this friend of the court attempted to begin his first lecture at the Ecole des Beaux-Arts in 1864. A riot raged for thirty minutes before the dignitaries surrendered the platform, only to be followed on foot to the Louvre by a hooting, nose-thumbing procession of students.[14]

13. Maxime Du Camp, *Souvenirs d'un demi-siècle,* Paris: Hachette, 1949, I, 214–216.
14. Roger L. Williams, *op. cit.,* pp. 247–249.

Student opposition to the Second Empire was widespread and not limited to those at the Sorbonne, and it helped to give the Opposition from the Left a much more militant, vigorous spirit than that ever developed from the Right. This student opposition was grounded more in scientific ideas than on a thorough study of politics or social problems. Students criticized the social order, not primarily because it created social abuses, but because it was based on a theological interpretation of the universe; in place of which they preferred, not merely a mechanical interpretation, but a materialist view of reality. The new authorities most eagerly read were Charles Darwin for his views on the mechanics of evolution; the Hessian philosopher and physicist Friedrich Büchner for his extreme views on matter and energy which were grounded in thermodynamics; and M.–P.–E. Littré, the positivist, who was favored over Comte for resisting turning positivism into a religious cult.[15] Nature was seen as purely physical, with life having no purpose or will, affected not at all by any supernatural will or power. Logically, many of these students defended the doctrine of spontaneous generation of life, denying the validity of biogenesis which Louis Pasteur was then revealing in his laboratory.[16]

Only one political form could house such philosophical and scientific ideas: the Republic. The various monarchical forms, whether from conviction or convenience, had reached an accommodation with the Church; while Republicans, if not necessarily atheistic, had denied Roman Catholic fundamentals and confiscated ecclesiastical properties. Those caught up in the intellectual novelties of the 1860s, therefore, rejected Bonapartism for its equivocal religious and clerical policies, and often saw the regime's censorship as a device to protect religion from scientific attack.

All Republicans worshipped the great Revolution of the eighteenth century. Studying it, commenting on it, they revealed through their heroes their particular political views. It may seem

15. Georges Weill, *Mouvement social en France, 1852–1910,* Paris: Alcan, 1911, p. 119.
16. Georges Weill, *Le Parti républicain de 1814 à 1870,* Paris: Alcan, 1900, p. 470.

paradoxical to speak of the development of a revolutionary tradition, since revolutions are aimed at upsetting tradition. Nevertheless, as the nineteenth century developed, the ideals of 1789 became a tradition, essentially that of democracy or the sovereignty of the people as expressed in the well known device "Liberty, Equality, Fraternity." Because of the failure of liberal monarchy between 1814 and 1848, this revolutionary tradition became exclusively associated with Republicanism and Bonapartism. Then, with a Bonaparte manufacturing a dictatorship in 1851, a majority of Republicans not merely rejected all association with Bonapartism, but became for the first time hostile to the principle of strong executive power.[17]

It needs to be emphasized, on the other hand, that the Republican movement, like the Revolution, had its nuances; and under the Second Empire the Republicans were hardly a unified group. One major distinction developed between those who had been politically active in 1848 and those who came of political age under the Empire. Of the former group, some had been in prison as early as the beginning of the reaction in 1848—Auguste Blanqui and François-Vincent Raspail, for example. When imprisonments continued into 1849, other radicals fled to avoid that fate, notably Louis Blanc and Ledru-Rollin. The latter, in London, established an organization called La Révolution, which was soon countered by an organization called La Commune Révolutionnaire, directed by Félix Pyat. Both men were Jacobins, Pyat simply believing that Ledru-Rollin was too mild; and both kept aloof from socialist exiles like Louis Blanc and Pierre Leroux, largely because most of the Republicans were convinced that their political failure in 1848 was rooted in their association with the Socialists, which had produced a popular reaction, a view encouraged by Mazzini whom they met in London.[18]

The exiles were augmented following the *coup d'état* of 1851 and in general were inclined to believe that their residence abroad would be short-lived. Some sought refuge in Belgium, Spain, Switzerland, and the United States; but Britain was the principal haven where nearly one thousand settled. Because

17. David Thomson, *Democracy in France Since 1870*, 4th ed., New York: Oxford University Press, 1964, pp. 11–16.
18. John Plamenatz, *op. cit.*, p. 112.

there was no unified party, the exiles were really a revolutionary army characterized by "political messianism." [19] By and large, the Republicans among them remained deist throughout the period of the Second Empire. If they fought the Roman Catholic Church and were anticlerical, they also rejected atheism as a monstrous doctrine, holding it to be the source of political oppression and of intellectual and moral degradation. There was no unanimity, however, as to what system ought to replace Catholicism: some wanted a liberal, antitheocratic Catholicism, perhaps a modified Jansenism; others preferred a liberal variety of Protestantism, notably the Unitarianism of William Ellery Channing; still others favored a natural religion without dogma or cult.

The Jansenist Republicans were inspired by the philosopher Jean-Baptiste Bordas-Demoulin and his disciple François Huet; their movement may be seen as a continuation of the spirit of Lamennais. Among the Protestants, Jules Favre was a notable convert, and George Sand had her two granddaughters baptized Protestant.[20] Others were enthusiasts for Protestantism without becoming converts, the most influential of them being Edgar Quinet who equated Catholicism with national backwardness. In his view, political and economic advancement was historically associated with a break from Catholicism; thus he saw the Reformation as a libertarian movement at the end of the Middle Ages. Peoples who had not achieved that particular form of freedom in the sixteenth century had been unable subsequently to achieve any other form of freedom. More specifically, if the ideals of the French Revolution were being defeated in the nineteenth century, it was because the Reformation had earlier been defeated in France. Quinet sought a more modern Christianity for his generation as the basis for national education and social unity, but was balked by the realization that the emerging generation of Republicans was not merely anti-Catholic but had lost faith.[21]

The French government did not recognize the fine political

19. Howard C. Payne and Henry Grosshans, "The Revolutionaries and the French Political Police in the 1850's," *American Historical Review*, LXVIII, #4 (July 1963) , 954–955.
20. Georges Weill, *Le Parti républicain*, pp. 452–454.
21. Richard H. Powers, *Edgar Quinet: A Study in French Patriotism*, Dallas: Southern Methodist University Press, 1957, pp. 140–155.

and religious distinctions that meant so much to the exiles, simply labeling the various opposition sects Republican and equating that status to socialism or communism. Despite the disapproval of his police, Napoleon III was inclined to grant pardons and amnesties during the 1850s, returning to France men whom the police knew to be unrepentant subversives; and on August 16, 1859, the Emperor decreed a general amnesty for political offenses, excluding only Ledru-Rollin. Some, like Victor Hugo and Louis Blanc, refused the amnesty, but the great majority returned home by 1860. After roughly a decade of feeding their expectations a rarefied diet of illusions, those returning discovered that they had become political curiosities. Their bold words, fired from the security of exile, had been reaching no significant section of the French population, the Emperor was dismayingly popular, and a new generation of Republicans had emerged that, as we have seen, had been reared not on the idealism of 1848 but in admiration of science.[22]

Unlike the older generation, the younger generation of Republicans had forsaken deism and all spiritual belief, so that the gulf between the generations was much vaster than a decade. As Mazzini wrote to Edgar Quinet, "[The younger generation] has no faith; it has opinions. It denies God, immortality, love, . . . all that is good, great, beautiful, and holy in the world, the entire heroic tradition of great religious thinkers from Prometheus to Christ, from Socrates to Kepler, in order to kneel before Comte. . . . As an inevitable consequence [this generation] is Machiavellian, opportunist, given to maneuvers and stratagems, deprived of moral sense, without a religion requiring an oath, without awareness of the sanctity of religious works or of the power of truth." [23] It might be argued, on the other hand, that a few young Republicans, despite their loss of faith, at least sought a substitute church in Freemasonry. Though the Grand-Orient de France maintained a pro-government attitude during the Second Empire, its Republican members, Jules Ferry, Léon Gambetta, and Isaac Crémieux being the most prominent, took ad-

22. Payne and Grosshans, *op. cit.,* pp. 970–973.
23. Georges Weill, *Le Parti républicain,* p. 470, quoting from Mme. Edgar Quinet, *Mémoires d'exil,* II, 434.

vantage of the secrecy of the order to work through it for the overthrow of the empire. In process, they also worked to alter the structure of the order, especially its religious principles. In 1865 they proposed to replace the belief in God with the doctrine of "the inviolability of the human person." Not adopted by the order at the time, the proposal nevertheless suggests that Freemasonry was drifting in the direction of Republicanism.[24]

If young Republican ideas primarily derived from science, those ideas were given a more political and social focus by a variety of intellectual influences under the Second Empire. Of first-rank significance was the anarchist Proudhon whose greatest work, *De la Justice dans la révolution et dans l'église* (1858), taught that the love of justice is the mother of every virtue and, moreover, that justice and religion are irreconcilable. Radicals influenced by Proudhon were often suspicious of Republicans in the Jacobin tradition, for the master criticized what he called the demagogic behavior of the nineteenth-century Jacobins, thus irritating some Republicans. In 1859 two books appeared that were also influential: Jules Simon's *La Liberté* and Etienne Vacherot's *La Démocratie,* for which Vacherot received a jail sentence. Histories of the great Revolution by Jules Michelet and Edgar Quinet also provoked Republican discussion, Michelet championing Robespierre and the Jacobins, Quinet the Girondins. As a result, Auguste Vermorel began to republish the works of Robespierre, Mirabeau, and Marat; while Arthur Ranc republished Buonarroti's account of the Babeuf conspiracy of 1796. The Hébertists, too, had their enthusiast in Edme Tridon, who produced an *apologia* in 1863, condemning the Jacobins for their indifference to social problems and justifying force rather than reliance upon legality.[25]

In 1861 Elias Regnault published *La Province ce qu'elle est, ce qu'elle doit être,* a work espousing political decentralization and demanding a complete reorganization of provincial administration. Two years later Pierre-Joseph Proudhon went further in

24. Jacques Freymond, "La France de 1870," *Etudes de Lettres,* XVIII (April 1944) , 64–66.
25. John Plamenatz, *op. cit.,* pp. 120–122; and Georges Weill, *Le Parti républicain,* p. 468.

his *Du principe fédératif* by presenting the federal system as the only proper one for a Republic. Many Republicans, raised in the tradition of the one and indivisible Republic, could not accept the principle of decentralization despite the obvious fact that the high degree of centralization had made the establishment of a dictatorship relatively easy. The decentralization principle, nevertheless, proved to be a rallying point for various factions of the Opposition. For in 1865 a small group in Nancy advocated such a program and received encouragement from some prominent Republicans—Jules Simon, Hippolyte Carnot, and Antoine Garnier-Pagès among them—along with the support of the Comte de Montalembert, the Comte de Falloux, François Guizot, and Antoine Berryer, Monarchists of different degrees.[26]

The imperial constitution of 1852 had not only provided for a highly centralized state, but did so in confirming and guaranteeing "the great principles proclaimed in 1789." Since several of those principles had been condemned by the Holy See, there could be no accord in principle between Church and Second Empire. It was otherwise in practice because the laicity of the state, as created by the Revolution, had been subsequently modified (long before 1851), and the state in fact could not be regarded as neutral between believers and nonbelievers. Three major cults were recognized and protected by the state; divorce had been abolished; the observance of Sundays was commanded by law, if never enforced; the law punished offenses to public and religious morality; religious instruction was obligatory in primary schools; God was invoked in legal oaths; and the constitution charged the Senate to protect the liberty of cults and religion itself. In the attempt to provide a bridge between old and new France, no Bonapartist ambiguity was less satisfactory to both Leftist and Rightist Opposition than a religious policy that was lay in principle but not in practice. And since Bonapartism was of revolutionary origin, this ambiguous religious and clerical policy was seen by most Republicans as proof that their most serious enemy was the Church. In other words, that Bonapartism was a form of Republicanism corrupted by the Church.[27]

26. Georges Weill, *Le Parti républicain*, p. 488.
27. Jean Maurain, *La Politique ecclésiastique du Second Empire*, Paris: Félix Alcan, 1930, pp. 941–945.

Beyond the realm of political and religious philosophies, one can see the evolution of Republican attitudes and divisions by examining actual political behavior. The elections of 1852 were the first to be held under the new dictatorship, and virtually all Republicans were agreed not to take the oath to uphold the Empire, thus resigning what few seats they contested and won. But the wisdom of this righteous stance was soon questioned by the leading moderate Republican sheet in Paris, *le Siècle,* then edited by Emile de Girardin. Why not take advantage of the constitution and introduce a few independent voices into the servile assembly of Bonapartists? By 1857, the date of the second elections to renew the *Corps législatif,* the younger Republicans favored active participation over high-minded sulking in salons.

In the first round of balloting, seven Republicans were elected. Of them, one died before the opening of the new Parliament, two of the older generation refused to take the oath and resigned their seats, and one soon abandoned his Republicanism for the governmental majority. Emile Ollivier, Alfred Darimon, and J.–L. Hénon took their seats, the latter only after exhibiting a proper amount of public reluctance to do so. A Jacobin from Lyon, Hénon was a scholarly physician and botanist, a virtuous man with no political ambitions or experience. Ollivier was the youngest of the group and a moderate, antirevolutionary Republican; while Darimon, a disciple of Proudhon, really served as a front for both Proudhon and Emile de Girardin. In the by-elections of 1858, two more Republicans were returned: Jules Favre, a former Saint-Simonian Socialist become a moderate, humanitarian Republican; and Ernest Picard, a well-to-do bourgeois with a background of Voltairian scepticism. These five deputies (they were known as *les Cinq*), in taking the oath, represented a break with graybeard leadership, but were so highly individualistic as to be neither the leaders nor the representatives of the Republican party at that moment.

If not much of a unified party, *les Cinq* were consistent in pleading for greater liberty which meant, in fact, they could not systematically oppose governmental policy. Jules Favre, for instance, in his maiden speech on April 30, 1859, made it clear that there could be no pact between the Republicans and the Bonapartist majority on domestic affairs. "But," he added, "if you wish to destroy the Austrian despotism, to deliver Italy from her wrongs, my heart, my blood, my body and soul are with you." [28] And, Favre added, once the Italians should be granted their liberties, the victor ought to restore them to the French. In 1860 Emile Ollivier spoke against protectionism and for Napoleon III's low tariff treaty with Great Britain—again for freedom. *Les Cinq* also consistently protested the financial speculation which was a handmaid of the expanding economy, harping on the presumed lowering of public and private morality tacitly encouraged by governmental enthusiasm for business and industry.

In this, at least, the Republicans of the 1860s were successful, for they established the cliché that the Second Empire was an unusually corrupt period when politics had simply become a racket for adventurers seeking money. Such a cliché was not only consistent with the intellectuals' alarms about civilizational decay, but had as a long-term example the rebuilding of Paris, which was easily misrepresented by the Opposition as a disguised plan to make Paris more easily commanded by troops and at a fantastic cost—thanks to the profits of speculators and corrupt officials. The cliché was the more acceptable because it portrayed men in power as reptiles and those out of power as paragons, a political truism of such longevity that it was beyond the need for proof. The revolutionary spirit was the beneficiary of these dark suspicions.

Perhaps the example of the Duc de Morny, the Emperor's half-brother and a notoriously successful speculator, was used to illustrate the lives of all other public officials. In any case, the cliché, if forever embalmed in textbooks, has not survived recent research. Even the Emperor left in his will approximately what he had inherited, and his ministers in general did not use politics to enrich themselves, though painfully aware of accusations to the contrary. Many members of Parliament were lawyers and gave up lucrative practices for politics, losing financially to gain the less tangible rewards of public life.[29]

In castigating the imperial regime for the reconstruction of

28. *Ibid.*, p. 424.
29. Theodore Zeldin, *The Political System of Napoleon III*, London: Macmillan, 1958, pp. 61–62.

Paris, the Republicans were equally successful in establishing the commonplace that the imperial motive was antirevolutionary. Certainly the imperial government was not indifferent to the problem of disorder in Paris, any more than previous governments had been! But anyone doubting the need to modernize a medieval city undergoing the early pressures of industrialization would profit from a vicarious promenade through the Paris of 1850 to experience in safety the hazards and inconveniences of that era along with the noxious odors, the epidemics, and the sordid slums. The question is not *why* the reconstruction was begun, but why it had not been started earlier! And the answer is that such a monumental undertaking required vigorous, determined leadership endowed with substantial political authority; along with an acceptance of the notion that the Industrial Revolution ought to be a boon for mankind, and that any government concerned for the welfare of its people needed to promote industrialization as well as to take measures to counter its evils. The opposition to reconstruction, an alliance of political enemies of the regime, aesthetes, and art historians, managed to obscure the need for reconstruction, turning it into a piece of political opportunism on the part of crass men indifferent to Parisian art treasures. And one can still fairly well gauge the predisposition of a writer toward the Second Empire by the emphasis he places on the political motives behind the reconstruction.

If one wishes to go beyond the need to modernize a medieval city to include the political considerations which every politician must have, then it is correct to note that Napoleon III was anxious to attach the Parisians to his regime through reforms which would destroy the causes for violent protest. And, as the Saint-Simonians had suggested, a public works program could provide full employment. To carry out the reconstruction of Paris required great energy and vision, contrasting favorably with that vision which saw the new wide boulevards as simply designed to facilitate cavalry charges. Baron Georges-Eugène Haussmann, in charge of the reconstruction as Prefect of the Seine, was accused by the Opposition of dangerous political ambitions, extravagance, graft, cynicism, and of having little artistic taste; so that the reconstruction of Paris, spanning nearly the entirety of the Second Empire, had the effect of joining both the political and cultural opposition to the regime.[30]

The unusual opposition that Haussmann faced, despite the Emperor's firm support, did force upon him unusual financial devices. Beginning in 1867, Jules Ferry wrote a series of articles on the matter in *les Temps,* which were republished as a book in 1868 under the title *Les Comptes fantastiques d'Haussmann,* a pun on *Les Contes fantastiques d'Hoffmann.* In fact, there was nothing fantastic about the financing except that it was unorthodox for its day, though consistent with the philosophy behind such new institutions as the Crédit Mobilier. That is, long-term borrowing against future income; in this case, the increased revenues to be realized from the growing population and the increased property values that the expenditures would create. In other words, the city would borrow money, "invest" it in public works, and pay off the debt from new tax yields.

By the 1860s unforeseen financial factors added to the controversy. Real estate values inflated quickly; courts tended to award inflated indemnities to those evicted—and there were lawyers who made a career out of such cases; so that construction costs rose to a point where they upset Haussmann's budgets, leaving him open to the charge that he had deliberately misled governmental committees about probable costs. As the *Corps législatif* obtained more political authority in that decade, especially more control of the budget, Haussmann was led to seek borrowing devices to by-pass parliamentary checks, angering Royalists and Republicans alike. Though the regime managed to protect him until 1869, it was necessary to sacrifice him as part of the formation of the Ollivier government. His achievement had been impressive, but his methods, his brutal energy, and his unorthodoxy left a dangerous legacy of hostility to the regime for its supposed financial irresponsibility and highhandedness.[31]

Under the constitution of the Second Empire, parliamentary elections were held every six years. *Les Cinq* had been elected in 1857; a much larger Opposition was elected in 1863, indicating

30. David H. Pinkney, *Napoleon III and the Rebuilding of Paris,* Princeton: Princeton University Press, 1958, pp. 33–45.
31. *Ibid.,* pp. 174–206.

that political life was reviving. The total of Opposition deputies elected was thirty-two, seventeen of them Republican, fifteen classified as Royalist or Catholic; and the Opposition vote was roughly two million out of over seven million, about double what the Opposition had received in 1857. Eight of the seventeen Republicans were returned from Paris, and a great majority of the successful Opposition candidates came from the larger cities. In the aftermath of the election, the Republicans tried to extend their influence into the rural areas, but were hindered by the absence of rural newspapers and by the tendency of provincial prefects to enforce security laws more rigidly than was the case in towns.[32]

Both the general spirit of opposition and the revolutionary spirit, therefore, remained largely confined to the larger cities, a restriction the more significant if we remember that France was still primarily an agricultural nation. From the point of view of most Frenchmen with their rural outlook, the city worker was an anomaly, a misfit, who could be counted on to take the opposite side from most of the French in political and social questions. But if few in numbers, the city workers were congregated in the centers of political power and were in a position to exert pressure out of proportion to their numbers. Their economic insecurity was apparently greater than that of the rural population, which contributed to making the city worker more "volatile" and susceptible to excitement and extremism. City workers were the most enthusiastic segment of the population for war against Austria in 1859 and for war against Prussia in 1870.[33]

The Bonapartists and the Republicans, each laying claim to the democratic principles of 1789, sought the political support of the urban workers; but, as the social movement developed in the 1860s, neither party was particularly successful in seizing the leadership. Prince Jerome-Napoleon, cousin of the Emperor, was well known for his radical views and his activity on behalf of workers. He was a friend of Armand Lévy, a former radical, who published *l'Espérance,* a newspaper which came to champion

32. Georges Weill, *Le Parti républicain*, p. 506.
33. Lynn M. Case, *French Opinion on War and Diplomacy During the Second Empire*, Philadelphia: University of Pennsylvania Press, 1954, pp. 274-275.

imperial democracy. The Prince was also a friend of Henri-Louis Tolain, one of the most influential of the Parisian workers who was active on behalf of Polish liberties in 1863. Lévy seems to have been the originator of the project to send a group of French workers to London in 1862 for the Exhibition in the Crystal Palace, hoping to broaden their horizons; and he worked out the arrangements with Prince Napoleon's aid. Napoleon III favored the trip and contributed 200,000 francs to make it possible.[34]

The consequent encounter with British labor provided the spark for further confrontations, and the French group soon abandoned its Bonapartist support. In 1864 Tolain led another delegation to London for a meeting at Saint Martin's Hall, where the constitution of the International Association of Working Men was completed on September 28. The Association named Tolain and two other delegates the official French correspondents, and toward that end they opened an office in Paris on July 8, 1865, intending to function publicly. The International, as it came to be known, was meant to be a platform for the cooperation of all labor and radical leaders, from Mazzini to Marx, from Proudhonists to English trade unionists; and the French correspondents hoped to make it clear in France that the new association was neither a Bonapartist agency nor intended for direct political action, but was organized as a study group for workers. This line was intended to allay the suspicions of radical workers and to avoid interference from the imperial police. "Study groups" in a number of provincial towns were subsequently opened: in Le Havre, Lille, Rouen, Lyon, Roubaix, and St. Etienne as examples. Their growth was small though the adherence of Auguste Vermorel gave the movement his newspaper, le Courrier français.[35]

Proudhon was the chief philosophical influence upon Tolain and his band. Thought to be an extreme revolutionary and anarchist because of the tone and wording of his pamphlets directed against bourgeois society, Proudhon was in fact a moder-

34. John Plamenatz, op. cit., p. 126.
35. Robert C. Binkley, Realism and Nationalism 1852–1871, London and New York: Harper, 1935, pp. 120–121; and Georges Weill, Le Mouvement social, pp. 99–102.

ate and practical reformer whose works further misled because they were complex and often contradictory. The well-known opening passage of his *Qu'est-ce que la Propriété* (1840) is a case in point with its revolutionary slogan to the effect that property is theft. All he meant to denounce was the use of property to exploit others, particularly in the forms of interest, usury, and rent. He was unopposed to property as possession and regarded it as a necessary guarantee of personal liberty, hence his opposition to communism. Proudhon claimed to build no system: He wanted an end to privilege and to slavery in all forms, and the establishment of a more perfect justice through the rule of law.[36]

Anarchy—for Proudhon was the first man to call himself an anarchist—meant something considerably milder to him than organized chaos. He saw mankind, having emerged from Nature to organize society and government, increasingly rebellious against these authorities as human reason and experience developed. Having emerged from the state of Nature in search of greater liberty and justice, liberty and justice continue to be man's goal; and rational man will ultimately recognize that true liberty will come only when men reorganize society so that authority becomes self-imposed rather than imposed by the state. Authority, in other words, would become completely decentralized. Because these ideas were published before Proudhon had made any observations of the Industrial Revolution, it would force him to change some of his views later in life.[37]

Proudhon was also known as a mutualist. The mutualists were originally a secret society in Lyon led by workingmen, notably Joseph Benoît, who participated in the labor uprisings of 1831 and 1834. When Proudhon visited Lyon in 1843, he found that both the mutualists and he were anti-Jacobin. Whereas the Jacobins argued that social and economic changes followed political revolution, the mutualists argued for the primacy of social and economic change. This set Proudhon to work on his *Contradictions économiques* (1846), a rambling work which happily contained a brief résumé in the final chapter. Here he developed

36. George Woodcock, *Pierre-Joseph Proudhon*, London: Routledge & Kegan Paul, 1956, pp. 45–46; and Weill, *Le Mouvement social*, pp. 41–42.
37. Woodcock, *op. cit.*, pp. 50–51.

his celebrated thesis that God is evil, that is, anticivilized, anti-liberal, and antihuman; and here he presented his mutualist theory: ". . . a society not merely conventional, but real, which changes the division of labour into an instrument of science, which abolishes slavery to machines and halts crises before they appear, which makes competition a benefit and monopoly a pledge of security for all, which, by the power of its principle, instead of demanding credit from capital and protection from the State, submits both capital and State to labour." [38] In political terms, mutuality was expressed as federalism, and he emphasized voluntary association.

In 1865 the Parisian correspondents of the International returned to London on the anniversary of its founding and for the first time discovered Marx's hostility to their master Proudhon. The following year, in Geneva, they were further confronted in the Association by the Blanquists. The Parisian delegation had increased to eleven members that year, and they carefully prepared a memorandum to be read, the nine points of which were clearly Proudhonist:

1) To date, democracy has been checked by the bourgeoisie. The International has been founded to lead, by scientific and peaceful ways if possible, the proletariat to political freedom.

2) Since labor is the source of all wealth, and capital is simply labor accumulated, there is no conflict between labor and capital—except when it comes to *interest* which has no legitimate defense, since it can provide the livelihood of someone who does not produce.

3) Free and obligatory education is not good, for it allows the state to impose uniformity and immobility. The proper instruction, which truly develops the individual, comes through the family; and without the family, humanity becomes only a collection of hostile beings. Mothers must be kept out of the workshops and at home.

4) Association is good so long as it assumes the cooperative form which respects the right of the individual.

5) Strikes are bad; they can only produce a diminution of the necessities of life. Far better to introduce a system which

38. *Ibid.,* p. 100.

makes change of job easy, both through technical apprenticeships and through ready statistics which reveal the better *métiers*.

6) The tax system is reprehensible, because it places the burden almost entirely on the workers. Until a radical reform of taxation is possible, taxes ought to be as direct as possible.

7) Standing armies contribute nothing to production and condition the soldiers to idleness. Their disappearance would be beneficial.

8) The question of protection and free trade is simply a quarrel between capitalists.

9) Religion is a respectable manifestation of the individual conscience as long as it remains a personal, individual matter.

This memorandum was greeted courteously by the delegates in 1866, though it was obvious that the Proudhonist program was at variance with Marxian fundamentals. The English delegates stood for immediate, practical goals such as the eight-hour day; consequently they favored the right to strike, while the French delegates were proposing a society based on universal cooperation.[39] The Proudhonist position in the International was no more uncomfortable than it became at home. The posture of being an educational organization could not conceal the fact that the majority in the International increasingly favored collectivization or communism, leading the imperial government in 1868 to dissolve the organization in France by court order. French Communists then tried to take direction of the movement— Varlin, Malon, and Combault in particular—but the government also prosecuted them, so that French influence in the International vanished.[40]

In the process, mutualism was giving way before communism and the revolutionary method in France, though it would be wrong to assert that the revolutionary method dated only from 1868. Mutualism had its brief domination in the '60s, but the revolutionary spirit had been nursed in the working districts since 1848. What is more, while the International addressed itself solely to workers, the revolutionary spirit could also be found among some members of the poorer middle class. Blanqui, for

39. Weill, *Le Mouvement social*, pp. 103–107.
40. *Ibid.*, pp. 108–114.

example, a communist revolutionary long before the Second
Empire, found his disciples in that group.[41]

Napoleon III, who in his younger days had written about
the extinction of pauperism, had financed the workers' trip to
London in 1862 and had not been displeased by the formation of
the International. Only when that organization began to champion principles intolerable for the imperial regime was there
retaliation. Before the dissolution of 1868, the government tried
for a compromise with the French delegation, agreeing to allow
the delegation's reports on the International to be published in
France if the delegates would include a brief statement of praise
for the Emperor for having done so much for the working class.
But the delegation refused, fearful of being regarded as a Bonapartist front. This failure to reach an understanding meant that
the Empire lost touch with the social movement, meant the defeat of the moderates and the victory of the extremists, and probably delayed the realization of the social advances which the
workers demanded—for the early Third Republic would show
itself more indifferent to social reform than the Empire had
been.[42]

In the papers found in the Tuileries after the fall of the
Empire, there remained a bare draft of a novel in the Emperor's
hand, probably a project which he hoped to commission a professional writer to develop. The simple plot concerned a man who,
having been abroad for most of Napoleon III's reign, returned
home to be amazed at the social and economic advances made
during his absence. This may suggest that the Emperor felt his
efforts were not appreciated; and, having been a pamphleteer
before achieving power, he was continuing to advance his program in the old way, hoping to attract support.[43]

The Republicans elected to the *Corps législatif* in 1863 were
hardly more acceptable than Napoleon III to the socialist leaders
(and we here lump mutualists and communists together as so-

41. *Ibid.*, pp. 117–118.
42. Hendrik N. Boon, *Rêve et réalité dans l'oeuvre économique et sociale de
Napoléon III*, The Hague: Martinus Nijhoff, 1936, pp. 153–154.
43. *Ibid.*, pp. 154–155; and *Papiers et correspondance de la famille impériale*,
Paris: Garnier, 1871, I, 218–219.

cialists). The average Republican, whether of the older or the younger generation, was primarily concerned for political form; and beyond that he was more likely exercised by religious and clerical issues than by social or economic abuses. By 1868, as the Empire was cracking down on radicalism, the socialist leaders urged the Republicans in Parliament to sponsor public discussions about social problems in order to lessen popular fears about socialism. Since 1848, after all, socialism was associated with Republicanism in the popular mind and had done much to wreck the Second Republic. If the Republicans were to succeed, then, it implied a reduction in popular fears about socialism. Jules Simon was the only Republican deputy who responded to the invitation to present and debate issues publicly. Consequently, in the parliamentary elections of 1869, Republicans faced not only the Bonapartist candidates but socialist candidates in a number of constituencies.[44] In the popular mind the socialist and Republican movements were generally confounded because of their mutual hatred of the Empire; but the schism between them was real and provides one more example of the deep divisions within the Opposition.

A long-awaited liberal press law, part of the general liberalizing of the imperial institutions in the 1860s, was promulgated on May 11, 1868, abolishing the licensing of journals and lowering the stamp taxes. Governmental officials lost the power to warn, suspend, and suppress journals, which displeased the more conservative Bonapartists. But the law fell short of pleasing the Left, because it did not provide for jury trials in the case of press offenses.[45] A spate of new journals were founded in the wake of the reform, some of them dedicated to encouraging the development of a liberal Empire. The majority, however, including the one which eclipsed them all, Henri Rochefort's *la Lanterne*, proved that the spirit of opposition was very much alive despite the imperial concessions. Eugène Ténot put out a book, *Paris en décembre 1851,* designed to inform that generation too young to have remembered the *coup d'état* of the Emperor's iniquity, and there were several political gatherings that year at the graves of

44. Weill, *Le Mouvement social,* p. 125.
45. Irene Collins, *op. cit.,* pp. 148–151.

notable opponents of Napoleon: that of General Godefroy Cavaignac, who had been the provisional President of the Second Republic, and that of a deputy named Dr. Victor Baudin who had fallen in defense of a barricade on December 2, 1851. Soon after, several newspapers promoted a subscription to raise a monument to Baudin, which led the government to prosecute Charles Delescluze of *le Réveil* and Alphonse Peyrat of *l'Avenir national* under the general security law. Though the two editors were found guilty, their trial on November 13, 1868, served as another sounding board for Republican intransigence.[46]

Beginning in 1868 the government also allowed many more public meetings where social and economic questions were discussed by a great variety of liberal and radical speakers. Orthodox liberal economists like Jean-Gustave Courcelle-Seneuil, Jean-Jules Clamageran, Frédéric Passy, and Henri Cernuschi, all Republicans, defended the right to private property and proclaimed the legitimacy of interest. Jérôme Langlois, the disciple of Proudhon, often spoke, as did Louis Tolain; and the communists were represented in their various systems by men like Gustave Lefrançais and J.–B. Millière. Whatever their differences, they were men of the Opposition, irreconcilable to the Empire.[47]

That Empire was on the verge of even more far-reaching reforms that would gratify and reconcile more moderate members of the Opposition, but not those whose principles shunned all compromise. "We are told," wrote Henri Rochefort in mid-1868, "that the early heat from which we are suffering may be attributed to the presence of a comet not yet perfectly visible. It is common knowledge that in all epochs the appearance of a comet has preceded a great event. I am only waiting for one particular great event in the world, but I have so little luck! You will see that it will not occur this year." [48] Given the actual strength of the regime, Rochefort's pessimism was justifiable, but the "great event" was closer upon them than the irreconcilables dared to hope.

46. Weill, *Le Parti républicain*, pp. 500–506.
47. Weill, *Le Mouvement social*, pp. 122–123.
48. *La Lanterne*, #5, June 27, 1868.

TWO

The Revolutionary

Situation

France has thirty-six million subjects, not counting the subjects of discontent. —*Henri Rochefort*

———————————————————————————

THE REESTABLISHMENT of Empire in 1852, widely held to be the restoration of public order, contributed to making the reign of Napoleon III an era of business confidence and industrial prosperity. France had not experienced the transformation to an industrial economy during the first half of the nineteenth century, but after 1848 the rate of industrial growth was spectacular and reached its peak before 1859. Thus, with both an established agriculture and a booming industry, France under the Second Empire was the wealthiest of the continental nations.[1] The revolutionary situation was rooted in this good fortune, promising paradise just around the corner, but fulfilling the promise for the few and providing compensatory crumbs for the many. Only where there is no hope are burdens silently borne, but ignite great expectations and anger often flares as hopes become dimmed.

This new enthusiasm for industrialization was by no means universally shared in France, and historians of France commonly

1. Rondo E. Cameron, "French Finance and Italian Unity: The Cavourian Decade," *American Historical Review*, LXII (April 1957), 552.

and correctly picture the French backing reluctantly into the twentieth century [2] as if to conduct a rear-guard defense of individualism and rusticity against the advance of the machine and the anonymity of urban factory work. Science was fine as long as its application was philosophical or anti-Catholic, but became sullied if harnessed to promote technology. Perhaps such an attitude was easier to maintain in a country where the population increase was tiny and the humane uses of technology were not widely perceived, leaving exposed only the abuses of early industrialism. Other factors, too, are cited to account for the retarded modernization of France: the limited supplies of coal, for example, and the morselization of the land rather than enclosure. Despite notable economic growth in the nineteenth century, the economy of France, when compared to that of Britain or Germany, reveals relative economic stagnation.[3]

Capital for economic development was not lacking, but an amazing proportion of it was exported. Under the Second Empire capital exports amounted to roughly twelve billion francs, somewhere between one-third and one-half of net savings; and this was accompanied by an equally large outflow of industrial and organizational skills, mainly to continental nations. Such a proportional outflow has never been exceeded by any capital exporting nation,[4] but the negative aspects of this prosperous performance are immediately evident. Available capital was neither being invested at home to expand the national economy nor to create jobs.

Those who favored industrialization, railway building, and the modernization of Paris made the question of raising capital more complex by their willingness to indulge in unorthodox methods. Saint-Simonian in origin, the new finance was, in a very

2. Lynn M. Case, *French Opinion on War and Diplomacy During the Second Empire*, Philadelphia: University of Pennsylvania Press, 1954, p. 274.

3. Rondo E. Cameron, "Economic Growth and Stagnation in France, 1815–1914," *Journal of Modern History*, XXX (March 1958), 1–13. Charles P. Kindelberger, *Economic Growth in France and Britain 1851–1950*, Cambridge: Harvard University Press, 1964, pp. 324–332.

4. Rondo E. Cameron, "The Crédit Mobilier and the Economic Development of Europe," *Journal of Political Economy*, LXI (December 1953), 461. Also see his *France and the Economic Development of Europe 1800–1914*, 2nd ed., Chicago: Rand McNally, 1965, pp. 51–68.

elementary way, Keynesian. Before 1848, the Bank of France was the only significant financial institution operating under a corporate charter and enjoying complete limited liability. Ordinary banking functions were carried on by a group of conservative, private bankers known collectively as *la haute banque*, many of them also regents of the Bank of France, the central bank of issue. As a group they were less than enthusiastic about industrialization and represented what was then called sound finance, meaning balanced budgets in particular.[5]

After 1848 and notably under the Second Empire, new corporate banks were chartered for both commercial and investment banking. Heavy borrowing and investment by private individuals and government against long-term profits and increased tax returns amounted to the promotion of industrialization and public works, along with the creation of jobs. The Emperor was such a promoter and earned the enmity and distrust of *la haute banque*. Some of the new institutions were lending agencies founded by the government, others private institutions encouraged by the government. The first was the Comptoir d'Escompte (1848), largely a commercial bank. Then, in 1852, the government founded the Crédit Foncier de France, a land bank to provide cheap credit for rural improvements, which soon expanded into municipal development, including the transformation of Paris.

The best-known of the new banks was the Crédit Mobilier, a private investment bank given its charter by Napoleon on November 18, 1852, shortly before the proclamation of Empire. Its promoters were Emile and Isaac Péreire, former Saint-Simonians, and they were backed by a major investor, B.–L. Fould et Fould-Oppenheim, between them controlling about 60 per cent of the initial capital invested. The Rothschilds, pillars of *la haute banque*, did not buy in, and for the first decade of the Second Empire, the Crédit Mobilier dominated French finance. Its profits were spectacular, paying 30 per cent dividends the first year; and in 1855 the bank earned thirty-one million francs on a capital investment of sixty million.[6]

5. Dennis W. Brogan, *The French Nation from Napoleon to Pétain 1814–1940,* New York: Harper and Row, 1963, pp. 125–130.
6. Cameron, "Crédit Mobilier," pp. 462–464.

The reaction against the new finance made itself felt in the second decade of the Empire when His Majesty felt obliged to placate the conservative financial interests, outraged anew by his low tariff treaty with Britain; and because the liberalizing of the Empire meant the increasing subjugation of the imperial budget to parliamentary committee. Regardless of party, the gentlemen of the *Corps législatif* favored orthodox finance and a reduction in government spending. The appointment of Achille Fould, not to be confused with the Fould above, as Minister of Finance in 1861, a friend of the Rothschilds and of sound finance,[7] simply meant a reduction in the rate of economic development. It is probably not mere coincidence that one can date the rise of worker hostility to the Empire from that moment. The Péreire brothers gradually lost their preeminence and were faced with new competition, first in 1863 with the founding of the Crédit Lyonnais by a group of bankers from Lyon and Geneva; and then in 1864 when the Rothschilds backed the new Société Générale. Despite this apparent reconciliation between the Empire and orthodox business and banking, the Emperor was compromised in their eyes as a Saint-Simonian. Having favored by and large his dictatorship in the name of order in 1851, they soon came to see parliamentarianism as a necessary check upon the Emperor's social and economic ambitions.

If the Second Empire was an era of rapid economic development, it was also a period of rapidly rising prices, in part stimulated by the increase in world gold production of which France received a disproportionate share, thanks to an export surplus between 1852 and 1866. In the general increase in the national wealth, wages lagged behind prices, so that in fact a redistribution of income in favor of the propertied classes was in progress.[8] The poor were getting richer, but the rich were getting much richer. When Napoleon III signed a commercial treaty with Great Britain in 1860, ignoring the protectionist majority in the *Corps législatif,* he subjected French business to British competition and promoted the concentration of French industry. Con-

---

7. Louis Girard, *La Politique des travaux publics du Second Empire,* Paris: Armand Colin, 1951, p. 273.
8. Cameron, "French Finance," p. 553.

sequently, French industrialists lowered wages to meet the competition. Many inefficient enterprises were forced to close their doors, and many workers experienced bitterly hard times. Their desire to stem falling wages was in large measure responsible for their willingness to join their British counterparts in the International in 1864.

Economic troubles worsened in 1862 with the interruption of raw cotton from the American South during the Civil War, but, aside from the cotton industry, French employers really had much less to complain about than their employees. The treaty caused uneasiness and inconvenience, but the figures on French industrial production reveal that the treaty stimulated rather than retarded production, leading to great profits in the 1860s. This is not to say that French business saw the light and thanked the author of their new prosperity: they remained protectionist in economic philosophy while reaping the benefits of the freer trade and remained aggrieved that the treaty had been signed despite their opposition. Thus their political attitude paralleled that of the financiers, an uneasiness, a pessimism entirely unwarranted by economic realities, prophets of doom when profits were high, yet confident that they were the practical men of affairs and the Emperor a visionary. Their loss of confidence certainly affected business expansion by 1865 and contributed to the export of investment capital.[9]

A recent study of French workers' attitudes toward the Second Empire shows that they were not constant. In the early period of the Empire, 1852–1858, workers in general seemed to be neutral: they neither rallied enthusiastically to the Empire nor manifested much open opposition. Beginning in 1859 and lasting until about 1863, the Empire enjoyed its most widespread labor support. This was the period of labor's greatest prosperity, and the workers in general supported the reforms opening the shift toward the Liberal Empire and the policy of assisting suppressed nationalities.[10] This middle period was also the time

9. Georges Duveau, *La Vie ouvrière en France sous le Second Empire,* Paris: Gallimard, 1946, pp. 117–123.
10. David I. Kulstein, "The Attitude of French Workers Towards the Second Empire," *French Historical Studies,* II (Spring 1962) , 360–367.

when a significant, if small, number of officials, journalists, and employers made their concern to improve the lot of workers most evident—just as it was the moment before the Emperor's compromise to retain the confidence of financiers and employers seemed to betray his well-known solicitude for the poor.

The greatest student of French social problems after mid-century was surely the sociologist-engineer Frédéric Le Play, whom the Emperor held in great esteem, though not agreeing with all of Le Play's ideas. A governmental engineer, Le Play spent his vacations for nearly a quarter of a century traveling about Europe in search of material on the social condition of the working classes. He was first encouraged to publish his materials, emphasizing the social problems facing France, by the Minister of the Navy and War François Arago in 1848; but the first edition of his massive work, *Les Ouvriers Européens,* was not ready until 1855, when it was published by the Imperial Printery.[11]

Le Play was a Catholic who had no use for the "false dogmas" of 1789. He saw the Revolution as having advanced the rights of the individual at the expense of the rights of the family, and he believed that the family was the most essential unit in the nation.[12] By mid-century, the beginning of the industrialization was seen by many observers and moralists as the beginning of the breakup of workers' family life, which most of them, whether of worker or bourgeois background, deplored. Some more revolutionary observers, it is true, were pleased that industry would loosen family ties, which they saw as the preparation for a less confining moral order. If mothers were to be employed in factories, their children would have to get their primary education in the public schools, presumably a lay education in place of religious instruction.[13] But Napoleon III, if unable to deny the dogmas of 1789, desired to learn from Le Play and sought his support toward social reforms to preserve the family and paternal authority in particular, an authority which was consistent with his own role in French government.

11. Frédéric Le Play, *Les Ouvriers Européens,* 2nd ed., Tours: A. Mame, 1877–1879, I, 42.
12. Georges Weill, *Le Mouvement social en France, 1852–1910,* Paris: Alcan, 1911, pp. 23–24.
13. Duveau, *op. cit.,* pp. 434–436.

In 1855, he appointed Le Play to the Council of State and entrusted the direction of the Exhibition that year to him. Three years later, after the Emperor and Morny recommended social reforms to the Privy Council based upon *Les Ouvriers Européens,* His Majesty asked Le Play to expose his ideas in an abbreviated book form—since the original work comprised six volumes—more practical for popular reading, for the Emperor had discovered little interest in, or comprehension of, social problems among those in his entourage. The requested volume, *La Réforme sociale en France* (1864), failed to impress a parliamentary majority already dubious about the Emperor's schemes and not of a mind to increase paternal authority. When Le Play dined at St. Cloud in November of 1869, he saw the coming changes in the governmental climate and predicted that the Emperor would soon succeed in pushing social reform. The Emperor, on the other hand, recognized indifference and prejudice on all sides and did not expect much progress in his lifetime, leading Le Play to criticize the Emperor for his "benevolent timidity" in not putting more pressure on his servants.[14]

We have already noted the imperial assistance to get workers to London for the Exhibition in 1862. A committee of ten workers, encouraged by Prince Jerome-Napoleon, developed a plan to provide for the election of a delegation of workers to be drawn from the different trades; and between July 19 and October 15 about two hundred workers, in small groups, made the trip to London. Upon their return, they prepared and published reports of what they had seen, which constitute the first real *"cahiers de doléances"* of the Parisian working class in the nineteenth century. In sum, they had found better working conditions in Britain and thus complained of long hours, low wages, and high prices in France; and the one consistent reason they cited for better conditions in Britain was the workers' right to combine and discuss their grievances on an equal legal basis with employers. French workers must obtain the right to form combinations, they concluded, and not a few added the prediction that strikes would soon become a feature of the French labor scene. Many asked for a ten-hour day, saying that if better working conditions

14. Le Play, *op. cit.,* I, 43–45.

were not soon realized in France the better workers would emigrate. Despite these grievances, there were numerous patriotic, even chauvinistic, phrases in the *cahiers,* leaving no one the right to question the loyalty of the workers.[15]

The length of the working day under the Second Empire depended upon industry and region; but if one had to generalize, the rule would be an average of eleven hours a day in Paris and an average of twelve hours a day in the provinces. Quite evidently the miners endured the longest hours, sometimes being kept working underground for extra hours without extra pay. Most workers did not work on Sundays, though this was not without exception; and in several industries workers preferred to have Mondays off, the reasons for this not being clear.[16] Recent research confirms the French workers' observations that British workers enjoyed somewhat better working conditions in that era, but adds that the French workers enjoyed notably better health. Since industrialization had begun earlier in Britain, the British had by 1850 gone through the worst phases of unregulated factory-town life and were taking steps to ameliorate the lot of workers. At the same time, British workers were by then the physical products of several generations of factory-town life, whereas most French factory workers still got a heartier start in the rural areas before seeking work in towns.

Working conditions in France began to improve after 1850, sometimes because of technical inventions which spared laborers the most arduous tasks, and in some cases because of improved sanitary conditions. In the first years of the Second Empire, a miner at Anzin was considered beyond usefulness by age forty, whereas by the end of Napoleon's reign it was not unusual for miners to be able to work until the age fifty. All studies of mining conditions and mortality rates make it quite plain that working and health conditions in the 1850s and 1860s were superior to what they had been under the July Monarchy. On the other hand, humane conditions had not been achieved; labor remained fatiguing, unhealthful, and dangerous, and not simply in the mines. The textile industries, for instance, required

15. Weill, *op. cit.,* pp. 60–67.
16. Duveau, *op. cit.,* pp. 239–243.

temperatures and liquids which were dangerous and debilitating; and industries generally took few measures to protect workers from moving machinery.[17]

Once improvements were evidently possible, the labor movement reflected increasing dissatisfaction that reforms were not coming fast enough. This irritation coincided with the economic dislocations following the commercial treaty with Britain, the gradual decline in investor confidence, and the decline in real wages. In finding itself forced to make gestures toward those favoring "sound finance" in the 1860s, the imperial government also sought to prove that it was not abandoning labor. But industrial workers began turning away from the regime and, as noted earlier, governmental candidates generally lost out to Opposition candidates in towns of over 40,000 in the elections of 1863.

The following year the Emperor, supported by his half-brother the Duc de Morny, presented new labor legislation designed to modify the restrictive provisions of the Chapelier Law of 1791 which had been incorporated into the Napoleonic Code. Morny persuaded Emile Ollivier, an original member of *les Cinq,* to become the reporter for the legislation. They proposed to repeal the article in the Code in which the word of an employer took precedence over that of an employee in a legal dispute; and they proposed to allow workers the right to form coalitions, if not unions, giving workers in coalition the right to strike for "justifiable grievances" so long as they avoided violence and did not use the strike for political ends. Coalition meant a temporary organization with a specific grievance in mind, and the regime hoped that this expedient would serve to improve working conditions without admitting the principle of unions that could call forth the determined opposition of business and industry.

The reforms passed easily, thanks to official pressure from the Emperor and Morny, then presiding officer of the *Corps législatif;* but the reaction to them revealed how difficult it had become, by 1864, for the regime to arouse anything but resentment. Since the new law prohibited unions, much of labor was

17. *Ibid.,* pp. 270–280.

more resentful for what had not yet been granted than grateful for what had just been given, while the conservative Bonapartists were furious at the Emperor for allowing the bill at all and gave him no credit for avoiding permanent labor unions. Eugène Rouher, their leading figure, remarked that apparently the Emperor had just joined the International. The parliamentary Republicans, equally annoyed that one of their own had publicly joined the government on the issue, claimed the bill was inadequate. But Ollivier, suspecting the futility of systematic opposition, preferred to take what was possible rather than to dwell upon the impossible. It marked his public break with the Left.

A small faction of the labor movement, however, remained loyal to the Emperor. It included some of the most intelligent and class-conscious workers, as well as some of the Parisian artisans who were apt to be the heart of any insurrection. They accepted Bonapartism at its face value—as a regime of revolutionary origin which was above class or party interest—because it sought to reconcile the warring factions in France; because the Emperor seemed not to rule simply for the bourgeoisie, as was the case of the older parties; and because too many of the parliamentary Republicans seemed bourgeois in their social and economic outlook. Furthermore, the Second Empire demonstrated a sensitivity to public opinion unknown to earlier regimes, giving promise that it would respond to demands to complete the half-realized social reforms.[18] The Emperor knew that he had this minority support and continued to ponder further reforms despite his recognition of the odds against them. He wished to abolish the *livret,* the workman's certificate which all workers resented having to carry, but which the *Corps législatif* wished to retain; and, at the time of the outbreak of the war in 1870, he had his long-time friend, Hortense Cornu, working on a plan to experiment with profit-sharing for workers in the mining industry.[19]

The antigovernmental attitude of the majority of workers after the reforms of 1864, however shortsighted it might seem in

18. Kulstein, *op. cit.,* pp. 368–375.

19. Hendrik N. Boon, *Rêve et realité dans l'oeuvre économique et sociale de Napoléon III,* The Hague: Martinus Nijhoff, 1936, pp. 157–162.

retrospect, seemed justified at the time, not merely because the reforms fell short of worker aspirations, but because legislation which did exist was often not effectively enforced by either employers or government officials. And when there was labor agitation, army officers seemed only too eager to engage in a pitiless repression in the name of order. Industrial accidents, particularly accidents in mines, if less frequent than under the July Monarchy, were still all too common; and management, which did so little to protect workers from accidents, too easily concluded that the imprudence of the miners or the normal risk of the mines were the causes of most accidents. While it had become general to establish funds for those widowed by accidents, retirement funds were practically unknown. The workers themselves, between 1864 and 1870, sometimes organized mutual aid groups to provide retirement funds beyond company control.[20]

Both management and government tried to meet growing labor hostility by providing instruction in liberal economics for workers. The intention was to demonstrate the benefits of competition and the free economy, to combat socialism and unionism, and, particularly after 1864, to show the proper use of the strike. Such efforts largely failed, partly because workers tended to suspect instruction from above.[21] But what must these men, notoriously hardworking for little return, have concluded about instruction which sought to prove that the solution to their poverty was harder work and a life devoid of vice! To their credit, they remained unconvinced.

This question of worker morality was a lively issue in the later nineteenth century. It was common to assume that industrialization was a moral disaster, not only because it could lead to the vulgarization of French civilization, but because it was presumably leading to the degradation of workers and increasing class consciousness and hostility. Family discipline and instruction evaporated as mothers went to the factories where they were exposed to debauchery, ill fitting them to teach their children the

20. Fernand L'Huillier, *La Lutte ouvrière à la fin du Second Empire*, Paris: Colin, 1957, pp. 11-15.
21. David I. Kulstein, "Economics Instruction for Workers During the Second Empire," *French Historical Studies*, I (1959), pp. 225-233.

benefits of virtue that the social order presumably requires. These concerns of that day have been preserved for us by the greatest literary descriptions of life under the Second Empire, which were portraits in unrelieved black. Charles Baudelaire and Emile Zola, for instance, painted much darker pictures of life in the 1850s and 1860s than Balzac and Eugène Sue have left us of life in the 1840s.

Immediately after the fall of the Second Empire, Zola sketched out a series of twenty novels through which he intended to describe all aspects of life under the fallen regime: *Les Rougon-Macquart, histoire naturelle et sociale d'une famille sous le second empire,* which he completed in 1893. Many of the social and moral conditions of that era which Zola portrayed were undoubtedly wretched, but he ignored happier situations which also existed. Zola was similar to those employers and officials of the time who described drunkenness, libertinism, and crime in such a way as to make it appear that all abuses and all perversities were the possession of all workers. Their class presumably knew all the vices and none of the virtues. Let the workers expel vice from their homes if they would reap the material advantages of virtue!

No doubt it is too much to expect perfect objectivity from a generation of writers who found the Second Empire and its promotion of economic expansion objectionable. These literary descriptions are not confirmed by recent scholarship, which suggests that the moral condition of the workers in general improved— especially during the 1860s—over what it had been in the time of Balzac. This improvement was seen by some writers, most of them long forgotten, who had a more balanced view of reality than Zola. Even Victor Hugo, for all his hostility to the regime, saw Parisian worker life more fairly than Zola, as did Denis Poulot in his *Question sociale, Le Sublime, ou le Travailleur comme il est en* 1870, a study published in 1872.[22] What was revolutionary about the workers' situation was not its total depravity, but its improvement and the hope for even greater advances.

And the workers could be irritated because the bourgeois

22. Duveau, *op. cit.,* pp. 527–535.

were advancing financially even more rapidly and because the financial discrepancies promoted a growing rift between workers and bourgeois. The rift was not so much a matter of money as a matter of attitude. Michel Chevalier, the Saint-Simonian who negotiated the commercial treaty of 1860 for the Emperor, complained that "an abyss separates the bourgeois from the peasant and the worker. . . . The bourgeois feels nothing in common with the proletarian. It is convenient to regard him as a machine that one rents, by which one is served, and that one pays only so long as he is needed. On the other hand, in the eyes of a great number of proletarians, the bourgeois is the enemy, whose superiority is accepted only because he is the stronger." [23]

An earlier tradition would have it that this rift was the creation of the Second Empire or, more specifically, of Napoleon's and Baron Haussmann's plans for Paris. We are given a quaint picture of pre-reconstruction Paris, a city with a few quarters where bourgeois or workers lived exclusively, but where most workers and bourgeois lived in the same houses—the bourgeois occupying the first- and second-floor flats while the workers occupied the smaller, less expensive apartments of the upper stories. Such cohabitation was supposed to have blurred class distinctions while the constant familiarity personalized class relations. Then came the modernists to pollute this fraternity. Their improvements raised the price of lodgings in the heart of the city, forcing the workers toward the *faubourgs*. The dislocations not only left bitter memories, but separated workers from bourgeoisie; and once separated physically the workers developed myths about bourgeois life which were both unrealistic and antagonistic.[24] This tradition, unchallenged by either common sense, sophistication, or the memory of class hatred in 1848, has persisted until very recent times when the notion of neighborhood solidarity, with the poorer neighbors helped out by the richer, has been demolished.[25]

23. Edouard Dolléans, "Vie et pensée ouvrières entre 1848 et 1871," *Revue historique*, 197–198 (July–September 1947) , 68.
24. Duveau, *op. cit.*, pp. 206–207; and Dolléans, *op. cit.*, p. 68.
25. David H. Pinkney, *Napoleon III and the Rebuilding of Paris*, Princeton: Princeton University Press, 1958, pp. 8–9.

It is true, of course, that the reconstruction of Paris forced up rents and that many workers moved to the *faubourgs* that were annexed to Paris in 1860; and no doubt the conservative Baron Haussmann believed that the expulsion of industry and workers from the heart of Paris was desirable, both for political and aesthetic reasons.[26] On the other hand, he also desired to destroy slums, to create parks and open spaces, to improve the water supply and sewage disposal, and, though his critics have rarely realized it, to make the city more beautiful. His work was made unexpectedly difficult by the increase of the municipal population during the reconstruction. The natural increase was not large, but the annexation of the *faubourgs* and provincial immigration to Paris nearly doubled the population. Most of the immigrants were young, poor workers. Their presence was irritating to many Parisians, not to speak of the fact that they were potential revolutionaries.[27]

Haussmann's record was mixed. He did destroy slums, but the government failed to provide controls to prevent the rise of new slums, both in the old city and in the peripheral quarters where so many of the slum-dwellers moved. Building regulations were probably too much concerned with the appearance of buildings—with their maintenance and cleaning. In his water program, Haussmann more than doubled the supply available *per capita;* still, by 1870 more than half the city's houses lacked water, suggesting that his regulations had failed to provide more equitable use of the water he was providing. The sewage disposal system was greatly improved, which meant that the pollution of the Seine was greatly reduced.[28]

On balance the record was a notable one, perhaps the most durable achievement of the Second Empire. Yet it fed both the revolutionary spirit and situation. The need for the reconstruction was so obvious that many of Haussmann's critics limited themselves to attacks upon the financing of it, calling the financial burdens not merely onerous but of doubtful legality.[29] As

26. Theodore Zeldin, *The Political System of Napoleon III*, London: Macmillan, 1958, pp. 76-77.
27. Pinkney, *op. cit.*, pp. 151-154.
28. *Ibid.*, pp. 93 and 126.
29. Girard, *op. cit.*, p. 400.

for the rifts in society that had existed before the Second Empire and which were deepening because of the redistribution of wealth under the Empire, no doubt they were widened by the expulsion of the workers to the *faubourgs*. On the other hand, it is impossible to calculate to what degree the hard times and the hard feelings were exacerbated by the fortuitous immigration, increasing the competition for workers' jobs and for rentals. In 1862 Haussmann estimated the population of Paris to be about 1,700,000, and of those about 1,070,000 to be in a state of real poverty. Since the total worker population of the city would have been between 1,250,000 and 1,300,000, it simply meant that very few laboring families escaped real indigence. Given the increasing wealth of the upper classes, the figures reflected the seriousness of the social problem.[30]

The government experienced general opposition in a new form following the battle of Sadowa in 1866, when Prusia unexpectedly emerged as a powerful military state. Through its procurers-general, the government knew that public opinion favored greater military preparedness, but opposed any idea of general conscription, something the French had not been subject to since 1814. After that date, the army had been fixed at 240,000 men, to be recruited as a professional force, and a limited draft law was passed to provide auxiliaries. The size of the army and the annual contingents of conscripts were occasionally modified, but the professional system remained in principle as of 1866. The Emperor, as heir to the military principles of the Revolution and Empire, preferred a system of universal military training, especially when he began to take seriously the improvement of the Prussian army in the 1860s; and he estimated that the trained men available for service, as regulars and reserves, ought to total 800,000. Such an increase meant general conscription and after Sadowa there was widespread fear in France that the government would introduce it. Indeed, the procurers-general reports implied that general conscription would endanger the popularity and the stability of the regime.[31]

The limited draft then in effect was highly inequitable but

30. Duveau, *op. cit.,* pp. 216–217.
31. Gordon Wright, "Public Opinion and Conscription in France, 1866–1870," *Journal of Modern History,* XIV (1942) , 28–30.

generally popular. Of the annual class eligible for conscription, generally fewer than 15 per cent were called up—and many of them were excused for physical disabilities or family obligations and could not be replaced. Thus the system produced fewer than 20,000 recruits a year. The remainder of the class was legally exempt and could not be called up even in time of war. Since upper-class and bourgeois conscripts could purchase substitutes under the system, and many urban workers evaded service through physical disability or family obligation, the army received its conscripts largely from the peasantry. Therein lay the system's popularity. Even the peasants favored it because of the likelihood of drawing a "good number" in the draft.[32]

For some months the Emperor delayed pursuing the necessary military reforms in deference to public opinion. When a compromise proposal, the Niel bill, was made public in 1867, it was coldly received. Its opponents, especially the Republicans, recalled the successful tactics of Valmy and accused the Emperor of plotting war. Again the Emperor delayed pushing the bill, hoping to make its need better understood by the public as well as to allay fears that he might be planning a war. Bonapartist legislators were as opposed to conscription as the Republicans, fearing that Opposition candidates would greatly benefit in coming elections. What was left of the government's proposal passed the *Corps législatif* early in 1868, and its effectiveness may be measured by the fact that France had a mere 60,000 trained reservists by midsummer 1870. Instead of the 800,000 men the Emperor had hoped for, the army would number about 300,000 at the opening of the war. As a military reform the Niel bill proved to be of negligible value, but it was a source of political weakness contributing to the decline of the Empire.[33]

The year 1869 proved to be the year of strikes. Contemporaries were inclined to call these strikes "unexpected," either because they were biased against the workers or because they had been indifferent to the growing labor ferment after 1864. In those years, despite the Emperor's concern for industrial condi-

32. Richard D. Challener, *The French Theory of the Nation in Arms 1866–1939*, New York: 2nd ed., Russell & Russell, 1965, p. 18.
33. Wright, "Public Opinion," pp. 33–45.

tions, his officials tended to share the employers' preoccupation with order, reinforcing employer resistance to the demands of workers. All the while there had been developing in the labor movement after 1864 a new sense of confidence and strength and a new sensitivity to the plight of fellow workers. The clash between blind intransigence and the frustration of these laborers produced acts of violence in 1869—in Paris, in Lyon, in Carmaux, and in the mines of Aubin, culminating in the strike at Le Creusot in 1870. At Aubin soldiers threatened by the strikers fired into a mob, killing fourteen and wounding about twenty,[34] a catastrophe for the Empire.

During the strike at Le Creusot, some workers were heard to shout for the Republic, and the strike committee openly adhered to the International. But as their employer, Eugène Schneider, was then presiding officer of the *Corps législatif,* one cannot be sure how many of the shouts for the Republic were really republican and how many were meant to intimidate Schneider. Looking at electoral results for that industrial arrondissement in 1869 and 1870, one could conclude that there was not yet any mass profession of faith in republicanism amongst the workers. On the other hand, the number of workers who voted in 1869 but abstained in 1870 meant that the Empire could not count on the workers with any confidence.[35] Industrial workers, however, were a tiny slice of the French population, and the general electoral results of 1870, favoring the regime seven to one, proved that Napoleon III, after twenty years of power, still enjoyed the loyalty of the masses.[36]

34. Pierre de la Gorce, *Histoire du Second Empire,* Paris: Plon, 1894–1905, V, 508–509.
35. L'Huillier, *op. cit.,* 47–74.
36. Duveau, *op. cit.,* p. 56.

THREE *Liberal Empire: Prelude to Revolution*

The history of England cries out to kings: March at the head of the ideas of your century and these ideas will follow and support you. March behind them, and they will drag you after them. March against them, and they will overthrow you. —*Louis-Napoleon (on William III)*

I F ONE REDUCES the traditional notions about the Second Empire to a few generalities, the following outline appears: A *coup d'état* in 1851 established a presidential dictatorship that was converted into Empire the next year. This regime, the first modern police state, made an echo of Parliament and destroyed all political opposition through prosecution and censorship, but catered to public opinion with promises of prosperity and grandeur. Beginning in 1860, the government endeavored to silence mounting criticism of the autocracy by granting political concessions. But each concession simply swelled the opportunity for criticism until, by 1870, the Emperor had shorn himself of authority without materially placating the Opposition. His defeat and capture at Sedan merely facilitated the destruction of his discredited and doomed regime.

These traditional generalities have been reduced to half-truths at best in recent years—especially after 1945 when the Second Empire enjoyed a revival of historical interest. No doubt the shocking collapse of the Third Republic in 1940 produced reconsiderations of its political and moral record, and the clichés of the Third Republic about its predecessor were called into question. And certainly the emergence of General Charles de Gaulle, representing both strong executive authority and the traditions of 1789, has conjured up the image and institutions of Napoleon III.

Of all the ambiguities that can be found in the politics of the Second Empire, there was one in which all the others were rooted. The existence of the Second Empire and its institutions obviously depended upon those of the First Empire, and both regimes were accepted by the French in the name of order after a period of revolutionary dislocation and change. Yet the Second Empire was no mere restoration of the First, because the second Emperor was more progressive and more humane than the first. More than a generation separated the "crowned Jacobin" from "Saint-Simon on horseback." While founding a naked dictatorship, Napoleon III publicly insisted that authoritarianism was a temporary expedient. "Liberty," he said, "has never helped to found a lasting political edifice; it crowns the edifice when time has consolidated it." [1] How much time that consolidation would require was unspecified, and opinion varied then, as ever since, as to whether the liberal concessions after 1860 were sops to hostile opinion or the gradual crowning of the edifice.

Opposition political cartoons of that day often pictured the Emperor as a mustached eagle grasping the bloodied body of France in its talons, gore dripping from the curved Napoleonic beak; his entourage a menagerie featuring avaricious, stupid, and serpentine beasts. While some writers, even recently, seriously advanced the idea that had not that era patronized Offenbach, the outcome of the War of 1870 would have been different. The success of the Republican Opposition in portraying Paris as a gaslit Gomorrah was such that during the siege of Paris in 1870 Prussian officers were astonished to discover that French husbands and wives were as devoted to one another as their virtuous Prussian counterparts. Ludovic Halévy remembered reading an item in a Cologne newspaper late in 1870 about the arrival of

1. Theodore Zeldin, *The Political System of Napoleon III*, London: Macmillan, 1958, p. 102.

Princess Murat at Wilhelmshöhe to visit the imprisoned Napoeon III, and the great surprise of the Germans that she was not a *cocodette,* but dressed simply and behaving like a proper woman, something, from their reading of French realistic novels, they believed to be impossible in a French woman. "The fault belongs to those of us who write," he noted, "and also to the public that reads us." [2] Indeed one almost hates to insist, for fear of disappointing the reader, that the legends of the political and moral horrors of the Second Empire are a bit too lurid. And like Halévy we must wonder why the public prefers stories about people who resemble it the least!

Consider, to begin with, the tradition of the authoritarian Empire as a police state: Even though Napoleon III's assumption of dictatorial power was generally welcomed in France, he knew perfectly well that important political factions furiously resented the *coup d'état* by which he consolidated all executive, legislative, and judicial initiative in himself. Most everyone knew that the Republic of 1848 was already imperiled by its unsatisfactory constitution and that a monarchical restoration was a distinct possibility. Napoleon, in fact, presented himself not as tyrant, but as tyrannicide, pointing his finger at the Royalists, but not consoling or placating the Republicans—for he was the one man who had sworn to uphold the constitution that he had suppressed.[3] Expecting vigorous opposition from both Left and Right, the new regime supplemented its censorship of the press with "extraordinary" police measures.

Political police were a legacy of the First Empire to all the regimes governing France after 1815. Police theory was based on the idea that public administration was an exclusive prerogative of the executive in his responsibility for the maintenance of order and security. Thus the police function included what we could call political duties: the intention was to defend the integrity of the centralized state, subjecting local life to Parisian control, and to promote order even at the expense of liberty. We have already noted that the censorship, arbitrary as it was, de-

2. Ludovic Halévy, *Notes et Souvenirs, 1871–72,* Paris: Calmann Lévy, 1889, p. 272.
3. J. P. T. Bury, *France 1814–1940,* New York: A. S. Barnes, 1962, pp. 88–89.

pended more upon legislation already on the books than it did upon the legislation of 1852. Indeed, press prosecutions between 1852 and 1860, the more arbitrary period of the Second Empire, were fewer in number than under Louis Philippe or the Second Republic. Similarly, the Second Empire innovated very little in police practice. Extraordinary police measures were taken after the *coup d'état* of December 2, 1851, but on March 27, 1852, the President ordered the police not to make any more arrests or prosecutions "except in conformity with the laws." [4]

Even the secret police were not notably increased in number over the previous regimes. Opponents of the regime then and since protested the omnipresence of secret agents, a protest based not upon actual fact but upon an assumption that the dictatorship required them. And, except for the moment of the *coup d'état* and its immediate aftermath, there is little evidence of police brutality. As a police state, the Second Empire fell far short of the twentieth century,[5] its strength based not upon its police but upon the consent of the governed.

Undoubtedly suppressed in 1852 were the powers of the legislature. Yet, in granting a legislature at the outset of the regime, it was only a matter of time before such a body would demand greater responsibility, especially in the control of finances. What Napoleon III meant to destroy was not representative government, but parliamentarianism. Once the executive authority was established and respected to guarantee order in society and to represent the nation as a whole, in place of the squabbling factions he thought parliamentarianism implied, then the legislative liberties might safely be revived to support the executive. But he did not have in mind the British system (unless it be the system of William III) where the monarch reigns but does not rule.

A British-style government would have permitted only one faction at court and in the government at a time, and hence only

4. Howard C. Payne, "Theory and Practice of Political Police During the Second Empire in France," *Journal of Modern History*, III (March 1958), 14–18.

5. *Ibid.*, 19–23. Also see Payne's *The Police State of Louis Napoleon Bonaparte*, Seattle: University of Washington Press, 1966, pp. 274–288.

one policy. During the Second Empire two contradictory factions (authoritarian and liberal) always existed at court, and Napoleon never banished one or the other until 1870. He listened to both, in his conduct of personal government; and he had a well-known penchant for by-passing his ministers to correspond directly with ambassadors, officials, and journalists. Such a governing technique, reputed to have derived from his many years as a conspirator, perplexed observers at home and abroad. It also meant that the Empire was not exclusively authoritarian in its more arbitrary period, just as it confused and hampered the gradual drift toward liberalism in the '6os.[6]

Aside from the Emperor's stated intention to crown the edifice with liberty, the advantages of legislative cooperation were not long in appearing. Imperial expenditures for public works and the granting of subsidies for railway development provoked sharp criticism, while the economic devastation from the floods after the Crimean War and the depression of 1857 suggested the practicality of a greater financial cooperation with the deputies. The fact that the Emperor's ministers were not members of the *Corps législatif,* therefore not present to explain and defend imperial policies, was a liability seen by both the Duc de Morny, the presiding officer, and Gustave Rouland, a senator and Minister of Public Instruction.[7]

By 1860 the Emperor felt ready to make needed changes in his system, and one can see a variety of factors which indicate why the first liberal measures were inaugurated that year. In the first place, initiative belonged to him because of his unusually strong position both at home and abroad, so that he could move from strength rather than from weakness. Having helped to bring liberty to the Romanians and the Italians, it seemed consistent to be its champion at home; while the territorial acquisitions born of the Italian intervention lent luster to the dynastic prestige. Had Napoleon III been authoritarian in spirit, he might well have employed his prestige to deepen the dictatorship. Instead he grasped the opportunity to liberalize the regime,

6. Pierre de la Gorce, *Histoire du Second Empire,* Paris: Plon, 1894–1905, IV, 603–605.
7. Zeldin, *op. cit.,* p. 103.

suggesting that he saw that course as the most promising way to consolidate the regime and insure the succession of his son.[8]

Some of the personal factors behind his decision, if more illusive, were no less important. Just as he had begun to seek more sincere support from the *Corps législatif,* so was he in need to escape from the awesome burdens of absolute power, for the signs of premature aging were unmistakable. He suffered from the isolation of his rank and from the failure, because of the dictatorship, to recruit the ablest statesmen in the realm. Only Morny was first-rate; but he was the Emperor's half-brother rather than a recruited politician. In a crisis Napoleon was alone, not even able to turn to his family for counsel or consolation.[9] The heir to the throne was only five; Prince Jerome-Napoleon, the Emperor's irresponsible and irrepressible cousin, was unreliable; while there were aspects of his marriage to Eugénie that he had considerable cause to regret.

The marriage had taken place in 1853 when he was forty-five and she twenty-seven. The age difference was less critical than the fact that the marriage united a devout and conservative Spanish Catholic with a liberal nonbeliever. Their first months together were seemingly passionate and caused embarrassment to some of the courtiers; and the Emperor was made joyful by the birth of the Prince Imperial in 1856. By then, however, her ardor had cooled, disturbing His Majesty and affecting his health.* He valued her as an ornament for the Empire, as she was a great beauty, and tried to ignore their differences in religion and politics; while she worked to preserve the imperial authority as her son's rightful inheritance. Theirs became a passionless but loyal relationship, that revived only after 1871, when Eugénie rediscovered to cherish in defeat those qualities of character which had won him the throne. Napoleon had a particularly bad time

---

8. *Ibid.,* pp. 104–108; and N. W. Senior, *Conversations with Distinguished Persons during the Second Empire from 1860 to 1863,* London: Hurst & Blackett, 1880, II, 115.

9. La Gorce, *op. cit.,* V, 37.

* Author's note: I am currently at work on a study of Napoleon III's health. This is not the place either for the details of his difficulties or for an estimate of their political effects. Suffice it to say that his deterioration was real and cause for his alarm.

with her in September 1860 after a state visit to Algeria, during which he felt compelled for reasons of their public obligations to conceal temporarily from her the death of her beloved sister Paca, the Duchess of Alba. She could not forgive him, suffered a terrible emotional storm, and fled briefly to Scotland in her grief and anger.[10] Only weeks later he signed the first of those decrees which produced the Liberal Empire and for which the Empress had so little sympathy.

One might argue that the "half-turn to the Left," to use Proudhon's words, which Napoleon made in November of 1860, had been forecast by the intervention in Italy the previous year, a venture on behalf of a subject nationality besides being anti-clerical. Then, early in 1860, came the low tariff treaty with Great Britain which was liberal in its emphasis on freer trade. But the first decree directed toward reviving legislative authority was that of November 24, 1860. It reestablished parliamentary right to respond to the speech from the throne, and reopened parliamentary debates to publicity. Henceforth, the ministers without portfolios were to be present in the *Corps législatif* to defend governmental projects in debate. Early in 1861 Emile Ollivier, leading light among *les Cinq*, thanked the Emperor for his "courage and generosity" in the course of a parliamentary speech, evidently attracted to Napoleon III because he seemed to be restoring representative, rather than true parliamentary, government. Since most of the younger Republicans had been converted to parliamentarianism after 1850 to combat the dictatorship, one can see in 1861 the beginning of the wedge which could ultimately split Ollivier from his colleagues.[11] A second legislative reform followed in 1861 when the Emperor granted the *Corps législatif* the right to vote the budget by sections, rather than *en bloc* as had been the case since 1852, a concession particularly to orthodox finance, so that it was a reform which appealed to conservatives and liberals alike.

10. T. A. B. Corley, *Democratic Despot, a Life of Napoleon III*, London: Barrie and Rockliff, 1961, p. 237; and Harold Kurtz, *The Empress Eugénie 1826–1920*, London: Hamish Hamilton, 1964, p. 153.
11. Theodore Zeldin, *Emile Ollivier and the Liberal Empire of Napoleon III*, London: Oxford, 1963, pp. 67–70.

After 1860 the imperial government also somewhat relaxed its attempt to manage parliamentary elections. Official candidates were still recognized and blessed by the government, but Opposition candidates were, for the first time, allowed to hold public meetings in every commune. Moreover, the mayors, who had been the chief instruments of governmental influence in towns and villages, were asked not to stand for parliamentary election, a disappointment for many that was reflected in a reduced zeal in backing the official candidates in their localities. The evidence is that this revival of political life particularly assisted local schoolmasters and priests, the former likely to campaign for Republicans because of their anticlericalism, the latter for non-Republican Opposition candidates in retaliation for the Emperor's Italian policy.[12]

We have already noted the gains made by Opposition candidates in the elections of 1863, when the total Opposition vote roughly doubled what it had been in 1857. At this late date it is difficult to know how much of that gain reflected a change in public opinion, how much of it owed to the greater liberty the Opposition enjoyed, or to what extent the electorate was offended by the clumsy electioneering of the Duc de Persigny, then Minister of the Interior, whose gerrymandering and purchase of votes certainly cost the government votes and who was removed from office several days after the election. The government, with 250 seats, was hardly in danger, but the Opposition had grown from five to thirty-two. To the authoritarian Bonapartists, the election results proved the folly of liberalizing the Empire, and their pressures upon the Emperor probably account for the postponement of further legislative reforms. Instead, he shifted his liberal program into different realms.

After 1860, when the Emperor needed relief from the cares of government, he sought relaxation in scholarship, something he had neglected since his imprisonment at Ham for an attempt on the July Monarchy in 1840; and, in the course of his researches for a life of Caesar, he was introduced to a substantial Roman historian, Victor Duruy. A scholar who had opposed the *coup*

12. Zeldin, *The Political System of Napoleon III*, pp. 92–95.

d'état, a liberal and an anticlerical, Duruy was shocked to discover that he had been named Minister of Public Instruction in 1863, without any prior consultation with the Emperor, a part of the cabinet shake-up following the elections. He decided to accept office only because he was being given a free hand in public education and inferred that the Emperor meant for him to promote a liberal and anticlerical program. For the six years of his ministry he struggled against clerical opinion and conservative finance, achieving less than he had hoped, but notably extending public education. The law of June 22, 1866 recognized the principle of free and *compulsory* primary education and required all communes of over five hundred inhabitants to maintain a primary school for girls, as the law of 1833 had provided for boys. He also worked to modernize the classical secondary schools and succeeded in founding a secondary curriculum emphasizing vocational training for students unable to benefit from the traditional curriculum. His attempt, in 1867, to extend secondary education to girls brought on a furious clerical attack that he survived only because of imperial support. In his memoirs, Duruy paid tribute to the Emperor's humane and liberal spirit: "Posterity will not be as unjust to Napoleon III as his immediate successors have been." [13]

The major liberal innovation of 1864 was the Coalitions Law, the labor reform for which Emile Ollivier served as the legislative reporter. For him to serve imperial legislation in such a manner was the last straw for many Republicans and, in fact, the Duc de Morny hoped to induce Ollivier to leave the Opposition and accept an official appointment. Ollivier was not prepared to do so, however, until a substantial liberal party, loyal to the regime, could be created in the *Corps législatif;* and the sudden death of Morny in March of 1865, removing the Emperor's chief liberal advisor and a remarkably effective politician in the *Corps législatif,* undoubtedly contributed to delaying the development of such a party for five years. His death was perhaps the most disastrous event experienced by the Second Empire in the

13. Roger L. Williams, *Gaslight and Shadow, The World of Napoleon III,* New York: Macmillan, 1957, pp. 213–226.

60's.[14] The very few Republicans inclined to follow Ollivier, Jules Ferry and Léon Gambetta in particular, known as the "little Olliviers," drifted back into the Republican camp, leaving Ollivier apparently isolated. Several weeks later he voted in favor of the speech from the throne for the first time, "a vote of expectation," he called it, leading one of the young Republicans to write: "It is more than capitulation, it is a betrayal." [15]

But Ollivier's expectation was not rewarded in the remainder of 1865 and 1866. Not only were there no more significant legislative reforms, but the news from abroad was uniformly bad. The attempt to seat Maximilian on the Mexican throne soured and had to be abandoned, while Prussia emerged from her war with Austria sufficiently powerful to reject a French claim for territorial compensation in gratitude for French neutrality. When, on January 19, 1867, the Emperor made a further gesture to his legislature, it was logical to assume that he was eager to appease the critics of his failures, especially since the gesture aroused the wrath of his conservative entourage.

The decree of January 19 required *all* the cabinet ministers to participate in parliamentary debates, and promised that new laws to provide greater freedom of assembly and of the press would be forthcoming. Even the Empress was totally surprised by the announcements. The Emperor had made clear to her that the democratization of the regime must ultimately come, but she had been led to believe that this unpleasant eventuality would only occur upon the accession of the Prince Imperial. That event would not take place until 1874 when he reached his majority, at which time the imperial couple would abdicate in his favor and retire to Pau for the winters and Biarritz for the summers. Whether that became Napoleon's intention after the death of Morny, or whether it was a ruse to pacify the household, we may never know for sure. What is certain, however, and what the Empress only realized after the fall of the Empire, is that the

14. Alfred Cobban, *A History of Modern France*, Baltimore: Penguin, 1961, II, 185.
15. F.–H.–R. Allain-Targé, *La République sous l'Empire, Lettres (1864–1870)*, ed. by Suzanne de la Porte, Paris: Bernard Grasset, 1939, p. 20.

Emperor's physical maladies had multiplied during 1866. He no longer felt capable of bearing the supreme power much longer, so that he must pursue the development of the Liberal Empire in order to guarantee the succession of his heir.[16]

This revival gave serious promise that some of the Bonapartist majority in the *Corps législatif* would now shift to the moderate liberal camp, called the Third Party; and that possibility meant that the Republicans could become swamped in a burgeoning Opposition that would not be revolutionary. As a result, most of the Republican deputies felt it necessary to stand apart from the Third Party after January 19 to demonstrate that there could be no accommodation between Republic and Empire: the irreconcilables. Calling the Third Party "bourgeois France . . . dreaming of conciliatory contradictions," Allain-Targé predicted that France would yet see a democratic and social Republic, an egalitarian and free society. "Everyone will participate in human dignity and be equal. . . . It will be the regeneration of the World." [17]

In the many months between the decree of January 19, 1867 and the parliamentary elections of 1869, Napoleon III was virtually besieged by those determined to prevent the consummation of the Liberal Empire, the conservatives led by the Empress and Eugène Rouher—and those months must have been bitter ones indeed. The ministers in whom he had confidence, most of whom had favored the liberal evolution, were dead or dying: Billault, Morny, Thouvenel, and Fould. Comte Walewski did not survive 1868, the Marquis de Moustier shortly followed him, and R.-T. Troplong, President of the Senate since 1852, died early in 1869. Napoleon knew that the Empress desired to put him out to pasture because of his illness and age, to become Regent herself; and he experienced the increasing silence around him that is the fate of old age.

New men came into the administration to replace the older generation after 1867, but they were generally not Bonapartists

16. Maurice Paléologue, *The Tragic Empress: Conversations of the Empress Eugénie, 1901–1919*, New York and London: Harper, 1928, p. 78.
17. Suzanne de la Porte, "Autour du 19 janvier. Tiers parti et opposition républicaine," *Revue historique*, 179 (1937) , 144–145.

and could only enjoy the hostility of the conservatives. Some, like Clément Duvernois, were purely opportunistic, he being an unprincipled and poverty-stricken man who had called himself Republican, a skillful journalist who gave himself to the Empire in 1868 for money and position. A second group of recruits came from the ranks of the younger lawyers, most of whom were liberal and Republicans in principle, but ambitious to rise and willing to follow Emile Ollivier if he could bring liberty without revolution. Finally, a third group was available: The younger generation of Royalists who had not known the *coup d'état* first hand and whose traditional vocation was to rally to the throne. As the Empire liberalized its institutions, they were available for service, really a new generation of Liberal Catholics led by Louis-Joseph Buffet. These factions contained men of ability, but their factionalism meant petty hatreds and jealousies which the Emperor, by temperament and physical condition, could not control.[18]

The electoral picture of 1869 was, under such transitional circumstances, much less clearcut than that for the previous imperial elections, and was made no less complex by the rifts within Republican ranks. Though the results of the various elections have naturally been compared as a measure of the growing opposition to the Second Empire, the oddities of the elections of 1869 do not, in fact, provide a very satisfactory comparison. The government, for instance, did not uniformly apply the old system of official candidates. Roughly twenty-four constituencies had no official candidates, including those of Paris where it was only too evident that the Republicans would win, and in Var where the Emperor refused to permit official opposition to the candidacy of Ollivier. In such constituencies the government gave official blessing to men running as Independents.[19] As for the Republicans, their divisions on social and economic issues produced a variety of schisms and alliances; and the very fact that Republican victories in Paris were assured brought forth more numerous candidates than usual. There most constituencies had two Republican candidates, a socialist opposing a moderate (bourgeois)

18. La Gorce, *op. cit.*, V, 446–473.
19. Zeldin, *The Political System of Napoleon III*, p. 141.

Republican, the same situation pertaining in Lyon. In some regions, where there was little hope of defeating the official candidate, Republicans sometimes coalesced with the liberal Monarchists, the candidate usually being known as Independent. In Marseille the socialist and moderate Republicans achieved unity to back the candidacy of a young firebrand, Léon Gambetta.[20] Another unique feature of the elections of 1869 is that they were fought with a far freer press than before, thanks to the long-awaited press reform of 1868. If some of the subsequent new journals favored the development of a liberal Empire, the great majority of them represented the radical Opposition and poured abuse on the regime.

The confusing electoral campaign was no more misleading than the electoral results. Forty Opposition deputies were elected, only eight more seats than in 1863, giving the government a heavy majority. But as thirty of the forty Opposition seats were Republican, it meant that the Opposition was more unified than before. On the other hand, most of the Independents elected would support the government if it pursued the liberal course and were thus only a temporary Opposition. The popular vote for Opposition candidates was significantly larger in 1869 than it had been in 1863 when the Opposition got roughly two million of the seven million votes. In 1869 the Opposition totaled 3,355,000 to 4,438,000 for governmental candidates. But there is reason to believe—not merely because of the confusion of the campaign, but because of the figures that would emerge the following year in the constitutional plebiscite—that many of the Opposition votes in 1869 were votes for a Liberal Empire. An even safer conclusion is that public opinion was overwhelmingly moderate: the Monarchists, whether Legitimist or Orleanist, suffered a major disaster; and the more radical Republicans were defeated by the more moderate Republicans. An exception was the radical François Raspail from Lyon, but his was a personal rather than an ideological victory.[21]

The conservative Bonapartists saw in the government's

20. Georges J. Weill, *Le Parti républicain de 1814 à 1870*, Paris: Alcan, 1900, pp. 508–511.
21. Georges J. Weill, *Le Mouvement social en France, 1852–1910*, Paris: Alcan, 1911, p. 126; and Zeldin, *The Political System of Napoleon III*, p. 142.

heavy majority of seats a mandate to continue authoritarian government; while Emile Ollivier, seeing that the old Bonapartist system was dying, rallied 116 deputies who signed a petition favoring responsible government, the 116 being the new Third Party and not including the Republicans. For the moment the Emperor continued with conservative ministers, though dropping Rouher as Minister of State; but on July 12 he signaled the coming Liberal Empire by granting the *Corps législatif* new powers of initiation and amendment. To which Gambetta replied, revealing his anxiety, "This is not a government which makes concessions; this is a government that is in flight. . . . Its previous reforms have satisfied only the timid; they irritate pure parliamentarians; they make no sense to the people. Besides, it is notorious that the government has obscured the meaning of universal suffrage which, a few years ago, it skillfully caressed and corrupted with the aid of equivocal theories and democratic procedures. Today the government even turns its back on democracy. Authoritarian, it begins to be parliamentary." [22]

Republican uneasiness reflected not merely the possibility of a liberal regime that would sidetrack the Republicans into oblivion, but implied their inability to recast society according to scientific principles. One of the profoundest objections the Republicans had to Bonapartism was its equivocal clerical policy, which the Republicans construed to be a pro-Catholic policy. And when they reviewed the names of those deputies of the Third Party, the 116 who had signed Ollivier's petition for responsible government, they found that sixty of them were clericals. It made little difference to a Republican that they were liberal; their Catholicism implied a Catholic revival, that the state which had been lay in principle but not in practice would become exclusively clerical.

By and large, the Liberal Catholics had had a bad time during the Second Empire. A majority of the clergy had openly supported the suppression of public liberties after 1851, a line the Liberal Catholics refused to follow, earning them the enmity of the Gallican Church, the state, and the Papacy. The position of the Gallican Church, however, was less comfortable than its

22. Léon Gambetta, *Lettres, 1868–1882*, ed. Daniel Halévy and Emile Pillias, Paris: Grasset, 1938, letter to Clément Laurier, July 15, 1869.

enemies often assumed, beginning with the fact that the regime adhered to the principles of 1789. And because the Papacy, in the time of Pius IX, seemed bent upon pontifical infallibility, the Gallicans were not in complete accord with Rome and needed the support of the French state. Yet they could not be the Emperor's allies when his Italian policy threatened the temporal authority of Rome. Finally, while a great majority of the French observed the forms of Catholicism, only a small minority of them accepted the teaching of the Church in its entirety. To side with despotism, as the Gallican Church did in 1851, against the liberties of the people, meant serious and lasting consequences for the Church; and, as the Empire began to shed its despotism in the '60s, the Liberal Catholic minority was in a position to assume the leadership of French Catholics in politics. The Liberal Empire they sought would be a Liberal Catholic Empire, precisely what the Republicans feared.[23]

On July 12, Napoleon III had taken the third step in abdicating his absolute powers, and before the month was out he summoned the senators from vacation to consider the necessary constitutional changes. To carry out the promise of July 12, he asked that the powers of initiation and amendment be granted to the *Corps législatif*, and that both houses have the right to elect their own officers. As for the ministers, they could be members of either house, would deliberate in council under the presidency of the Emperor, and would be dependent upon him. He evaded the question of true ministerial responsibility to Parliament in defense of some executive authority. In reporting the imperial project to the Senate, the conservative Senator A.–M. Devienne remarked: "If History preserves any truth, it will say that Napoleon III alone initiated the liberal movement, not only without coercion, but surrounded by considerable resistance and vulnerable to that ingratitude with which it is our habit to greet at the outset the most courageous actions." [24] A generous piece of praise which assisted a reluctant Senate to sanction the requested reforms without incurring responsibility for them.

23. Jean Maurain, *La Politique ecclésiastique du Second Empire*, Paris: Félix Alcan, 1930, pp. 939–959.
24. La Gorce, *op. cit.*, V, 501.

Senate debate began on September 1 under the new presiding officer, Eugène Rouher of all people, and Prince Jerome-Napoleon rose to praise what was in the imperial project, but to complain that it did not go far enough, being ambiguous about ministerial responsibility and not turning the Senate into a true legislative body. But the great majority, grateful that the project had not been so radical, accepted it on September 6 with only three dissenting votes. As far as the necessary legislation was concerned, the Liberal Empire was founded. It remained only to find the men to staff it.

Gambetta was increasingly anxious. Vacationing in Switzerland, he heard rumors of Prince Jerome's speech, favorable remarks about it on all sides, making a "lively and disagreeable impression on me." [25] Next day, having read it, he found it very serious.[26] Why, he wanted to know, had not Jerome's speech made a greater sensation in Paris? "Either I am losing my mind or Paris is incomprehensible. I believe that this is the program of January 19, 1867." This, in other words, was the Emperor's real intention for France within a year or two: A responsible ministry, universal suffrage for election to the Senate, and the mayors to be elected by the municipal councils. "No longer able to checkmate the Revolution," Gambetta complained, "[the Napoleons] want to marry and exploit it." [27]

Republicans more radical than Gambetta profited from the press liberties to preach revolt, notably in *le Rappel* and in *le Reveil;* and they strained for pretexts to justify violence against the regime. They found such a pretext by insisting that the government was constitutionally liable to summon the new Parliament within six months of the dissolution of the old. In preparation for the elections of 1869, the old *Corps législatif* had been dissolved on April 27; meaning, the radicals argued, that the new *Corps législatif* must be installed no later than October 26. Since the by-election for seats not filled in the first balloting were not scheduled until November 21, there seemed every likelihood that Paris would experience radical uprisings on October

25. Gambetta, *op. cit.,* #56, to André Lavertujon, September 5, 1869.
26. *Ibid.,* #57, to Clément Laurier, September 6, 1869.
27. *Ibid.,* #60, to André Lavertujon, September 9, 1869.

26. Indeed, many conservatives hoped for just such an attempt, thinking that it would force the Emperor to restore the dictatorship. Came the day and the revolutionaries kept to their dens, aware that the government was ready with troops. An eccentric poet reading verse to a small gathering in the Place de la Concorde was the only disturbance of the peace, and the police disdained to disperse poetry.[28]

Four Parisian seats were to be filled by the by-elections of November 21, and once again the moderate Republicans triumphed over the more radical candidates. Emmanuel Arago, Adolphe Crémieux, and A.–O. Glais-Bizoin won three of the seats, though the fourth was won by the radical Henri Rochefort, former publisher of *la Lanterne,* who was permitted to return from exile to campaign. His victory gave him parliamentary immunity, and he founded *la Marseillaise* to renew the assault upon the Empire. The general failure of the radicals in the fall of 1869, however, did little to dispel the liberals' fear of them; and the attack upon authority, whether political or religious, drew former liberal opponents of Napoleon III closer to his regime.[29] A notable example was Anatole Prévost-Paradol, journalist and essayist, whose first attempt at public office came in the elections of 1869 when he stood for the *Corps législatif* from Nantes against an official candidate, a democrat, and a Legitimist. He came in a very bad last. In the runoff, the official candidate beat the democrat by a narrow margin. The experience was shocking to Paradol, partly because of the ignominy of his defeat, but also because he realized for the first time in the course of the campaign the extremism of many radicals. As the Emperor moved to establish parliamentary government after the elections, Prévost-Paradol began his rally to the regime which would end with his request for a diplomatic appointment.[30]

28. La Gorce, *op. cit.*, V, 507–512.

29. Charles Chesnelong, *Les Derniers jours de l'empire et le gouvernement de M. Thiers*, mémoires publiés par son petit-fils, Paris: Librairie Académique Perrin, 1932, p. 8.

30. Pierre Guiral, *Prévost-Paradol (1829–1870)*, *pensée et action d'un libéral sous le Second Empire*, Paris: Presses Universitaires de France, 1955, pp. 634–648.

Meanwhile, the Emperor had already renewed correspondence with Emile Ollivier about the formation of a liberal ministry and, during an interview at Compiègne on October 31, Ollivier stated his terms for entering the government, terms which he had earlier spelled out by letter to Clément Duvernois. Several members of the current cabinet were acceptable to Ollivier, but by and large he wanted new men for the new era, men drawn from the 116. He also wanted it understood that the time for halting Prussia had passed, and that all questions dividing the two countries ought to be settled peacefully; finally, that the occupation of Rome ought to continue at least until the Vatican Council had completed its deliberation. The weeks plodded past as both Emperor and prospective minister pondered the problems of a new government, when, on November 29, the Emperor opened the new *Corps législatif* with the words: "France wishes liberty, but with order. As for order, I am responsible for it. Help me, gentlemen, to establish liberty." [31]

In response, a new petition favoring responsible government attracted 136 signatures, and the Republicans grudgingly granted their support, giving the Emperor a clear mandate to dismiss his conservative ministers. One faction of the Republican deputies, headed by Ernest Picard, felt that the time had come to show less intransigence and to cooperate more openly with the deputies favoring the Liberal Empire. A second group, led by Jules Simon, thought that such cooperation made the Republicans dupes of the Empire, but were persuaded by Jules Favre to be less stiff-necked for at least the moment.[32] On December 27, Ollivier received the following from Napoleon: "The ministers having given their resignations to me, it is with confidence in your patriotism that I ask you to designate the men who can form a homogenous cabinet with you, which will faithfully represent the majority in the *Corps législatif,* which will be resolved to apply—both in letter and in spirit—the *sénatus-consulte* of September 8. I am counting on the devotion of the *Corps législatif* to the major interests of the country, as on yours,

31. La Gorce, *op. cit.,* V, 520.
32. Weill, *Le Parti républicain,* p. 516.

to aid me in the task which I am undertaking to make the constitutional regime function correctly." [33]

The new government was formally installed on January 2, 1870, and was "homogenous" only in that it did not contain any conservative Bonapartists or Republicans. Otherwise, the cabinet comprised several different elements in the attempt to make it a ministry of reconciliation. As the Emperor himself would continue to preside over the cabinet, no prime minister was designated. Ollivier took the ministries of Justice and Cults with the title Keeper of the Seals. He brought with him two faithful political allies: J.–P.–N. Chevandier de Valdrôme, a former instructor at the Ecole Centrale become an industrialist and a deputy since 1859, who took the Interior post; and Maurice Richard, first elected to the Corps législatif in 1863 to become a member of the Third Party, who became Minister of Fine Arts.

Two ministers came from the former liberal Opposition: Comte Napoleon Daru, in the Chamber of Peers under Louis-Philippe, but elected to the Corps législatif only in 1869, now took the Foreign Affairs ministry; Louis-Joseph Buffet, Liberal Catholic Opposition since 1863, became Minister of Finance. Three ministers represented Bonapartists who had been converted to the idea of Liberal Empire: As Minister of Public Instruction, Emile-Alexis Segris, a lawyer first elected to the Corps législatif in 1859 as an official candidate, but one of the 116 petitioners. Joseph de Talhouët, a parliamentarian who had protested the coup d'état of 1851, but who had rallied to become an official candidate in 1852, then reverting to favor the Liberal Empire, to become Minister of Public Works. And Louvet, the third convert, took the Ministry of Agriculture.

The Emperor had argued that the ministers charged with national defense ought to be above party consideration and should be subject to his choice because he was commander-in-chief. Thus, Admiral Charles Rigault de Genouilly, a senator since 1860 and Minister of the Marine since 1867, retained his portfolio in the new government. Similarly, Marshal Edmond Leboeuf, who had succeeded Marshal Niel at the War Office in 1869, kept the Ministry of War. The only new minister not to fit

33. *Le Moniteur*, December 28, 1869.

the category of friend of Ollivier, Bonapartist convert, or member of the parliamentary opposition, was Esquirou de Parieu, who became Minister-President of the Council of State. No satisfactory explanation for his choice has been given.[34] But while he had not been a deputy in the *Corps législatif,* he had been Minister of Public Instruction in 1850 when the Falloux Law was passed, a compromise educational measure prepared chiefly by Liberal Catholics. He was, in short, a congenial colleague to the men of January 2.

The Emperor, who had seemed unsure and indecisive for the previous six months, believed that he had forced a revolution upon his entourage; and the pessimism and depression he had revealed to many observers in the later 1860s suddenly gave way to optimism with the formation of the liberal government. "Nothing has been more interesting nor more extraordinary," noted Ludovic Halévy, "than this perfect calm on the Emperor's part during this parliamentary crisis. Here is a man who, six months ago, one can say had France in his hand. . . . He has calmly let it all go. Those around him are dismayed, the Empress irritated. Around him the Emperor sees only somber and anxious faces. 'What is the matter,' he says to everyone, 'never has it been so orderly during a revolution.' The word is apt and true." [35]

While the court and most of the Republicans remained sulky, the government of January 2 was generally well received by the nation. The Orleanist *Revue des Deux Mondes* mirrored the change of heart of the old liberal Opposition: "If this is not the greatest of all revolutions, it is at least one of the most interesting, one of the most salutary and most opportune." [36] The dying Comte de Montalembert, greatest of the Liberal Catholic writers, greeted the new ministry favorably despite his personal dislike of Napoleon. Adolphe Thiers was somewhat more reserved, hating Napoleon and accusing him of compromising French independence with his foreign policy, yet letting it be known that he would henceforth support the regime if it carried out its promised reforms. Other former Orleanists like François

34. Zeldin, *Emile Ollivier and the Liberal Empire of Napoleon III*, p. 117.
35. Ludovic Halévy, *Carnets*, Paris: Calmann-Lévy, 1935, II, 36–37.
36. Zeldin, *Emile Ollivier and the Liberal Empire of Napoleon III*, p. 120.

Guizot and Odilon Barrot also lent support; and the old Duc de Broglie, if pessimistic about the success of the new regime, favored it nevertheless and urged his son to accept a diplomatic post.

Even the opposition of the intellectual and literary world began to melt, the election of Ollivier to the Academy being the most stunning example of the new climate. Individuals, too, let their approval be known: Jean-Jacques Weiss, literary historian and liberal journalist, rallied and was made the secretary-general of the Ministry of Fine Arts; Prévost-Paradol solicited a diplomatic post and accepted appointment to represent France in Washington; E.-R.-L. de Laboulaye, Professor of Jurisprudence at the Collège de France, dropped his opposition and was appointed to a commission to study the government of Paris and the Seine; Ernest Renan, historian and philologist, did not receive public appointment, but welcomed the liberal advances as a defense against the radicalism which had alarmed him during 1869; the liberal poet Victor de Laprade, member of the Academy since 1858, ceased his opposition; and the Republican George Sand announced herself as both enthusiastic and satisfied. Others were more cautious publicly, but the favorable drift was unmistakable.[37]

Though not prime minister, Ollivier was clearly the principal minister in the government of January 2, and he introduced a British-type system of commissions—really committees of experts—to examine major problems and to recommend legislative solutions. One commission was established to recommend ways to reduce the high degree of centralization in France as a means to grant greater liberty; another to formulate a system of self-government for Paris; another to investigate the state of public education and the monopoly enjoyed by the Université; and still another to advise on vocational education which Duruy had recently inaugurated. There was a commission for public works, one for revision of the criminal code with a special view to ending the inquisitorial system which placed the burden of proving innocence on the defense, and a labor arbitration commission to promote industrial and agricultural peace.

37. Guiral, *op. cit.*, pp. 668–670.

The principal merit of the commission system was also its chief liability. If reforms required lengthy study by experts, such study also delayed their legislation and ran the risk of arousing the animosity of politicians in the *Corps législatif*, jealous of their newly won prerogatives. Perhaps Ollivier could have coped with the program somewhat more shrewdly by staffing his commissions with more parliamentarians, but he was no Morny and too often employed his eloquence when nothing short of political groundwork would do. As an unhappy result, many of the projected reforms were still projects when the war broke out in midsummer to destroy them. Other reforms did get before the *Corps législatif* for consideration before the war, and in reviewing them one is struck by the probability that this reformist regime, in its zeal to demonstrate its good intentions, bit off more than it could effectively manage. The government moved, for example, to repeal the General Security Law of 1858, which had been passed following the Orsini attempt on the Emperor's life; it moved to reestablish jury trials in press cases and to eliminate the stamp tax on newspapers. Ollivier proposed to abolish the *livrets,* those identification cards so hated as discriminatory by workers; and the right to authorize public works was to be transferred from the Emperor to the *Corps législatif,* a final slap at the fallen Baron Haussmann, but an important measure of parliamentary financial control.[38] The record, in sum, was mixed; but Pierre de la Gorce's judgment of it seems fair: "This work, even though interrupted at its onset, though somewhat impaired by excesses of optimism and by some inexperience, deserves not to be forgotten. It was one of the best attempted in the nineteenth century." [39]

That there was general recognition in 1870 that the Empire had been renewed and strengthened by the coming of the Liberal Empire, and that the Ollivier ministry responded to popular desires for both liberty and progress,[40] should not blind us to the

38. Zeldin, *Emile Ollivier and the Liberal Empire of Napoleon III,* pp. 123–129.
39. La Gorce, *op. cit.,* VI, 20.
40. Jacques Freymond, "La France de 1870," *Études de Lettres,* XVIII (April 1944) , 54.

fact that the victory of the liberals that year sharpened the hostilities of both Left and Right, made desperate by the possibility of impotence. The Emperor took his new position as parliamentary sovereign seriously, but was no longer the vigorous man he once had been and was unable to inspire his new ministers, just as he was feeble in the face of court bickering and disaffection. The Empress officially supported the reforms, but was indiscreetly critical of them, while Prince Napoleon continued to press for greater liberties, liberties which that restless, equivocal, and unstable personality would likely not have granted had he had the supreme power for which he hankered. Rouher, no longer a minister but presiding over the Senate, kept ostentatiously aloof, ready to resume power when this liberal aberration should end.[41] "This representative regime," wrote Prosper Mérimée, a close friend of Her Majesty, "is hardly an amusing comedy; everyone in it lies shamelessly, and yet allows himself to be taken in by the latest word. . . . People were stupid in 1848, but they are infinitely more so now." [42] Such sentiments from courtiers were hardly reassuring.

As for the Left, its more moderate members watched the progress of the Liberal Empire in tacit dismay, anticipating the probable necessity of adhering to the regime; while the more radical members kept up their shrill abuse of the Empire and of those Republicans thought likely to rally to the Empire. One of them saw the new government as a Bonapartist-Orleanist-Legitimist conspiracy against the Republican ideal, predicting that, unless the Republicans succeeded in establishing a Republic within eighteen months, they would all be in Cayenne.[43] Another, Henri Cernuschi, the Republican economist of *le Siècle*, feared more from the moderate Republicans: "On the Left there is a set of people who want nothing more than to be in the saddle, all of them ready to succeed Ollivier when he is thrown into the ditch. There will be few who have taken the oath who

41. Augustin Filon, *Recollections of the Empress Eugénie*, New York: Cassell, 1920, p. 81; and Maxime Du Camp, *Souvenirs d'un Demi-Siècle*, Paris: Hachette, 1949, I, 247.

42. Prosper Mérimée, *Lettres à une Inconnue*, Paris: Calmann-Lévy, 1874, II, 362.

43. Allain-Targé, *op. cit.*, pp. 204–206.

will be capable of remaining irreconcilable to the end. . . . We shall see, my dear [Edmond] Adam, if God gives life to the Empire, Picard after Ollivier, Jules Ferry after Picard, Gambetta after Jules Ferry. That will be *le pont d'Avignon.*" [44]

The ministers of January 2 had hardly settled to their task of reforming the Empire when they were confronted with one of those peripheral issues which can be the salvation of an otherwise bankrupt Opposition. Prince Pierre Bonaparte, on January 10, shot to death a minor employee of Henri Rochefort's *la Marseillaise,* giving the radical Republicans the prospect of a political funeral. No matter that Prince Pierre was a family outcast, a *persona non grata* at the Tuileries and without official employment. He was a Bonaparte, and Rochefort had written of him just the day before the murder, "scratch a Bonaparte, find a ferocious animal." [45] The unfortunate incident occurred while arrangements were being made for a duel between the Prince and another editor of *la Marseillaise,* and the seconds of the latter behaved in a manner which provoked the attack. Ollivier at once ordered the arrest of Prince Pierre, who turned himself in; but Rochefort, the radical deputy elected the previous November from Paris, did not intend to let this opportunity slip by: "I have been so weak as to believe," he wrote, "that a Bonaparte could be other than an assassin! I dared suppose that a straightforward duel was possible in this family where murder and snares are tradition and custom. Our collaborator, Paschal Grousset, shared my error, and today we weep for our poor and dear friend, Victor Noir, assassinated by the bandit Pierre-Napoleon Bonaparte. For eighteen years now France has been held in the bloodied hands of these cut-throats, who, not content to shoot down Republicans in the streets, draw them into dirty traps in order to slit their throats in private. Frenchmen, have you not had quite enough of it?" [46]

If Ollivier meant to see that the murderer was brought before a court of law, he just as clearly meant to punish appeals for insurrection; and he began by seizing *la Marseillaise.* On the

44. Guiral, *op. cit.,* p. 671.
45. *La Marseillaise,* January 9, 1870.
46. *Ibid.,* January 11, 1870.

floor of the *Corps législatif,* where Rochefort predicted a whitewash of Prince Pierre, Ollivier replied: "A murder has been committed by a highly-placed person: We shall prosecute him. . . .
As for these exhortations designed to inflame popular sentiment, we are unmoved and unfearful. We are the law, we are *le
droit,* we are moderation, we are liberty, and, if you stand in our
way, we shall be force." [47] Nevertheless, radical leaders raised a
large mob which met at the Noir home in Neuilly for the funeral;
but, in the face of determined military preparations by the government, the radicals fell to bickering. Gustave Flourens and
Auguste Vermorel insisted on challenging the government by
directing the funeral procession through Paris to the cemetery of
Père-Lachaise, while Rochefort and Charles Delescluze preferred
to give way and have the body buried in the Neuilly cemetery
where they would be unmolested by troops. In the end, the Noir
family insisted on Neuilly, caring more for the deceased than for
insurrection. In the collapse of the attempted revolt, its organizers were revealed to be indecisive and inept, noisy windbags in
the eyes of the more moderate Republicans who had taken no
part in the attempt.

In the aftermath, the government successfully prosecuted
Rochefort for inciting revolt and for contempt for the Emperor,
and hoped that Prince Pierre would also receive a prison sentence to avoid the appearance of a whitewash.[48] Unfortunately
for Ollivier, however, the defense effectively showed that Prince
Pierre had been deliberately goaded to commit violence by the
staff of *la Marseillaise,* and he was acquitted. Probably justice
was done, but the case left a bad taste.[49]

By April 1870 the Ollivier government was ready with a new
constitution. Because it was intended to be a measure of national
reconciliation, the new constitution was deliberately designed to
include meritorious elements from a variety of previous consti-
tutions. If it resembled any one previous constitution more than

47. La Gorce, *op. cit.,* VI, 16.
48. Emile Ollivier, *Journal 1846–1869,* ed. Theodore Zeldin, Paris: René
Julliard, 1961, II, 417–419.
49. Eugénie de Grèce, *Pierre-Napoléon Bonaparte 1815–1881,* Paris: Hachette,
1963, pp. 334–375.

the others, it was that of 1848; for the new constitution provided for representative government rather than true parliamentarianism, allowed the executive considerable authority, and rested upon the sovereignty of the people. The Emperor remained the active head of government, appointed his own ministers, and presided over their deliberations. And he retained veto power. Absolutism was to be prevented by a series of checks: he was required to govern with the cooperation of his ministers and a bicameral parliament, and he remained responsible to the people through plebiscites, a modified democracy given the nature of a plebiscite. Legislative initiation was shared by the executive and parliament, and the earlier ambiguity was preserved by making the ministers both "dependent" upon the Emperor and "responsible" to parliament. The Senate became a legislative house for the first time under the Empire with the right to veto bills of the lower house, but senators continued to be appointed by the Emperor. Because the senate had to abandon its constituent power to the people, henceforth the constitution could only be altered by plebiscite at the Emperor's initiative.

Ollivier quite clearly wished to retain a strong executive and to avoid true parliamentarianism where the executive would be a figurehead. Accordingly, the Republican Left, converted after 1852 to parliamentarianism, would not support such a settlement and feared that the plebiscitary system left the nation in constant danger of another *coup d'état* as in 1851. Thus, Republicans like Gambetta revived their open opposition, regarding the Liberal Empire as only a bridge between the Republic of 1848 and the Republic of the future.[50] For their part, the liberal reformers did not view the Liberal Empire as a transitional stage between autocracy and parliamentarianism. They sought to reconcile liberty and democracy, to reconcile strong government with liberty; and they abhorred parliamentarianism as a form which could only make France weak through factionalism.[51]

On April 20, 1870, the Senate issued the *Senatus Consultum* which revised the constitution of 1852 and transferred the constit-

50. Freymond, *op. cit.*, p. 55.
51. Zeldin, *Emile Ollivier and the Liberal Empire of Napoleon III*, pp. 141–151.

uent power from the Senate to the people. Most of the senators were conservative and disliked—in 1870, as in 1869—to be shoved in a liberal direction. At their instigation, therefore, a plebiscite was suggested as necessary to ratify so radical a constitutional change, the *Senatus Consultum* alone being insufficient; for, being remote from public opinion, these ancient gentlemen expected the public to veto the liberal constitution in favor of the autocracy. The government fell in with the plan, realistically expecting success. Furthermore, they worded the plebiscite in such a way as to force the conservative Bonapartists to vote for the Liberal Empire, otherwise to vote against the Empire: "The people approve the liberal reforms of the Constitution by the Emperor in effect since 1860, done in conjunction with the principal governmental bodies, and, thus, ratify the Senate Decree of April 20, 1870."

Not even the most optimistic member of the government, after the electoral disappointment of 1869, expected the magnitude of the governmental victory in the plebiscite of May 8, when the new constitution was approved 7,358,786 votes to 1,571,939. What is the more remarkable is that many supporters of the reforms had voted No or abstained on grounds that the plebiscite was antiparliamentary, and Daru and Buffet had resigned from the cabinet before the plebiscite as a gesture of Center-Left disapproval. The Republicans, of course, had campaigned vigorously against the constitution, and very possibly the extremism of their campaign forced many moderates into the government camp, especially the religious who might otherwise have had little enthusiasm for the Liberal Empire and might have abstained.

Plebiscites, it is true, can be misleading elections, for a choice between Yes or No can obscure shades of opinion. On the other hand, we are especially suspicious of plebiscites because of their use by twentieth-century dictatorships in which abstention or negation has been dangerous. Their results may reveal nothing about the true state of public opinion. The elections of the Second Empire, particularly the votes of 1869 and 1870, were quite something else: The Opposition had a press, it campaigned openly, and one could vote No or abstain without fear of retaliation. Indeed, roughly a half million voters, who did exercise their right to abstain in 1869, evidently cast votes for the Liberal Empire in 1870.

But they alone cannot account for the increase in the governmental vote from 4.3 million to 7.3 million. Part of the problem is solved if we reverse the time-honored interpretation that classified the electoral results of 1869 as a true picture of public opinion and those of 1870 as deceptive. The best bet is that 1869 saw a large protest vote, either for local issues or because greater liberty was wanted; but that those votes were not directed against the Empire, far less against a Liberal Empire. His Majesty's Catholic and monarchical supporters may have been lukewarm; but their likely alternative was hardly monarchy but a Republic, and that was unthinkable. As for the Republicans, they have been regarded as the party closest to the social and economic realities bred by industrialization and thus bound to be the ultimate party to govern France despite the Empire's triumph in 1870.[52] Yet the electoral results of that year show that many employers voted against the Empire because of its free-trade philosophy, leading their employees to vote for the Empire. In point of fact, the social and economic record of "Saint-Simon on Horseback" compares favorably with that of the Republicans who governed for several decades after him, suggesting that they were not necessarily closer than he to social and economic realities.

In the plebiscite, the Emperor received 67.5 per cent of the vote as against the 74.5 per cent he had received in 1851. If he was not stronger than ever, as Gambetta feared he was, he had at least won a notable triumph.[53] His victory, however, neither reconciled nor silenced two determined groups, the Republicans and the conservative Bonapartists. The latter, led by the Empress Eugénie, were the more dangerous for Ollivier, as they were courtiers at the center of power and skilled intriguers; and because they were determined to regain paramountcy in Europe which France had lost by 1866. They no more condoned the

52. Freymond, op. cit., pp. 69–71.
53. Zeldin, Emile Ollivier and the Liberal Empire of Napoleon III, pp. 153–162.

liberalism than the pacific foreign policy of the ministry of January 2. What that ministry most needed under the new constitution was time to inaugurate its reforms and the opportunity to prove that the liberal monarchy was the form most likely to calm the warring factions at home. And that time was to be denied.

One of the conditions laid down by Ollivier in taking office was that the Prussian gains of 1866 in the German world were to be regarded as legitimate, and he refused to agree with the conservatives that French failure to obtain compensation along the Rhine or in Luxembourg should be cause to seek revenge. Indeed, the new French government proposed to Lord Clarendon that he recommend disarmament to Berlin; and, as a measure of good faith, Comte Daru successfully proposed a reduction of 10,000 men from the already small contingent to be called up from the class of 1870. Berlin rejected the British suggestion, as the Francophile Clarendon expected would be the case, but even so the French government seems to have anticipated no trouble from that quarter. On June 30 Ollivier told the lower house that peace seemed assured.

Perhaps a government so intent upon constitutional and domestic reform too easily turned its back upon the foreign scene; and the Duc de Gramont, appointed Foreign Minister after Daru's resignation, was not the equal of his British or Prussian counterparts. Certainly the Earl of Clarendon had greater insight into the dangers confronting the French than the French themselves did. The Anglo-French alliance, sometimes called the Crimean alliance, had been allowed to collapse in 1863 by the British. Their suspicions had been aroused by the French annexation of Nice and Savoy in 1860, and in 1863, at the time of the Polish revolt, they failed to support Napoleon in his desire to help the Poles and refused to attend an international congress which he wished to call to deal with the problem. It proved a mistaken policy which would have long-term consequences, and was the more wrongheaded as Napoleon III had by then proved himself a consistent friend of Britain.[54]

54. W. E. Mosse, *The European Powers and the German Question 1848–1871*, Cambridge: Cambridge University Press, 1958, p. 366.

Most of the British preferred, by 1863, an understanding with Prussia that could serve to check Russia in the East as the Crimean alliance had done, but which had the additional advantage of defending Belgium against an anticipated French attempt at annexation. Rumors of such French intentions were current in the 1860s, and how serious such intentions were has remained controversial ever since. Napoleon III clearly valued the British alliance above all others and knew that Belgian independence was a cardinal feature of British policy. He also sympathized with aspirant nationalities and backed the desire of Prussia to expel the Hapsburgs from Germany. After 1863, the question of Belgium emerged in Franco-Prussian discussions about the future of south Germany, and Clarendon believed that Prussia sought to promote French annexation of Belgium as a compensation for Prussian annexation of south Germany, but really to prevent a revival of the Anglo-French alliance and to keep France isolated. Clarendon, one of the few who expected Germany to become a greater threat to British security than France, worked in vain after 1867 to revive the Anglo-French alliance and his death, on June 27, 1870, was greeted with relief by Bismarck.[55]

Shortly after, July 2 to be exact, the complacency of the ministry of January 2 was shattered with the announcement that the vacant Spanish throne had been offered to Leopold von Hohenzollern-Sigmaringen, brother of Carol I of Romania. The French cabinet, naturally inferring that Bismark was engineering a new humiliation for France and anxious to avoid a charge of spinelessness from the conservative Bonapartists, promptly protested the candidacy to Prussia rather than to Spain. This turned the affair into an international rather than a localized crisis, which Bismarck could exploit. If, to the majority of the French, the Hohenzollern candidacy was reminiscent of the intolerable Hapsburg encirclement of the sixteenth century, there is no reason today to believe that the candidacy had long been plotted by Bismarck as a diabolical scheme to enrage them. He favored that candidacy when it became a possibility, and the actual offer of

55. *Ibid.*, pp. 300–303.

the crown provided him the means to create a European crisis.[56]

Ollivier and Gramont simply fell into his trap by protesting the candidacy to Berlin on July 3, and made the matter worse in an official statement to Parliament on the sixth by using threatening words: "[But respect for the rights of Spain] does not oblige us to stand aside while a foreign power, by placing one of its princes on the throne of Charles V, threatens to upset the present balance of power in Europe to our detriment and to imperil the interests and the honor of France. This eventuality, we ardently hope, will not come to pass. To prevent it, we count on both the wisdom of the German people and on the friendship of the Spanish people. If it be otherwise, fortified by your support, Gentlemen, and by that of the nation, we shall know how to fulfill our duty without hesitation and without weakness." The government wanted peace, in other words, but not at the expense of honor, and an aroused French public saw that national honor was the issue and clamored for its defense.[57]

Even these ministerial mistakes, however, did not guarantee that Bismarck would have his war, for Napoleon III was opposed to its declaration. On the evening of July 7, the French Ambassador to Prussia, Comte Vincent Benedetti, was ordered to go to Ems where the King of Prussia was vacationing, and to induce him, in his dual role as sovereign and head of the Hohenzollern family, to secure the renunciation of the Spanish throne by Prince Leopold. That same evening, Napoleon received Olozaga, the Spanish Ambassador to Paris, who opposed the Hohenzollern candidacy because he believed it would lead to a French-inspired civil war in Spain that could be ruinous. Thus he went to ask Napoleon whether peace would be assured if Prince Leopold would withdraw. "That is a question," the Emperor responded, "which does more honour to your patriotism than it is flattering to my intelligence. It is clear that if the Hohenzollern candidature were out of the way, peace would be assured, but how can

56. Lawrence D. Steefel, *Bismarck, the Hohenzollern Candidacy and the Origns of the Franco-Prussian War of 1870*, Cambridge, Mass.: Harvard, 1962, p. 244.

57. Zeldin, *Emile Ollivier and the Liberal Empire of Napoleon III*, pp. 174–176.

you imagine that Count von Bismarck, who has engineered all this *de longue main* to provoke us, will let the opportunity slip?" [58] Olozaga received the imperial authority to inform Prince Leopold that his withdrawal would avert a disaster.

The King of Prussia, meanwhile, received Benedetti on July 9 at Ems and three days later Prince Karl Anton, father of the candidate, withdrew his son's acceptance of the Spanish throne. It seemed that the French had won a striking diplomatic victory. On the same day, Prince Karl Anton wrote to the Prussian King: "July 12, 1870, Sigmaringen: Of Napoleon's *personal* desire to keep the peace I have today striking proof. Namely he has expressed it as his wish to King Leopold of the Belgians and requested him to press us for a withdrawal. . . . It now rests with the French Government to prove itself in earnest about the preservation of peace now that the *pretext* for war has been removed. If not, then it is clear that Napoleon is the submissive tool of the war party, which he is obliged blindly to obey for dynastic reasons." [59]

Prophetic words! Yet the matter should have been settled then and there. In fact, cold reason on the part of the Ollivier government would have prevented the candidacy from reaching crisis proportions in the first place. Not only was France unprepared militarily and diplomatically for war, but the new regime needed peace to complete its revolution. And that is precisely what the authoritarian Bonapartists sensed in taking a militant stand against the Hohenzollern candidacy. Had the Ollivier ministry contained men of great experience in foreign policy, they might well have played down the significance of the candidacy. Prince Leopold, if a Hohenzollern in name, was a great grandson of Caroline Bonaparte and a grandson of Stéphanie Beauharnais, more recently related to these families than to the Hohenzollerns.[60] Instead, the ministry, too much aware of the vociferous conservatives in the wings, sought to prove itself no less

58. Georges Bonnin, *Bismarck and the Hohenzollern Candidature for the Spanish Throne,* London: Chatto and Windus, 1957, p. 258.
59. *Ibid.,* p. 250.
60. A. Mels, *Wilhelmshoehe, souvenirs de la captivité de Napoléon III,* Paris: A Dupont, 1880, p. 58.

patriotic and vigorous in the face of Prussian arrogance. Militant pronouncements only inflamed public opinion, and that proved to be lethal for a government that was philosophically committed to representing public opinion.

Thus, to satisfy public opinion and to fend off the authoritarian Bonapartists, Napoleon permitted Gramont to instruct Benedetti to get the King of Prussia to associate himself more directly with the renunciation by assuring France that "he would never again authorize this candidacy." The King properly rejected the invitation as implying that he had been guilty of wrongdoing initially. In his report of the interview to Bismarck, he concluded by saying that "[the King] had nothing further to say to the ambassador. His Majesty leaves it to your Excellency whether Benedetti's fresh demand and its rejection should not be at once communicated both to our ambassadors and to the press." [61] Such latitude was all Bismarck needed! He published the King's report, but in an abbreviated form which made it appear that Benedetti had made an insulting demand upon the King, who had thereupon dismissed the Ambassador in an insulting manner. It was the last straw for the French Parliament, which voted for war without even examining Benedetti's account of the Ems interview. Bismarck had his war on July 19. More, he had maneuvered the French into declaring it, costing them overnight the sympathy of world opinion and sentencing them to isolation. Emile Ollivier might think that he was defending the honor of France and representing opinion at home, but his government had essentially lost control of affairs under pressure from the public and the conservative Bonapartists, fatally compromising both the integrity of France and the moderate reforms under way.

Since it has long been established that Napoleon III did not want war with Prussia, and since he obviously had a clearer idea than most of his generals of French military deficiencies, historians have had to deduce that he was incapacitated by his illness to account for his failure to stem the drift toward war. To such a deduction there are a variety of objections beyond the absence of medical proof. (And are we to infer that good health is a guaran-

61. La Gorce, *op. cit.*, VI, 281.

tee against political error?) Like Ollivier, Napoleon III was committed to the liberal reforms and victim of the same political pressures that gave the liberal ministry its precarious toehold in office. Daring not to have their courage or integrity called into question, the cabinet and the Emperor felt compelled by circumstances to force the issue with Prussia. Whether deservedly or not, they won a great victory in Prince Leopold's withdrawal; then pressed their luck into disaster. Reporting the outbreak of the war to his government, the British Ambassador in Paris came to the correct conclusion: The war had been forced upon the Emperor by the Right and by his ministers. He was in a poor position to resist because of the line he had taken at the time of Sadowa and could not afford the appearance of "truckling" to Prussia.[62]

The Parisian population may have been wildly enthusiastic for the war, but all eyewitnesses to the Emperor's departure from St. Cloud attest to the gloom and pessimism of the occasion. Knowing that the outcome of the war was so doubtful, aware that he was unfitted by experience to be generalissimo, and as conscious as anyone that his health was undermined, why did Napoleon III not choose to rest on the laurels of Solferino and Magenta and give supreme command to Marshal Bazaine who expected it? Probably because he believed that the nation expected him to do his Napoleonic duty, because he wished to subject the young Prince Imperial to battle in order to demonstrate that he was worthy of his name and position; and because the experience of the Crimean War with its bickering generals had suggested to him that the necessary unity of command could only be imposed by an Emperor's orders.[63]

The significance of his decision to go to the front proved more political than military. If he was not the strategist or tactician his uncle had been, neither were any of the senior subordinates who might have commanded in his place, notably Bazaine who was given supreme command only on August 12 after the

62. Lord Newton, *Life of Lord Lyons*, London: Longmans, Green, 1913, I, 301–302.
63. Fernand Giraudeau, *Napoléon III intime*, Paris: Paul Ollendorff, 1895, pp. 409–410.

initial reverses along the Rhine had forced a general retreat. And no matter who had commanded at the outset, he would have been hamstrung by the Minister of War's logistics. Marshal Leboeuf had given the cabinet his well-known assurance that the army was ready "down to the last gaiter button," but Napoleon III was somewhat closer to the mark when he telegraphed the Empress that he had found nothing ready. Assembling the French units at the frontier was so chaotic as to be demoralizing, and so time-consuming as to cost the French all opportunity to strike before the numerical advantage of the Prussians became decisive.

But, by his departure from the capital, the Emperor left Ollivier and his colleagues exposed to the hostility of the Empress, now Regent. Bad news was not long in coming from the front; Alsace had to be abandoned by the end of the first week of August, and Lorraine was on the verge of Prussian occupation. The Republicans demanded that the Parisians be armed and that the Parisian deputies in Parliament be named as a special committee of defense. Some of the cabinet members thought it was high time to arrest the Republican leaders, and Ollivier urged the Empress to recall the Emperor as the only person who could keep the Left in check. She refused the requested arrests on the grounds that they were more likely to incite insurrection than to contain it; while the Right, which certainly did not want the Emperor to return to Paris to strengthen the liberal ministry, convinced the Empress that his return without a victory would be fatal for the dynasty. Whatever merit may be found in her reasoning, it had the immediate effect of abandoning Ollivier and his colleagues to the Left and the Right, and led to subsequent military decisions which cost France what chance remained for victory.

On August 9 Clément Duvernois, the ex-Republican who had espoused the Liberal Empire but who had lately readjusted his principles to join the Right, moved a want of confidence vote in the lower house. Ollivier got ten votes, the ministers voting for themselves, and the liberal experiment collapsed with them— identified with national disaster. Napoleon was dismayed at the news.[64] The authoritarian Bonapartists were again in control, and the Empress put the new cabinet under the direction of the new Minister of War, the aged and undistinguished General Comte de Palikao. The Empress of course had never enjoyed public confidence, the new ministry had little to recommend it, which suggested to the Republicans—aware of their strength in Paris—that their moment had come. Yet they hesitated, fearful of being held accountable in case the armies should suffer a major defeat, fearful of imperial reprisals in the event of a victory. Many of the Bonapartist deputies vacillated too, uncertain whether to strike down the Republicans or to promote a revolution in the Chamber to forestall one in the streets. But too many of them were conscious of an unsavory analogy to provoke a royalist restoration: "If there be a morally condemned role in our history, it was the Senate's role in 1814," the Catholic deputy Charles Chesnelong wrote. He would have none of it, and knew that most others shunned such an action.[65]

The government desperately needed a victory in the field to bolster the home front against the Republicans and was dismayed to learn that the Emperor had given up supreme command and was planning to return to Paris to help prepare for its defense. Bazaine, the new generalissimo, had retired into Metz, and the plan was to gather the remnants of MacMahon's forces beaten in Alsace with the reserves available at Châlons, retreating on Paris to make the city a formidable fortress. Palikao and the Empress were entirely opposed to this strategy. Not only did they insist that Napoleon remain with MacMahon's forces, but that these forces go to the aid of Bazaine. The strategy of MacMahon and Napoleon was based on military reality, that of the government on the political crisis it faced in Paris: wishing at all cost to avoid the admission of serious defeat and the appearance of abandoning Bazaine who was popular with the Republicans. The upshot was that MacMahon felt compelled to move northeastward against his better judgment with his outgunned and

64. Zeldin, *Emile Ollivier and the Liberal Empire of Napoleon III*, pp. 180–182.
65. Chesnelong, *op. cit.*, pp. 218–220.

outnumbered army. And the Emperor, though disapproving, refused to interfere.[66]

The well-known end to the mistaken strategy came at Sedan, where the cornered army was battered beyond reasonable hope. Then Napoleon intervened, not as commander at Sedan, but as sovereign, to avoid further and useless bloodshed. For some weeks he had regarded the cause as lost because of the initial unreadiness and had so warned the Empress; [67] and now that the liberal ministers had fallen, taking with them the best hopes for his dynasty, there was little left for him but to seek death on the battlefield. All those who saw him at Sedan attested that he repeatedly and needlessly exposed himself to Prussian fire, complaining to an aide that his final failure was "not even to be able to get himself killed!" [68] Sedan was surrendered, along with the Emperor, on September 2, and two days later the Empire was gone.

66. *Enquête parlementaire sur le Gouvernement de la Défense Nationale,* Paris and Versailles: 1872–1875, Deposition of MacMahon, I, 29–32; and Léon Laforge, *Histoire complète de MacMahon,* Paris: Lamulle et Poisson, 1898, I, 248, 268.
67. Pauline Metternich-Winneburg, *Souvenirs de la princesse Pauline de Metternich, 1859–1871,* Paris: Plon-Nourrit, 1922, p. 197.
68. Général Prince de la Moskowa, "Quelques notes intimes sur la guerre de 1870," *le Correspondant,* December 10, 1898, pp. 969–970.

FOUR *September 4, 1870: The*

Reluctant Revolutionaries

Whereas the fatherland is in danger;
Whereas the national representatives have been given sufficient
time to decree the dethronement;
Whereas we are and do constitute legitimate authority deriving
from free universal suffrage;
We declare that Louis-Napoleon Bonaparte and his dynasty
have forever ceased to reign in France. —*Léon Gambetta, September 4, 1870*

DISQUIETING RUMORS of military defeat began seeping into
Paris on the morning of September 3, but Napoleon's
laconic telegram to the Empress reporting his surrender
and captivity did not reach the Ministry of the Interior until
four-thirty that afternoon. In the evening General Comte de
Palikao went before the *Corps législatif* to make the appalling
news official whereupon Jules Favre, for the Republicans, moved
that the imperial regime be declared overthrown and that a parliamentary commission be elected to assume responsibility for the
national defense. The shock and confusion were too great for
immediate action, and the deputies postponed all decisions for
the morrow.

By the morning of the fourth, the benumbed ministers
brought forth a counterproposal they hoped would save the imperiled regime. Aware that the unpopular Empress was no bul-

wark, they moved to revamp the Regency by asking the *Corps législatif* to elect a five-man Council of Regency and National Defense, naming Palikao Lieutenant-General of the Council. A third option—really a compromise—was then offered by Adolphe Thiers, who moved that a commission be elected to carry on government and the national defense, but that a constituent assembly be named *only* when circumstances would permit. His motion, in other words, implied the overthrow of the dynasty without specifying it and postponed a decision on a new form of government. A parliamentary committee was immediately appointed to consider the three alternatives, and a hasty verdict was expected.

The likelihood was that the committee would report favorably on the Thiers proposal, in which case the new commission might well be dominated by men who had rallied to the Liberal Empire. If the Empress had resigned herself to such a possibility, the Republicans and Socialists had not. The sparse evidence implies that some of the Republican deputies connived with more radical leaders in Paris—men like Blanqui, Delescluze, Millière, and Pyat—and that a mob from the poorer quarters was quickly mobilized around the Palais Bourbon. Gambetta was probably not one of the conniving deputies. But he knew of their maneuvers and believed that the presence of a mob, which he hoped to control, would force the deputies to take more revolutionary measures while maintaining a semblance of legality. In other words, that the deputies would see the need to vote for the Republic; but the Assembly would continue to function, insurrection would be checked, and the Republicans could get on with the unfinished business with Prussia. Gambetta's revolution, to be aided by socialist agitation, was not to be socialist, but to be directed against personal power.[1]

Mobs have a way of spoiling even well-laid plans, which Gambetta's were not. He spoke to the crowd and tried to keep order, not wanting the Assembly dispersed in the face of the enemy; but the Assembly was invaded and the presiding officer refused to continue the sitting. The Republicans feared to hesi-

---

1. J. Tchnernoff, *Le Parti républicain au coup d'état et sous le second empire,* Paris: Pedone, 1906, pp. 609–611

tate any longer, and Gambetta rose to announce that the Bonaparte dynasty had ceased to reign in France. Even this did not satisfy the mob. A new government must be formed at once and at the Hôtel de Ville, the traditional scene of revolutionary government. The Republican deputies, having lost control at the Palais Bourbon, had no further option but to abandon the Assembly and to lead the mob across the Seine to the Hôtel de Ville where they found the more radical leaders already assembled.[2]

A clash between the factions of the Left seemed imminent, but was avoided when Jules Ferry proposed that the Parisian deputies form the new government. As elected officials, they had some legitimacy. As Paris was then the principal Prussian target, these deputies could lay special claim to the responsibility for defense. (The radicals had no such effective argument.) It meant the inclusion of Henri Rochefort, the only radical among the Parisian delegation, but his exclusion might have provoked insurrection. And Gambetta was included on grounds that he had been elected from Paris in 1869, though opting for a seat from Marseille.[3]

"Citizens of Paris," their announcement ran, "the Republic is proclaimed. The government has been named by acclamation. It is composed of citizens: Emmanuel Arago, Crémieux, Jules Favre, Jules Ferry, Gambetta, Garnier-Pagès, Glais-Bizoin, Pelletan, Picard, Rochefort, Jules Simon. General Trochu [already military governor of Paris] is charged with full military powers for the national defense. He is called to the presidency of the Government. The Government asks the citizens to be calm. The people must not forget that they are in the presence of the enemy. The Government is, above all, a Government of National Defense." [4]

The executive committee having been announced, it remained to distribute ministerial portfolios, to appoint mayors for the government of Paris, and to dissolve officially the Council of

2. J. P. T. Bury, *Gambetta and the National Defense,* London: Longmans, Green, 1936, pp. 63–65.
3. *Enquête parlementaire sur les Actes du Gouvernement de la Défense Nationale,* Déposition de Jules Favre, I, 332.
4. *Défense Nationale,* Rapport Daru, p. 63.

State and the *Corps législatif*. In the scramble for places, the chief contest was between Gambetta and Picard for the Ministry of the Interior, with its control of the police, both men recognizing that it was the key position after a change in regime. Beyond that, if Picard should secure Interior, it meant continued cooperation between Republicans and liberals as under the Liberal Empire; if Gambetta, the administration would become exclusively Republican. Gambetta achieved the prize by getting to the ministry first, sending out telegrams to the prefects at once over his signature. When the ministries were allocated, late in the evening of September 4, Gambetta's priority was recognized, and the outmaneuvered Picard accepted Finance. Probably the right man was in the right place, for if anyone in the government could be a Danton, it would be Gambetta, a thirty-two-year-old firebrand with a taste for improvisation.[5] As for the remainder of the ministries, Crémieux took Justice, Jules Favre Foreign Affairs, and Jules Simon Public Instruction, to which were added Cults and Fine Arts. Four posts went to men not on the executive committee: Public Works to Pierre Dorian, Commerce and Agriculture to Joseph Magnin, and War and Marine to General Le Flô and Admiral Fourichon respectively.[6]

Etienne Arago was named mayor of Paris despite a popular clamor for Rochefort; and on the following day, September 5, Arago nominated twenty mayors for the arrondissements. Evidently Arago consulted only Gambetta before making the nominations public, enabling him to name some candidates further to the Left than pleased some members of the government. The nominations, however, were allowed to stand of necessity to avoid infuriating the radicals.[7]

For such an improvised, indeed haphazard, revolution as that of September 4 to have been bloodless seems remarkable in a city where revolutionary violence was already a tradition, especially since the factionalism within the old Opposition seemed to guarantee a struggle for power. The imminence of military

5. Bury, *op. cit.*, pp. 70–76.
6. Amaury Dréo, *Gouvernement de la Défense Nationale. Procès verbaux des séances du Conseil*, Paris: Charles-Lavauzelle, 1905, pp. 69–70.
7. *Défense Nationale*, Rapport Daru, pp. 102–104.

disaster probably restrained the hottest heads on the Left, while any thought of a Bonapartist *coup d'état* was rendered hopeless by the captivity of the Emperor. The Bonapartist edifice collapsed with hardly a whimper, the Senate and *Corps législatif* simply ceasing to sit so that their abolition was mere formality, and the Empress slipped out of the Tuileries on the fourth to beseech her American dentist to aid her escape from Paris and from France.* All parties found it expedient for the moment to think of the national defense first and to temporize about politics, thus creating a façade of unity.

The party most scrupulous in maintaining this patriotic façade was that headed by the Empress-Regent, now in British exile. Brought news that the Prussians might offer her more favorable terms than they were prepared to offer the Republicans in Paris, she firmly rejected all intrigues that might hamper the national defense and wept over the plight of the French forces which remained after Sedan.[8] Gambetta, meanwhile, was purging all Bonapartists from office as collaborators of the recent despot, replacing them with men thought to be moderate Republicans and devoted to the principle of strong central government. This naked party preference not only laid Gambetta open to the charge that he aimed at a dictatorship based upon loyal creatures, but made rather porous the façade of national unity desired by the Government of National Defense. In fact, Gambetta believed that a successful national defense required the leadership of a unified, disciplined party but, whatever the merits of his argument, his expulsions and appointments had both immediate and long-term significance.

No doubt, for instance, the Minister of the Interior was able to prevent the political disintegration of France by appointing prefects, on whom he could personally count, to trouble spots throughout the country. As a revolutionary regime the Government of National Defense was weakly based and dared not excercise its authority in a high-handed manner. Lyon, Marseille, and Toulouse were the main centers of radicalism outside Paris, and

---

* See the details in *The Memoirs of Dr. Thomas W. Evans: The Second French Empire,* New York: D. Appleton, 1905.
8. *Défense Nationale,* Déposition du Général Bourbaki, III, 345–346.

Gambetta sincerely believed that he faced secessionist movements in all three where commune governments, denouncing the new national government as bourgeois, were champions of social and economic radicalism.[9] Only the appointment of vigorous prefects, sustained by loyal National Guard units, sufficed to maintain Parisian authority; but at best the cities remained sources of anxiety.[10] In Paris itself, the radical leaders soon grew restless at seeing the moderates in possession of the offices and organized the Central Committee of the Twenty Arrondissements, ostensibly a patriotic pressure group but in reality a rival government impatiently waiting in the wings. But of this, more later.

In 1814 men who had followed Napoleon I helped to arrange the Bourbon restoration and were absorbed into the new regime. Known then as liberals, they mingled with Republicans and liberal Monarchists. Consequently no Bonapartist party in name existed right down to the election of Louis-Napoleon as President in 1848. Gambetta, by expelling the Bonapartists from office in 1870 as tainted men, made of them a party anxious to regain office and to have an opportunity to remove the stain of the humiliating defeat.[11] The Opposition under the Second Empire had easily labeled them corrupt men, perhaps making it easier to clean house in 1870, but setting an imposing standard of virtue for the men of the Third Republic that in time proved to be more than a liability.

As Minister of the Interior, Gambetta fell heir to responsibility for the revived National Guard, already reactivated on August 12 by the Regency as the military crisis became apparent. General Palikao had initially ordered the formation of sixty battalions in Paris, each containing 1,500 men divided into eight companies. On September 6, Gambetta ordered the formation of sixty additional battalions. The Parisian municipalities were responsible for carrying out his decree, and the battalions were given the right to elect their own officers. Traditionally the National Guard had been an unpaid service, largely recruited from

9. Lissagaray, *History of the Commune of 1871*, New York: International Publishers, 1898, pp. 3–4.
10. Bury, *op. cit.*, pp. 226–232.
11. Theodore Zeldin, *The Political System of Napoleon III*, pp. 3–8.

the middle class; but, with the principle of *levée en masse* revived on the sixth, Gambetta felt compelled to authorize a daily stipend for the assistance of guardsmen drawn from the very poor. Beginning at 1 fr. 50 per day the stipend was soon increased by 75 centimes for a wife and 25 centimes for each child. To the dismay of Generals Trochu and Le Flô, the workers flocked enthusiastically to the recruiting posts, ultimately providing manpower for 134 battalions instead of the proposed sixty. Untrained, the men were of doubtful military value and would have been of greater use in war industries.

The government, however, was caught in a dilemma of its own making. During the electoral campaign of 1869, the Republican candidates for office had generally favored a nation in arms over the professional army and were now in no position to restrict enlistment. Because many of the new battalions elected the most radical of the Parisian leaders to be officers (some of whom seem to have been self-appointed!), any governmental attempt to deny workers their right to the daily stipend would have been to risk insurrection. Not even a shortage of rifles could restrict recruitment: 280,000 were issued by September 30, and still twenty-four battalions were unarmed.[12] In its planning of military operations, the government was never free from the fear of armed pressure on the home front, a numbing effect upon men already tormented by the agonies of their military situation.

One army of regulars had been lost at Sedan, while Bazaine's army of five corps lay idle at Metz. Yet Trochu still had in Paris, at the beginning of the siege, 106,000 regulars; but only a small proportion of them were seasoned troops. Renault's XIV Corps consisted largely of recruits and had not yet been on campaign. Vinoy's XIII Corps contained several regiments which had missed reaching MacMahon at Sedan and had then been recalled to Paris. The navy contributed 8,000 sailors and 3,000 marines who were reliable, well-disciplined men. In contrast were the Garde Mobile, eighteen battalions of reservists brought back from Châlons by Trochu, where they had been notorious for an indiscipline that became worse when they returned to the influ-

12. *Défense Nationale*, Rapport Daru, pp. 112–121; and Bury, *op. cit.*, pp. 85–88.

ence of Parisian radical leaders. So much for the "regulars." The more undisciplined troops were the most insistent on the superiority of natural French *élan* over anything the disciplined Prussians could put against them.[13] We need not be surprised that the French professionals had little sympathy for such notions after their field experiences of the previous month.

At the outset of the siege, not one member of the Government of National Defense believed that Paris could hold out for more than a month. On the other hand, the defensive positions were in an excellent state, sufficient to inflict heavy casualties upon the assaulting army and to hold it at bay for at least a month. By that time, relief forces could presumably fall upon the German rear and relieve the city. Unfortunately for such strategy, the Germans did not waste their forces in assault, but were content to surround the city and lay siege to it.[14] Otherwise Trochu's strategy might well have succeeded, sparing him the public criticism for inaction that became his cross.

This initial expectation of a short siege enabled the members of the government to refrain from the tight controls in Paris that the crisis really demanded but that, as liberals, they were reluctant to decree. Considerable fuel and foodstuffs had been crammed into Paris in preparation for the siege, but strict measures to control consumption were not taken early enough. Equally important, these Republicans, who had made a career attacking censorship under the Empire, freed the press from all restraints including taxes and were jelly when confronted by insults and threats from the radical fringe.[15] Yet the men in the government were neither stupid nor mediocre, as they have been so often portrayed. Their talents were simply not those required for the time or place: mostly lawyers, not an experienced diplomat among them, their political careers spent wholly in opposition, and so conditioned against authority that, with the notable

13. Michael Howard, *The Franco-Prussian War*, New York: Macmillan, 1962, pp. 320–321.
14. *Défense Nationale*, Rapport Daru, p. 132.
15. Hazel C. Benjamin, "Official Propaganda and the French Press during the Franco-Prussian War," *Journal of Modern History*, IV, #2 (June 1932), 220.

exception of Gambetta, they were temperamentally unsuited to exercise it. In 1868, when Napoleon III and Marshal Niel were vainly trying to provide the regular army with large numbers of trained reserves, Jules Favre and Jules Simon had countered with proposals for a trained militia to replace the standing army.[16] Favre, in the *Corps législatif*, accused Niel of wanting to turn France into a barracks. Niel's response, "Take care that you do not turn her into a cemetery," [17] equally epitomized Favre's dilemma in 1870.

Beyond providing for the national defense, one of the earliest problems to confront the new regime was whether to hold elections for a national assembly. The issue was first formally tackled by the cabinet on September 8. Jules Favre presented a sound case for immediate elections, based as it was upon the current governmental assumption that a quick peace could be negotiated with Bismarck on the grounds that the war was merely Napoleon III's war. Now that the "aggressor" had been captured and overthrown, it simply remained to reestablish the peace—a moderate peace involving no loss of French territory. What the Government of National Defense needed, in Favre's view, was a legitimacy based upon national sanction in order to open negotiations. He had not yet spoken to Bismarck, nor would he for another ten days, so that he did not know that Bismarck had territorial ambitions, something the imperial generals had discovered when Napoleon III surrendered; nor did Favre's view show any awareness of Bismarck's responsibility in provoking the war.

The opponents of immediate elections, the more doctrinaire Republicans led by Gambetta, recalled the recent imperial successes at the polls and concluded that the Republicans were not likely to win an election. Consequently they favored preserving the revolutionary regime with a public explanation that it was unwise to carry on with politics in the face of the enemy. By a

---

16. Richard D. Challener, *The French Theory of the Nation in Arms, 1866–1939*, New York: 2nd ed., Russell & Russell, 1965, pp. 26–27.
17. Maxime Du Camp, *Souvenirs d'un Demi-Siècle*, Paris: Hachette, 1949, I, 258.

narrow margin, the cabinet voted against immediate elections, postponing them until October 16.[18] The inadequacy of the decision became apparent even before Favre had his first interview with Bismarck, for the Prussians revealed that they would not negotiate with a government which did not represent the whole nation. Gambetta, therefore, moved that national elections be advanced to October 2 and that municipal elections precede them, his motion passing.[19] The Parisian radicals were furious at the decision, convinced that the government was selling out the revolution to the provincial reactionaries; but two days later, September 18, Bismarck granted Favre an interview at the Royal Headquarters.[20]

If the radicals had initially agreed to tolerate the Government of National Defense for patriotic reasons, they did not mean to allow that regime free rein. On the very night of September 4, they proposed a Republican Central Committee of the Twenty Arrondissements, with headquarters on the Place de la Corderie-du-Temple, which was actually organized on the eleventh. Soon dominated by Delescluze, Pyat, Blanqui, and Flourens, the Central Committee began to consider the same problems then confounding the government: elections, national defense, and provisioning of the city.[21] The Central Committee was meant to be a potential government, its members knowing full well from long experience under the Empire that the men of September 4 were not revolutionaries and hating them as betrayers of the true Republic. *"Gambetta, un révolutionnaire manqué,"* said Flourens, *"un Danton, un Hoche et un Washington tout ensemble; en résumé une bruyante incapacité, un avocat qui ne doute de rien, so mêle de tout, et ne sait rien faire."* [22] By which he meant bourgeois. The intention was not so much to give the Government of National Defense a chance, but to be prepared to take advantage of its mistakes.

18. *Défense Nationale*, Rapport Chaper, pp. 12–13; Rapport Daru, pp. 113–137; and Howard, *op. cit.*, p. 227.
19. Dréo, *op. cit.*, p. 128.
20. *Défense Nationale*, Rapport Daru, pp. 146–147.
21. *Ibid.*, 85–87; and John Plamenatz, *The Revolutionary Movement in France, 1815–1871*, London: Longmans, 1952, pp. 133–134.
22. Gustave Flourens, *Paris Livré*, Paris: Librairie Internationale, 1871, p. 60.

The men in the actual government, if uneasy about the existence of the Central Committee, underestimated at the outset the danger from that source. They suffered initially from the illusion, honestly acquired after years of opposition to hideous despotism, that they were political and economic radicals, therefore kin of the men in the Central Committee. And were they not all Republicans, equally anxious not to injure the infant Republic? Political liberals the men of the government were, but radicals, no. And far from being economic radicals, they were not even truly liberal, having fought Napoleon III on free trade. In the few months that this regime was in power, its caution and restraint in economic and financial policy, its unwillingness to mobilize forcefully the national resources, its refusal even to confiscate the properties of former officials of the Empire may have been liberal in theory, but was intensely conservative in spirit.[23] Indeed, the economic conservatism of the early Third Republic was rooted in the conservatism of September 4; and as the autumn of 1870 deepened and the menace from the Left became more obvious, the government sensed its conservative role but was too harnessed to old attitudes to take unequivocal measures to defend itself against insurrection.

It is only too easy to list the mistakes of the government, ignoring the appalling task it had shouldered and belittling its efforts against demoralizing odds. Recognizing the imminence of a Prussian attack upon Paris, the cabinet began on September 7 to organize a governmental delegation to be established in the provinces. The nature of this delegation, including the question of whether the entire government ought to leave Paris, was hitched to the problem of national elections. Thus, on the eighth, when the cabinet rejected Favre's appeal for immediate national elections, it was sentencing the government to remain in Paris. For the government was Parisian, not national, and could not abandon its political base while the state of provincial opinion was so doubtful. This logic was officially recognized on September 9, and two days later Crémieux was the minister chosen

23. Edward L. Katzenbach, Jr., "Liberals at War: The Economic Policies of the Government of National Defense, 1870–1871," *American Historical Review*, LVI (July 1951), 805–817.

to go to Tours as the governmental delegate. Considering that his task was to begin mobilizing the provinces for the relief of Paris, one would think that youth and vigor would have been the desired qualities; but Crémieux was chosen because he was the oldest member of the government and least able to endure the rigors of a siege. Gambetta, meanwhile, had been receiving an alarming number of reports of local resistance to central authority and concluded that a stronger government was needed at Tours. On the fifteenth, Glais-Bizoin (another ancient) and Admiral Fourichon were designated to join Crémieux.[24]

The government took a further step to bolster its position. Jules Favre asked Adolphe Thiers if he would consent to take the French embassy in London to use his well-known talents to build up foreign sympathy and diplomatic assistance for France. Thiers agreed, on the eleventh, not merely to go to London but to seek support also in St. Petersburg and Vienna.[25]

Favre finally had his interview with Bismarck at Ferrières on September 18, the stupendous estate acquired by Baron James Rothschild during the Second Empire. Evidently Favre was taken entirely by surprise when he heard Bismarck's conditions for peace and was shocked out of his wits. Having expected an easy return to normal relations now that Napoleon III had been removed, Favre discovered that Bismarck meant to detach two provinces from France as well as to exact a large indemnity. The kindest thing to be said about Favre's response is that he had had no experience as a diplomat and was under great strain. Negotiating as he was from a position of obvious military weakness, his best line would have been to reiterate that the war had been Napoleon's, to insist that the new Republic wanted nothing but peace with the German world, and to offer a formal guarantee of the German frontier against further aggression. This would eliminate the German claim on Alsace and Lorraine, which were wanted for defensive purposes; and Favre could have offered a substantial indemnity as a measure of the Prussian victory.

No one knows whether Bismarck would have found such terms acceptable. But it is known that the Prussians were con-

24. *Défense Nationale,* Rapport Chaper, pp. 10–23.
25. Dréo, *op. cit.,* p. 105.

cerned about the length of their supply lines with winter coming on, that they had respect for the recuperative powers of the French, and that they had granted moderate terms to Austria in 1866 once their objectives had been obtained. Instead of such a proposal, Favre blustered that France would cede neither an inch of territory nor a stone of her fortresses, predicting an endless struggle between the two nations.[26] By chance, the investment of Paris was completed the following day.

Favre's failure to obtain terms from Bismarck that could lead to an armistice brought the dilemma of the French government into full focus for the first time. To have signed such harsh terms would have compromised the Republic, not the Empire whose defeat had made them possible, which meant that the war had to be pursued by men who had no confidence that it could be won. Perhaps a determined national resistance would force the Prussians to offer more lenient terms, but the military disparity suggested precisely the opposite, opening the possiblility of even harsher terms after a fight to the knife. The radicals of Paris, on the other hand, had no doubt that armed French citizens, if led by "true" Republicans as in 1792, would sweep back the Prussians. When they discovered that the government had been seeking an armistice without giving the people opportunity to win a certain victory, it proved what the radicals had believed all along: that bourgeois Republicans were not Republicans. No matter that the government had rejected disastrous terms; that it should seek something less than victory was intolerable.

On September 22, Gambetta had to confront this radical outrage. A delegation of twenty representing the arrondissements —mostly self-appointed, extremist busybodies—were joined by 107 National Guard officers, who were led to the Hôtel de Ville by Jules Vallès, Blanqui, and Millière, there to demand that resistance to Prussia be pursued vigorously, that national elections be postponed as prejudicial to the national defense, but that elections for the Paris Commune be held without delay. The demonstrators were so menacing that Gambetta could not control them, and they were only dispersed when Picard came forth

26. Howard, *op. cit.*, pp. 231–232.

with a false announcement about a Prussian attack upon Paris.[27] The civilians in the government finally learned what the military had known and feared all along: that it is folly to arm any group which cannot be effectively disciplined. This demonstration of September 22 of course revealed the association of the Central Committee and certain units of the National Guard.[28]

Next day the government reconsidered the problem of elections—not merely because of the demonstration favoring election of the Commune, but because there would be no immediate armistice, the original reason for calling national elections. Gambetta thought that it would be dangerous to postpone municipal elections, but the majority held that all elections should be postponed and all energies directed to the war. The radicals were pleased at the cancellation of national elections for, as Blanqui put it, "If elections take place, the reactionaries will certainly win. Representative Assemblies are outmoded, condemned, bad, not only in times of crisis, in time of war, but always." [29] But they continued to hold out for the Commune: "The people of Paris," Delescluze said on September 27, "must proceed alone in elections; and these elections should take place next Sunday whether the government likes it or not." [30]

Next, the Tours delegation made trouble by announcing that national elections would be held on October 15. Because of the investment of Paris, the Tours delegation had found itself weak in its isolation. Its decision to decree the elections despite Paris simply reflected the need to shore up its authority, but the decree was an assumption of autonomy that the government in Paris did not mean to tolerate. The cabinet debated the matter on October 1, ordering Tours to rescind its decree, then deciding that the Tours delegation must be brought to heel and that Gambetta was the man to do it.[31] The Minister of the Interior left Paris by balloon for Tours on October 7, a mode of transportation for which he had little stomach, but made necessary by the Prussian blockade.

27. Dréo, *op. cit.*, p. 151; and Bury, *op. cit.*, p. 89.
28. *Défense Nationale*, Rapport Daru, p. 87.
29. *Ibid.*, p. 147.
30. *Ibid.*, p. 91.
31. *Défense Nationale*, Rapport Chaper, pp. 32–33.

Meanwhile, the government faced a second armed demonstration at the Hôtel de Ville on October 5, this time led by Major Flourens at the head of ten battalions of National Guards. Demanding immediate municipal election, Flourens also asked that his battalions be armed with chassepots and that National Guard units be used to make sorties against the besiegers. For several days the cabinet debated the seriousness of Flourens' activities, coming to the easy conclusion that, if he perhaps aspired to govern Paris, his battalions were probably loyal to the government, and that it would be best to ignore the indiscipline on the fifth rather than provoke further confrontation. Thus, on the seventh, the government again announced the postponement of all elections until the siege could be lifted.[32]

Evidently the Central Committee anticipated the postponement and was already arranging further unpleasantness for the government. That very day Etienne Arago, the mayor of Paris, warned the government that another armed demonstration was in the making, and when Flourens appeared at the Hôtel de Ville on October 8 with about six battalions, the entire government had assembled to meet him. General Trochu was especially firm, refusing the chassepots, municipal elections, and mass sorties against the enemy, adding that the presence of the petitioners was a serious breach of military discipline. Charles Floquet, the deputy mayor, accused Flourens of jeopardizing the life of the Republic, after which most of Flourens' officers abandoned him, breaking the back of the demonstration. Flourens offered to resign his command, and his officers accepted it.[33]

Any hope that Flourens had become imbued with loyalty to the regime was quickly dissipated. Two days later the Prefect of Police, Kératry, reported that Flourens and Blanqui had just presided over a meeting of National Guard battalion commanders and had presented a resolution calling for the overthrow of the government. Though the resolution was beaten, 48 to 19, the meeting exposed radical intentions beyond dispute. Kératry and Trouchu were for arresting Flourens and Blanqui at once, but the cabinet members quibbled over whether sufficient evidence

32. *Ibid.*, pp. 37–38; and Dréo, *op. cit.*, pp. 191–193.
33. *Défense Nationale*, Rapport Daru, pp. 127–131, and Dréo, *op. cit.*, p. 194.

existed to secure conviction. One reads their debate with a growing realization that these men, whose lives had been spent in
opposition, were little aware that a government has both a right
and a duty to defend itself against subversion, particularly in
time of war. General Trochu finally prevailed over the reluctant
cabinet members in getting the arrest order voted, though
Rochefort separated from the majority on the issue.[34] The cabinet refused, however, to close down the meeting places where the
radicals gathered to foment insurrections, salving consciences
that were proving too delicate for the task at hand.

During the month of October, the hope of foreign intervention on the side of France gradually waned. On the first of the
month, Thiers had sent an optimistic telegram to the Tours
delegation, wire communication with Paris by then having been
cut off. He believed that Russia would exert pressure to obtain
an acceptable peace settlement, though he had not obtained any
formal guarantee.[35] Needing more precise information, the
Tours delegation asked the regular French representative in St.
Petersburg for clarification. He responded on October 14 with
the dismal advice that France ought not to expect any help from
the European powers, meaning that the Thiers mission had
failed.

Thiers himself arrived in Tours on October 21, the very day
that the British Ambassador read his government's proposal that
both belligerents agree to an armistice to permit the French to
conduct national elections, a proposal that was quickly supported by Russia, Austria, and Italy. The French at Tours felt
forced by circumstances to agree, and toward the end of the
month Thiers traveled to Versailles to reopen negotiations with
Bismarck. Upon arrival, he was smitten with the news that Marshal Bazaine had surrendered Metz on the twenty-seventh; and
the Prussians sent Thiers on to Paris with a safe-conduct pass
that he might give the government accurate news of Metz. Presumably Paris, like Tours, would now see the need to resume
negotiations.

34. *Défense Nationale,* Rapport Chaper, p. 40; and Dréo, *op. cit.,* pp. 201–
202.
35. François Charles-Roux, *Alexandre II, Gortchakoff et Napoléon III,* Paris:
Plon, 1913, p. 508.

The undeniable news that Bazaine had surrendered that the government thus received on October 30 came as a double shock to the cabinet. For the surrender of five corps released thousands of German troops for service against Paris and against the troops being trained by Tours. Furthermore, the government had just rebuked Félix Pyat for an inflammatory article in *le Combat* where he had published, as fact, a rumor of the surrender, claiming that the government was hiding the truth from the people "in its usual way." [36] Now the government had to admit the loss of Metz, and at the same time to announce the reopening of armistice negotiations with Bismarck.

Was further resistance in fact useless? The answer lay not alone in an appraisal of the military facts but in politics, for at stake was the future of the Republic. By October 30 both the military and political facts seemed to require an armistice, time to bring food into beleaguered Paris and to provide for national elections that would relieve the government from its precarious dependence on Paris alone. All sorties from the city had failed, Metz and 150,000 men were gone, and the potential effectiveness of provincial armies remained unknown, though Gambetta had plunged with the expected vigor into the task of raising relief forces upon his arrival in Tours earlier that month.

Gambetta, more Republican than liberal, authoritarian by nature, was more temperamentally qualified for the exercise of power than were his colleagues who remained in Paris. As Minister of the Interior, he was empowered to prevent the Tours delegation from holding national elections until Paris should sanction them. His next act was to take over the Ministry of War at Tours, which he did with Admiral Fourichon's approval, thus combining in his person the ministries responsible for raising and equipping the armed forces, and for employing them. He exercised a virtual dictatorship outside of Paris, yet always conducted himself as a man believing in liberty, insisting that he neither violated the law nor exceeded his instructions. Whether on September 4 or later, he worked to avoid revolutionary violence.[37]

---

36. Henri Rochefort, *Les Aventures de ma vie*, Paris: Dupont, 1896, II, 243.
37. Bury, *op. cit.*, pp. 224–225.

Almost at once Gambetta appointed Charles de Freycinet as his assistant, giving him the title of Delegate. Both Gambetta and Freycinet believed that civilians alone were competent to direct the mobilization of the national resources for total war. The professionals having bungled the first portion of the war, the amateurs would now take over. The military was unaccustomed to taking direction from a civilian Minister of War, but also inexperienced in matters of industrial production and national finance, so that the generals had no satisfactory alternatives to support their irritation at civilian control.

Considering that France lost about 500,000 men in casualties and prisoners from the imperial army, the total number raised for further service by the Government of National Defense was impressive—at least on paper. Paris contained roughly 260,000 troops, while the Tours delegation ultimately mustered 578,900 more by calling up only unmarried males between twenty-one and forty. The total was almost exactly what Napoleon III and Marshal Niel had projected in 1867 as adequate to contain the Prussians, so that the problem was not numbers but time to train recruits before Paris should fall. Perhaps in retrospect the effort appears to have been doomed at the outset, but it is also understandable that Gambetta, aware of the manpower available, convinced of the superiority of French *élan,* and determined not to compromise the Republic, sincerely believed in the possibility of victory.

Whatever the military crisis, political considerations never faded away because of Gambetta's determination, not merely to save the Republic, but to prevent its seizure by the extreme Left. When the provincial National Guard was mobilized by a decree of October 12, the Guard's traditional privilege of electing its own officers was confirmed. Each canton was responsible for raising a battalion, every arrondissement a legion, and every department a brigade. Officers of the Garde Mobile had been appointed by the Ministry of War under the Empire, but after September 4 these positions were made elective too. As in Paris, the elective principle proved not to be a source of political strength but of indiscipline, until the government ultimately felt obliged to revoke the elective principle on December 18.

The auxiliary forces also included the *francs-tireurs*—or free corps—raised locally and informally. Multiplying quickly, these bands of partisans were more often a political embarrassment than a military asset. Estimated to include over 50,000 men, they helped to convert the war into a terror and counterterror affair, and their freewheeling operations led Gambetta to try to reorganize them as Garde Mobile. Each partisan band had a distinct political hue, the spectrum running from the Legitimists to the extreme Left, and some comprised foreigners. In fact, the most notable of the partisan leaders was the Italian volunteer Giuseppe Garibaldi, whose assistance held the possibility of annoying French Catholics and conservatives, not to speak of the fact that he might end by demanding Nice and Savoy for Italy as the price of his cooperation. The provincial population as a whole, however, did not engage in partisan activity, but was inclined to accept passively whatever political or military authority was established in any given locality. Gambetta failed to fire rural patriotic fury, and rural desire for peace and order became a major reason why the radicals' demand for war *à outrance* made little sense. In fact, the longer Gambetta worked to build the national resistance, the more hostile the rural population grew to Republican idealism.[38]

Even in Paris, where popular desire to resist the Prussians was much greater, based both on support for the Republic and upon a simple faith in the invincibility of Parisians, a great majority still supported the moderate Republicans in office, not the radicals agitating for power. When that government announced on October 30 that it would again seek an armistice for the purpose of national elections and to revictual the city, the news was coupled with that of the loss of Metz and news of a minor military reversal on the northern side of Paris, setting off rumors of treason and heightening suspicions of incompetence. Those who had opposed the moderate Republicans from the start had little trouble equating armistice to treason and military defeat.[39]

On the morning of the thirty-first, a crowd began assembling

38. Howard, *op. cit.*, pp. 239–256.
39. *Défense Nationale*, Rapport Daru, pp. 171–174.

at the Hôtel de Ville to protest an armistice, its size variously estimated to have been between two and six thousand;[40] certainly a tiny minority of the Parisians, but large enough to be noisy and dangerous. Members of the government began arriving after one o'clock, and soon delegations of demonstrators were received. Attempts were made to explain governmental policies, but to little avail in the face of demands for immediate election of the Commune. Meanwhile, the mob began to occupy the Hôtel de Ville, and the government could do little to protect itself, knowing that many of the National Guard units were commanded by radicals. In desperation, the government permitted Mayor Arago to announce that municipal elections would be held, but did not specify a date. Consequently, Arago's announcement was rudely greeted by the mob, which may account for his private decision, in sending instructions to the mayors of arrondissements, to advise them that the elections would take place "tomorrow, Tuesday, at noon." [41]

By then the concession was useless as the radical leaders, seeing the government apparently defenseless, prepared to assume power. Late in the afternoon of October 31, Gustave Flourens—whose arrest had never been carried out for fear that he would be protected from the police by radical battalions— arrived at the Hôtel de Ville with a slate of names "unanimously elected" in the courtyard. The confusion was great when names were read out to the mob but we can be sure that Flourens meant to establish an emergency Commune council for Paris plus a Committee of Public Safety comprising five members: Flourens, Delescluze, Blanqui, Millière, and Ranvier. The regular government refused to resign, forcing Flourens to issue a decree announcing the government's resignation.[42]

Had the population as a whole supported Flourens, the insurrection might well have succeeded. Meanwhile General Ducrot, informed of the peril, was on his way with two brigades withdrawn from the front lines, while loyal battalions of Na-

---

40. *Ibid.*, pp. 233–235.
41. *Ibid.*, p. 187.
42. *Ibid.*, pp. 195–200; and Jules Simon, *Souvenirs du 4 septembre*, Paris: Librairie Illustrée, 1874, p. 331.

tional Guards were mustered in the Place Vendôme. By midnight between thirty and forty battalions were converging on the Hôtel de Ville. Flourens, with his usual feeble appraisal of a situation, tried to provoke a fight; but his own National Guardsmen seemed to panic, and all was over by five in the morning on November 1, Flourens escaping.[43]

At the height of the crisis, when the government had been forced to concede municipal elections, the Minister of Public Works, Pierre Dorian, further assured the insurgents that no reprisals would be taken against them once order was restored, giving this assurance without consulting other members of the government. Dorian's motives have remained doubtful: he claimed to have made the concession under duress.[44] But as his name also figured on Flourens' list for a new revolutionary regime, the taint of duplicity was never washed away. He provided a moral issue, however, for his ministerial colleagues who had great talent for indecision. Insurrection in time of war was patently intolerable, which even Rochefort, the most radical member of the government, saw in insisting upon the arrest of the radical leaders and in proposing that it was time for the government to evacuate Paris for a more secure provincial seat.[45] Moreover, as the recent concessions to the radicals had been made under duress, some members of the government argued that the government was not honor-bound to keep its word.

At its morning meeting on November 1, faced with the resignation of the new Prefect of Police, Edmond Adam, if it voted to arrest the radical leaders, the government voted against arrest by a narrow margin. Following which the government voted to postpone municipal elections from that day until the sixth, thus provoking the resignations of both Adam and Rochefort.[46] Next the government decreed a plebiscite for November 3 to ask the public if, in the light of the insurrection, the government still enjoyed popular support. The enthusiastic response—558,000

---

43. Simon, *op. cit.*, pp. 337–348; and *Défense Nationale*, Rapport Daru, pp. 207–213.
44. *Défense Nationale*, Déposition de Dorian, I, 527.
45. *Ibid.*, Déposition de Dréo, II, 62.
46. Etienne Arago, *L'Hôtel de Ville de Paris au 4 Septembre et pendant le siège*, Paris: Hetzel, n.d., pp. 241–248.

votes to 62,000—should have given the government courage to crack down on the extreme Left for its mutinous action, especially since the vote gave the government a firm legal basis for the first time.[47]

Indeed, the new Prefect of Police, Ernest Cresson, informed the government that its radical enemies were again hatching a *coup* and proposed the immediate arrest of the plotters. Jules Ferry on November 2 drew up a list of twenty-four Leftists whom the government could well have out of circulation. Then nothing was done until the results of the plebiscite could be known; and, even then, further debate obstructed action. When Cresson was finally granted authority to make the arrests, his principal targets, members of the would-be Committee of Public Safety, were safely in hiding. Of the rest, all but Jules Vallès were acquitted, certainly giving moderate government an appearance of spinelessness.[48]

Unlike Gambetta in Tours, no one in Paris had any taste for the emergency powers needed to unify the home front in order to face the enemy more efficiently. Under the Empire, the Republicans had come rather too easily to regard themselves as more virtuous than the politicians in power. In the autumn of 1870, the crisis these Republicans faced did not permit lengthy considerations of personal honor. Nor was it overly realistic for a regime that knew itself to represent only a minority in France to be concerned for the good opinion of a group that represented an even tinier minority in the nation. At least when the government went ahead with municipal elections on the sixth, it did not commit the suicidal folly of permitting the election of a Commune—of a rival government. The elections simply provided new mayors and deputy mayors for each arrondissement, men who had no common meeting place or unity.[49] Otherwise, the insurrection and its suppression settled nothing. A carping press was allowed to publish its abuse of the government, though the government did *protest* against the publication of rumors and

47. Simon, *op. cit.*, p. 270.
48. Dréo, *op. cit.*, pp. 271–272; and *Défense Nationale*, Rapport Daru, pp. 239–247.
49. *Défense Nationale*, Rapport Daru, p. 262.

polemics; [50] and radical groups were free to meet and to culti-
vate their grievances.

Whatever else it may be, a besieged city is fertile ground for
the growth of suspicions and hatreds. As the privations worsened,
experienced more thoroughly by the poor than by the well-to-
do, the population fed itself an unhealthful diet of rumor and
slander. The viler the imputation, the more likely it was to be
believed. The French in general have been accused of being at
once the most skeptical and the most gullible people in Europe,
and one can only wonder if the saying had its birth during the
siege of Paris.

Bismarck alone profited from the disorders in Paris, for they
allowed him to assume a harsher line with Thiers and thus
placate the Prussian military who had been accusing Bismarck of
being too eager to reach a peace settlement. Thus Thiers had to
report to his government that while Bismarck would agree to an
armistice for the purpose of convening a National Assembly, he
would not permit the revictualing of Paris during the armistice
unless a defensive fortress were surrendered in compensation.
Thiers urged acceptance of the terms, convinced that further
resistance could only produce harsher terms; Favre felt certain
that acceptance would provoke a new insurrection in Paris.[51] As
the Government of National Defense backed Favre, negotiations
broke down on November 7. This news was at once sent to the
Russian government by the Tours delegation in the faint hope
that the Russians would now decide to intervene to force peace.
Four days later the Russians denounced the Black Sea restrictions
of the Treaty of Paris, a fair measure of Russian concern for the
plight of the French.[52]

For the moment, nevertheless, the decision to break off negotiations seemed wise. On November 14 a pigeon from Tours
brought news of a provincial French victory on the ninth at
Coulmiers, which opened the way for French occupation of Orleans; and as Trochu had been organizing a massive sortie from
Paris, the city was overcome with confidence that its delivery was

50. Benjamin, *op. cit.*, p. 220.
51. Howard, *op. cit.*, p. 339.
52 Charles-Roux, *op. cit.*, pp. 520–521.

at hand. General Trochu was considerably less optimistic. Green troops might win local victories, but he thought they were unlikely to sustain an offensive against experienced regulars. He also knew that thousands of German regulars, released by the surrender of Metz, would soon be available for service around Paris and in the Loire valley. Trochu's original plan was to try to break out of Paris down the Seine valley toward Rouen, from whence he could cooperate with provincial forces either in the Loire or in the northwest. Evidently the popular clamor to break out in the south in order to link up with provincial forces surely marching northward from Orleans determined Trochu to alter his plans. Redeployment of troops and guns cost him every possibility of surprise by the time the main sortie was launched on November 30. Three days of fighting, and the French drive was contained, crushed, and had to be abandoned. Immediately after which Moltke had a message sent to Trochu notifying him that the Germans had also defeated French forces on the Loire and had reoccupied Orleans.[53]

One would think that a government, never optimistic about the outcome of the war, would have seen in this double disaster an indubitable sign that the game was up. Yet the straw-clutching continued. Trochu, so long criticized by the Parisians for inaction, argued at the beginning of December that the inaction had been necessary to conserve strength until the delegation could put a relief army in the field. That army was now in the field. Perhaps it had suffered a defeat at Orleans, but until Paris knew for sure that the relief army was destroyed, it was hardly the time to seek an armistice. Favre took a contrary view, dictated by political rather than military expediency. Noting that General von Moltke had offered a safe-conduct pass if the French government wished to send an agent to verify the loss of Orleans, Favre saw the offer as a veiled invitation to renew armistice negotiations; and he was for seizing this opportunity to get a National Assembly elected that could assume all further responsibility for making war or peace. A majority in the government, holding that it was necessary to avoid even a hint of readiness to

53. Dréo, *op. cit.*, p. 376.

capitulate, voted not to accept Moltke's invitation and to continue the uneven struggle.[54] Blind patriotism, Thiers called it; but not being a Republican, his political future was not in the balance.

Certainly the Prussians were not happy about their situation during December of 1870. They had every reason to believe that time was on Gambetta's side. His growing provincial armies were still ineffective that month, but German morale and efficiency tumbled as winter deepened and supply lines lengthened. Looking back at that month, the critical significance of the premature surrender of Metz for both sides becomes clear. Without the two armies thereby released for service elsewhere, the Prussians might well have had to settle on terms more congenial to Paris.[55] Even with these reinforcements, a stalemate persisted that drove the Prussians to the expedient of bombarding Paris into submission so that the siege troops might be freed for provincial duty.

Trochu, meanwhile, was preparing a new sortie, consistent with his argument that the provincial armies had to be supported as long as they were in the field. On December 21 he tried an attack upon the village of Le Bourget north of Paris, a seemingly vulnerable point. But German artillery was again too much for the French infantry; and after frantic fighting in the bitter cold, Trochu had to abandon the venture, well aware of the political consequences of his failure. Moreover, the city's food stocks were nearing an end, and a military success was absolutely urgent. Desperate for a solution, the ministers began revealing doubts about Trochu's military capacity. Perhaps new leadership would change French fortunes for the better.[56] A suitable replacement for Trochu was another matter, however, since few of the ranking officers were considered safely Republican, and a number favored making peace at once before the city should fall. Lacking a satisfactory replacement, the government had to persist with a commander who no longer enjoyed full confidence.

54. *Défense Nationale,* Rapport Daru, pp. 280–286.
55. Howard, *op. cit.,* p. 373.
56. Dréo, *op. cit.,* pp. 437–438.

The Prussians, meanwhile, completed their preparations to bombard Paris, and on January 5, 1872, lobbed their first shells at the city.[57]

If the bombardment failed to produce the anticipated damage, it also failed to crush civilian morale. Indeed, it stirred the fires of resistance, putting Trochu on the spot because he intended to shepherd his remaining forces. No more sorties until a decisive moment arrived or as a last resort. He was overruled by his civilian colleagues, a decision which has remained controversial ever since, and the plans for an attack upon the German lines had to be prepared by general officers junior to Trochu. The target was Versailles. The attack was to be launched from Mont Valérien and carried through Buzenval and Montretout, points where the German defenses were at their strongest. Nearly half of the troops for the assault were to be National Guardsmen. The sheer folly of the operation left room to suspect that it was designed, not in any hope of success, but in the realization that no armistice was politically possible without a sortie so bloody that even the most patriotic radicals in Paris would see the need to call a halt. Perhaps that was the case, especially in the minds of some professional army officers who had long since ceased to believe that victory was possible. Probably the civilian ministers, no longer confident that Trochu could distinguish between what was militarily possible and impossible, were willing to gamble on the impossible for a change. They knew full well that the Republic could not survive Parisian contempt if a determined sortie were not made in response to the bombardment.[58]

The assault began on January 19. It was poorly planned and, though it achieved limited success owing to the Germans' surprise, the battle was soon decided by German superiority in position and artillery. A chaotic retreat in rain and mud was the last act in the dismal fiasco. A majority in the government still believed that further sorties were possible, a fact that should have absolved them from the later charge that January 19 had been a calculated bloodletting. Trochu, insisting that no more large-scale sorties be planned, was asked to resign his command.

57. Howard, *op. cit.*, pp. 358–361.
58. *Défense Nationale*, Rapport Daru, pp. 312–316.

He refused, insisting that the government dismiss him to make the military and political issues clearer and to spare him the appearance of abandoning his duty. He retained the presidency of the government in giving up his military command to General Vinoy.[59]

In the meantime, the radicals were preparing another insurrection and took advantage of the defeat on January 19 at Buzenval to attempt a *coup*. The center of revolutionary activity after October 31 had been the XIXᵉ Arrondissement where Charles Delescluze was mayor and where those radical leaders who had escaped arrest had gone into hiding. Some of them were ultimately arrested by Cresson's inadequate police force, and Flourens was eventually turned over to the police by his own National Guardsmen.[60] On January 22 the insurrection began when a group of armed men appeared at the Mazas prison and forced the release of its political prisoners. But the government at the Hôtel de Ville, having learned to expect trouble after a military fiasco, was well guarded by troops. This time the insurgents had not come to parley. They opened fire, which was at once returned, and within fifteen or twenty minutes the mob was in flight. Next day Cresson obtained authorization to arrest Delescluze and Félix Pyat, and all radical groups and clubs were officially suppressed. Despite the quick collapse of the insurrection, the radicals had provoked the government to fire upon the citizenry and the government knew only too well what the consequences would be—sooner or later.[61]

On the evening of January 22 the council met in Jules Simon's office at the Ministry of Public Instruction, the majority agreeing that for both military and political reasons an armistice must be obtained at once. Otherwise, the government would be so weakened as to have to accept an unconditional surrender. The following day the council renewed its discussion of acceptable armistice terms, concluding that it would be best to see what Bismarck then had to offer, but to try to limit the armistice to Paris alone and not to include the provincial forces still in the

59. *Simon, op. cit.*, pp. 428–431; and Howard, *op. cit.*, pp. 364–367.
60. *Défense Nationale*, Déposition de Cresson, II, 40–41.
61. *Ibid.*, Rapport Daru, pp. 347–356; and Simon, *op. cit.*, pp. 432–436.

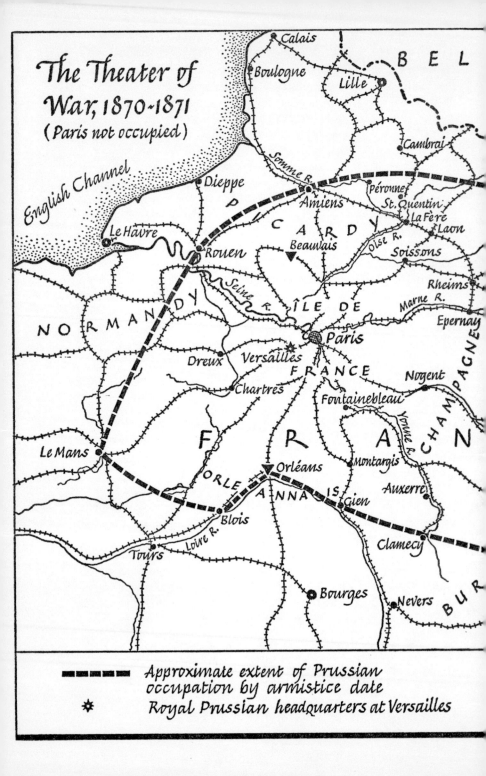

Main Prussian bases

Main French bases

field. The difficulties therein were recognized, especially since the government knew the necessity of national elections.[62]

Jules Favre called on Bismarck at Versailles later that same day to begin negotiations which culminated on the twenty-eighth. The terms, of course a measure of the Prussian victory, also reflected several compromises obtained by Favre to bolster the domestic position of the Government of National Defense. It was agreed, for instance, that the armistice must apply to the whole country, not merely to Paris, for the purpose of electing a National Assembly. Yet an exception was made for three eastern departments—Jura, Côte d'Or, and Doubs—where French military operations still continued and which Favre refused to endanger. (The Prussians, better informed than Favre, knew that those operations were on the verge of collapse and were conceding nothing of substance.) [63] As for Paris, Favre managed to prevent the occupation of the city during the armistice and persuaded Bismarck of the inadvisability of insisting that the French government disarm the National Guard. In exchange, Favre did have to agree to a Parisian war indemnity of two hundred million francs and to giving up the Parisian defensive forts. The armistice was to be of three-week duration, during which time the Germans agreed to assist in feeding Paris.[64]

With the armistice signed at 11:15 P.M. on January 28, Bismarck gave Favre permission to telegraph instructions to Bordeaux, where the Tours delegation had moved after the loss of Orleans. Favre committed an incredible blunder in drawing up the dispatch, a blunder which Bismarck must have recognized in countersigning it. "We are signing today a treaty with M. de Bismarck. An armistice of 21 days is agreed upon; an Assembly is to be convoked at Bordeaux for February 12. Make this news known to all France. Have the armistice put into effect; convoke the voters for February 8. A member of the Government will leave for Bordeaux." [65] Gambetta and his colleagues at Bordeaux

62. Dréo, *op. cit.*, pp. 569–577; and *Défense Nationale*, Rapport Daru, pp. 361–368.
63. Howard, *op. cit.*, p. 442.
64. *Défense Nationale*, Rapport Daru, pp. 372–384, 541.
65. *Ibid.*, p. 387.

logically assumed from the dispatch that the armistice applied to all France and proceeded accordingly.

Two days later, anxious for the details of the armistice, Gambetta telegraphed to Versailles; and, since Favre had returned to Paris, Bismarck answered Gambetta directly. Only then did Gambetta learn that the armistice did not apply in the three eastern departments. By then it was too late to prevent a German envelopment of the forces in the East, and the remaining French pawn became useless. Probably Favre's error was twofold: He ought not have tried to exclude the eastern departments from the armistice in the first place, leaving them exposed to the entire German strength. In any event, when the French command in the East learned that the armistice did not apply to them, its decision was to pass into Switzerland rather than surrender to the Germans. About 80,000 troops escaped across the frontier.

The armistice was, of course, a serious blow to the people of Paris after their dogged resistance in the belief that they were invincible. Some of the radical politicians still insisted that Paris had the means to prevail, but in general the population now accepted the idea of capitulation, in the words of the official inquiry, "with a profound weariness and a discouraged resignation." [66] The real political concern for the government at that moment was not Paris, but Gambetta. Communications being what they were between Paris and Bordeaux, it had not been possible for Gambetta to keep abreast of rapid political decisions in the capital, nor did Paris learn of his disapproval of an armistice until after it was signed.[67] He had, it is true, put the armistice into effect in the provinces, but it became clear that he regarded the armistice as merely a breathing spell. And he expected that a National Assembly would pledge itself to continuing the war *à outrance*. The members of the Government of National Defense, so long fearful of insurrection in Paris, suddenly feared that it would be Gambetta who would challenge their authority. Jules Simon was at once sent off to Bordeaux to reason with Gambetta and, when the two could not even agree

66. *Ibid.*, p. 411.
67. Bury, *op. cit.*, p. 248.

on the electoral procedures to be used on February 8, three more members of the government were packed off to support Simon. The danger of civil war was real, and the government knew that it would be a final calamity in the presence of the enemy.[68]

68. *Défense Nationale*, Rapport Daru, pp. 417–419.

FIVE

The Commune of Paris

The people of Paris are the most enlightened of all peoples. They are aware of their intellectual worth, knowing that when they speak the world gathers to listen, and that when they move the world hastens to follow. —*Henri Rochefort, March 12, 1871*

T HE TRUTH about Paris and her revolutionary Commune—its origins, its structure, its doctrines, and its myths—has been elusive and a maddeningly complex problem for those who sought to go beyond simplistic or doctrinaire explanations for the mid-spring madness that engulfed Paris in 1871. The siege of Paris had ended not in victory but with an armistice, the lengthy suffering evidently in vain. After months of privation, but fortified by the certainty of Parisian invincibility, the impossible—the intolerable—had happened; and Parisian nerves had little reserve for the fact. On March 18 Georges Clemenceau, then mayor of the XVIIIᵉ Arrondissement (Montmartre), witnessed some of the disorders that marked the schism between Paris and France. "Suddenly a terrific noise broke out," he wrote, "and the mob which filled the courtyard burst into the street in the grip of some kind of frenzy. Amongst them were chasseurs, soldiers of the line, National Guards, women and children. All were shrieking like wild beasts without realizing what they were doing. I observed then that pathological phenomenon which might be called blood-lust. A breath of madness seemed to have passed over this mob: from a wall children brandished indescribable trophies; women, dishevelled and emaciated, flung their arms about while uttering raucous cries, having apparently taken leave of their senses. I saw some of them weeping while they shrieked louder than others. Men were dancing about and jostling each other in a kind of savage fury. It was one of those extraordinary nervous outbursts, so frequent in the Middle Ages, which still occur amongst masses of human beings under the stress of some primeval emotion." [1] This scene capped the most memorable day in Clemenceau's life, a scene worthy of memory when one is tempted to see the origins of the Commune in a rational plan or conspiracy.

Nearly one hundred years have passed since those five weeks culminated in massacre and fire, but no impartial history of the Commune yet exists.[2] The fairest brief, and recent, remark about the Commune comes from Sir Denis Brogan: "The Commune was a folly; some of its leaders were criminals. But the greatest crime of its authors (of whom Thiers was one) was in making final that alienation of the workers of Paris from the official organization of the French State which the days of June 1848 had begun. The 'bloody week' of May 1871 was a wound that, if at times it seemed closed, was never really healed." [3] He might well have added that historical scholarship has been a faithful mirror of the running sore. Consequently, just as the social cleavages widened by the Commune have never been closed, so have the historical traditions about the Commune not been resolved, instead hardening into mythologies.

Moreover, in recent years the problem of understanding the issue of 1871 has been complicated by an easy analogy between 1871 and 1940. Because of the unsavory capitulation and collaboration of 1940, the *"capitalistes-capitulards"* of 1871 have been retarnished in retrospect. Thiers, having traditionally been seen as the man of the Rue Transnonain (a time-honored reference to the repression of 1834 when he had been Minister of the Interior), now became the safe-and-sane "patriot" of 1940. A new tradition was born which reduced all political history to the struggle between Fascists and anti-Fascists.[4] Anticommunards

1. J. Hampden Jackson, *Clemenceau and the Third Republic*, New York: Collier Books, 1962, p. 32.
2. Frank Jellinek, *The Paris Commune of 1871*, New York: Grosset & Dunlap, 1965, p. 435.
3. D. W. Brogan, *The French Nation*, New York: Harper & Row, 1963, p. 157.
4. For an example see "Heralds of Fascism," in J. Salwyn Schapiro, *Liberalism and the Challenge of Fascism*, New York: McGraw-Hill, 1949.

were reincarnated to staff the Fascist leagues of 1934, to be the men of Vichy and the collaborators with Nazi Germany, a simplistic pattern which ignored significant differences between 1871 and 1940—not to speak of events in between. Worst of all, historians who lived through the horrors of 1940 were enabled to participate vicariously in the earlier agonies with some degree of confidence about what their positions would have been under Napoleon III or in 1871.

In contrast to 1940, the French public of 1870 was enthusiastic for war and had considerable confidence that it could be won; France had no allies on whom to depend or, it must be added, to desert through a separate armistice; and she fought on, in 1870, after the initial catastrophes, well beyond what the military facts suggested and with a pronounced concern for national honor. No doubt that, when defeat came, it was humiliating and disastrous. Stupidity and lack of proper preparation there had been. But the lengthy resistance came within sight of forcing a moderate peace settlement. Surrender came only when all reasonable prospects were exhausted, something that cannot be said of 1940.

Indeed, in 1871 Gambetta seemed dangerously close to breaking with the Government of National Defense when he realized that the armistice was not to be a breathing spell but the prelude to surrender. His desire to fight on was fortified by the manpower figures he had on paper and by the advice of a tiny minority of the military, notably General Chanzy. Together they managed to ignore what the release of German troops from Paris would mean, to ignore the demoralization of their inadequately sheltered and repeatedly beaten troops. Gambetta and Chanzy also seem to have been unaware that to prolong the resistance was to run a grave political risk, so convinced were they that the Republic could only be saved with a military victory. They knew nothing of a conflict that had developed between Bismarck and the German military, the latter hoping for a continuation of the war to enable them to crush France completely. While Bismarck, fearing foreign intervention if the war continued much longer, was threatening to open negotiations with Napoleon III if the Republicans could not be brought to terms.[5] Thus Gambetta's

5. Michael Howard, *The Franco-Prussian War*, New York: Macmillan, 1962, pp. 442–445.

intransigence in Bordeaux horrified the members of the Government of National Defense. To follow his counsel would be to risk total defeat and a Bonaparte restoration. Those around Gambetta urged him to attempt a *coup* to become a dictator and to continue the war. Having already done much to preserve the honor of France, he did much for his own honor by rejecting such advice. On the other hand, in giving way to the majority in the Government of National Defense and allowing peace to come, he could not bear to participate in the peace making. Resigning from the government, he would soon move temporarily into Spain and out of the limelight.

Elections for the National Assembly were then scheduled for February 5 in Paris and for February 8 in the provinces. There was no time for electoral campaigns in the usual sense, and most voters understood that they were not so much voting for parties as deciding between peace and war. An exception would have been in the larger cities where, as under the Second Empire, the voters were more enmeshed in political controversies and likely to know and follow party lines. But the small rural freeholders were by far the largest social group in France. Conservative by instinct rather than in doctrine, they voted for the local notable who, in most cases, represented immediate peace with Germany.[6] All victorious candidates, of course, also represented a party of a political persuasion, so that the electoral results were inevitably measured in party terms.

The Parisians elected forty-three deputies to the National Assembly. Most of them were Republican or Socialist, many of them favored war to the end; and it is correct to conclude that their election was a vote both for war and the Republic. The rural voters, in contrast, in opting for peace only incidentally elected a monarchist majority to the Assembly. The Parisians logically concluded that the provinces were overwhelmingly monarchist in spirit, an assumption that contributed to the groundwork for civil war. That these rural voters were merely conservative did not become apparent until the formative years

6. J. Néré, "The French Republic," *The New Cambridge Modern History*, Vol. XI, *Material Progress and World-Wide Problems*, Cambridge: Cambridge University Press, 1962, pp. 300–302.

of the Third Republic when the possibility of a monarchist restoration led rural voters to indicate clearly that they favored a republic, a conservative republic. Meanwhile, the first of the myths was in the making. Of the 675 seats in the new Assembly, only about 200 were held by Republicans, the rest going to men espousing some form of monarchy. It seemed to be 1849 all over again.

The National Assembly convened on February 13 in the uneasy atmosphere of a Bordeaux that had only recently been under the spell of Gambetta and where pro-war sentiments were still strong. The Parisian contingent within the Republican minority soon made clear its feeling of having been betrayed by a defeatist peasantry, adding to that the air of city sophisticates in tedious intercourse with yokels. The provincial majority resented both the condescension and the indifference to the sacrifices made in vain attempts to relieve Paris. Many of the provincials could neither forget nor forgive those Parisian delegates like Félix Pyat and Charles Delescluze who had, in the face of the enemy, organized demonstrations and insurrections.

Adolphe Thiers had become by then the predominant figure, returned by twenty-six departments, a bourgeois liberal on good terms with both moderate Royalists and moderate Republicans, but resented in Paris as a man of peace and order. Urban workers had feared him since the days of Louis-Philippe when he had shown little understanding of social problems; but he had gained in prestige for his opposition to Napoleon III and for a speech in 1866 when he had warned of the dangers from German unity. Like the men of September 4, he was an antirevolutionary raised to power, by a revolution in 1830 and again in 1870. His diplomatic mission that autumn made him understand the consequences of French isolation. No foreign assistance would be forthcoming, and to preserve the French state he must negotiate with Bismarck to prevent dismemberment. Thiers was for the facts, as Zola put it, the Left was for principles.[7]

The Government of National Defense formally abdicated its authority to the Assembly as the Assembly began to organize a new government. It being understood that the Orleanist Thiers

7. Emile Zola, *La République en marche*, Paris: Fasquelle, 1956, I, 62.

would head the new government, Thiers thought it expedient to impose a Republican upon the Assembly as its presiding officer. His choice was Jules Grévy, a conservative Republican who had opposed the Empire, opposed Gambetta, and favored the summoning of a National Assembly.[8] Grévy was overwhelmingly approved by the Assembly, the extreme Left abstaining. It remained to settle Thiers' executive title. The monarchists were only too happy to retain the republican form of government through that period of national humiliation, but wished also to prevent the establishment of permanent republican institutions. Consequently they settled the title of Chief of the Executive Power on Thiers in the hope of suggesting the provisional nature of the regime.[9]

Thiers then presented his cabinet for approval: a coalition government composed of three moderate Republicans (Favre, Picard, and Simon) ; two Orleanists (Lambrecht and Dufaure) ; one Legitimist (Larcy) ; one former conservative Bonapartist (Pouyer-Quertier) ; and two professional officers (General Le Flô and Admiral Pothuau) . Since this cabinet did not reflect the monarchical preponderance in the Assembly, the provisional nature of the government was underscored. In fact, if one includes Thiers himself, then half of the new cabinet were associates of the retiring Government of National Defense.

The first order of major business was necessarily a peace settlement, and toward that end Thiers and Foreign Minister Jules Favre left Bordeaux on February 19 to meet with Bismarck in Versailles. Thanks to earlier negotiations for an armistice, the French knew the approximate terms they faced, the loss of Alsace and Lorraine plus an indemnity. By February 21, when Bismarck presented his conditions to Thiers and Favre, they were aghast to learn that the terms were even more severe: the indemnity had been raised one billion francs, and Bismarck wanted a military occupation of Paris until the treaty should be formally ratified. Thiers fought to scale down these demands, not merely the indemnity, but he wanted to retain the fortress of

8. Maurice Reclus, *L'Avènement de la 3ème République, 1871–1875,* Paris: Hachette, 1930, pp. 27–28.
9. *Ibid.,* p. 29.

Belfort in Alsace as a recognition of its valor in holding out successfully against the Germans, and he was only too aware of the political consequences of allowing Paris to be occupied. In the end he managed to reduce the indemnity to five billion and to retain Belfort in exchange for permitting German troops entry into Paris. This was bitterly resented by the Parisians as ingratitude for their heroic resistance—good Republicans sold out by monarchists. The convention terms were put in final form on the twenty-sixth and signed. Thiers kept his composure until he reached his carriage; then wept all the way back to Paris.[10]

While the Germans prepared to enter Paris on March 1, Thiers hastened back to Bordeaux, hoping for quick ratification of the terms in order to give the Germans only several days in Paris. He presented his convention to the Assembly on the evening of February 28, asking that it be accepted the following day. A succession of Leftists went to the rostrum to protest the terms, to which Thiers replied that peace was necessary and that he had obtained the best terms possible. One anguished deputy shouted that only Napoleon III should have to sign such a shameful treaty, leading the Bonapartist Conti, the Emperor's recent *chef de cabinet,* to deny to the throng of clenched fists that His Majesty would ever have accepted such terms. At once the Assembly took time to confirm the dethronement of Napoleon III and his dynasty, declaring him responsible "for the ruin, for the invasion, and for the dismemberment of the country." Following which the Assembly ratified the treaty terms 546 votes to 107, with 23 abstaining. The dismal scene concluded when the delegates from Alsace-Lorraine gave their resignations, professing unending filial ties with France. A handful of Republican delegates also submitted resignations: Gambetta, Félix Pyat, Ledru-Rollin, Rochefort, Tridon, Ranc, and Malon.[11]

In its few remaining days in Bordeaux, the new government took several steps that deepened the rift between Paris and the provinces. On March 3, General d'Aurelle de Paladines was appointed commander of the National Guard—badly received in

10. *Ibid.,* p. 35.
11. Roger L. Williams, *Henri Rochefort, Prince of the Gutter Press,* New York: Scribner's, 1966, pp. 97–98.

Paris because he was a Bonapartist and because he was popularly, if unfairly, held responsible for the loss of Orleans the previous December. General Vinoy, the army commander, exacerbated the matter by suppressing six radical newspapers in Paris that protested the appointment. Next a military court condemned Flourens and Blanqui to death *par contumace* and Jules Vallès to six months' confinement for their part in the insurrection of October 31, whereupon a number of the remaining Parisian deputies retaliated by proposing the arraignment of the Government of National Defense. Many Parisians, indeed, were convinced that the rural majority would not consent to reestablish the capital in Paris, and on March an informal committee drawn from National Guard battalions in Paris resolved to establish an independent Republic of the Seine should the Assembly decapitalize Paris.[12] Immediately thereafter Thiers did propose not to return the seat of government to Paris. Most likely Fontainebleau would have been the choice could it have provided adequate housing for the deputies and their families. Versailles proved to be more accommodating and was somewhat closer to Paris.[13] In any case, the rural deputies revealed their fear of all major cities, not merely Paris. Thiers intended to soften the blow to Parisian pride by putting his administration in Paris while keeping the Assembly beyond the reach of the mob.

The most impolitic measures adopted by the Assembly, however, were financial laws that reflected rural indifference to the economic hardships born of the siege. The first of these was a law of February 15 that limited pay to those National Guardsmen who could present an official certificate of dire poverty, on the logical grounds that the war had ended. In effect, many workers were suddenly deprived of 1 fr. 50 a day. On March 10 the Law of Maturities ended the moratorium on commercial paper, providing for the immediate collection of commercial bills outstanding since August 15, 1870.[14] The Parisian deputy Millière tried

12. Georges Bourgin, "La Commune de Paris et le Comité Central (1871)," *Revue historique,* 150 (December 1925), 33–35; and Zola, *op. cit.,* I, 83–84.
13. Zola, *op. cit.,* I, 77–101.
14. M. Winock and J. P. Azéma, *Les Communards,* Paris: du Seuil, 1964, p. 42.

to preserve the moratorium on rents as the war had destroyed the livelihood of many urban renters, but he was beaten flat by the conservative majority.[15] Such laws drew Parisian workers and bourgeois together in outrage against the Assembly, for the measures made no sense given the economic collapse of the city; and as it was known that many of the landlords and creditors who would benefit from the legislation had moved out of Paris to escape the siege, it appeared that those who had endured the siege were to suffer a second time.

The Assembly was scheduled to adjourn on March 11, to reassemble in Versailles on the twentieth. Before adjournment Thiers, concerned to halt this drift toward civil strife, begged the deputies to bury party issues in the interest of national recovery. Because he was warmly applauded, it was presumed that a pledge of political neutrality had been given, the so-called Pact of Bordeaux.[16] Good intentions aside, party issues were not the sole source of political conflict. Anger, hatreds, and suspicions are not dissipated with a round of applause, and particularly not when they represent both immediate and ancient grievances. By the time the Assembly packed its bags for Versailles, a new revolutionary spirit and a new revolutionary situation were perilously close to merging.

When Thiers and his ministers reached Paris on March 15, they found the city in an ugly mood that could be useful only to the avowed revolutionaries, and Thiers concluded that the National Guard would have to be disarmed. He began by ordering the seizure of National Guard artillery, about 227 guns then parked in Belleville and Montmartre, many of which had been purchased by public conscription during the siege. Their removal was scheduled for the night of March 17–18 while the city slept; but the maneuver was bungled by the army and not completed before daylight. An angry mob collected, some of the regulars deserted to the National Guard, and long pent-up frustration exploded into the frenzies that Clemenceau viewed with his

15. Jean T. Joughin, *The Paris Commune in French Politics,* Baltimore: Johns Hopkins, 1955, I, 26.
16. Jacques Chastenet, *Histoire de la Troisième République,* Paris: Hachette, 1952, I, 67.

physician's eye. No one planned an insurrection that day; emotion simply took over. Two generals, Lecomte and Clément-Thomas (the latter had recently resigned the command of the National Guard out of disgust for its indiscipline), were recognized by the mob, seized, and shot—again by nobody's order.[17] Thiers did not mean to repeat the geographical mistake of the Government of National Defense and moved his administration to Versailles that very afternoon. With him went all governmental authority, and the radical newspapers suppressed by General Vinoy reappeared almost at once and hardly in a conciliatory vein. The destruction of private property, Rochefort informed his readers in referring to the suppression of the journals, was begun by Thiers and, therefore, would justify demolition of Thiers's home in the Place Saint-Georges should the Parisians see fit.[18]

A recently formed committee called the Central Committee of the National Guard assumed provisional responsibility for government in Paris following Thiers's flight to Versailles. Formally constituted only on March 15 after a number of preliminary meetings, this committee included elected representatives from National Guard battalions in thirteen of the twenty arrondissements. Generally referred to simply as the Central Committee, the new organization was easily confused by those outside Paris with the Republican Central Committee of the Twenty Arrondissements established immediately after September 4. In fact, a careful reading of the reports of the parliamentary committee that later investigated the revolutionary movement of 1870–1871 leads one to believe that those who penned the official version of those chaotic months never managed to distinguish clearly between the two committees.[19] The consequent confusion of persons and issues laid the groundwork for the reactionary myth about the Commune.

For instance, the original Republican Central Committee of

17. John Plamenatz, *The Revolutionary Movement in France, 1815–1871*, London: Longmans, 1952, pp. 141–143.
18. Raymond Manevy, *La Presse de la IIIᵉ République*, Paris: Foret, 1955, pp. 47–48.
19. Bourgin, *op. cit.*, p. 2.

the Twenty Arrondissements included Jacobins, Blanquists, and men of various radical factions who had been, or were, affiliated with the International. The first call for such a committee seems to have been made by a Proudhonist named Dr. Dupas, a member of the International favoring *décentralisation fédéraliste*. His demand that a popular organization seize the Hôtel de Ville was signed by Chassin, Leverdays, and Edouard Vaillant, among others. In the effusion of radical pronouncements after September 4, many well-known names like Tolain, Varlin, and Johannard were evident, all affiliates of the International and having the advantage of prior association. But in short order many radicals not belonging to the International came into prominence in the revolutionary movement, and this Central Committee was soon dominated by Jacobins and Blanquists.[20] Between September of 1870 and March of 1871, in other words, not only was the membership of the Central Committee in constant flux, but the avowed revolutionaries soon outnumbered the antirevolutionary radicals. What they had in common was an awareness of the conservatism of the Government of National Defense.

A further legitimate ground for confusing the two Central Committees derived from the well-known fact that many members of the Central Committee of the Twenty Arrondissements got themselves elected to be battalion commanders in the National Guard. In such capacity, they were both the political and military instigators of those demonstrations and insurrections against the Government of National Defense which imperiled its existence and hampered the resistance to Prussia. Superpatriots in utterance favoring war *à outrance*, they were seen as anything but patriotic by men more conservative. When, in March of 1871, a new Central Committee of the National Guard was formed, soon to fill the governmental vacuum in Paris, the conservatives assumed that the same old troublemakers were at work and began referring to the events of March 18 as simply the third major insurrection since September 4.

The grounds for confusion of people and issues did not end there. When the February armistice provided time for election of

20. J. Dautry and L. Scheler, *Le Comité central républicain des vingt arrondissements de Paris*, Paris: Editions sociales, 1960, pp. 11–22.

National Assembly, many groups formed in Paris simply to elec-
tioneer, drawing up lists of candidates to be backed. Not only
might any given individual simultaneously be a member of several groups or committees, but his name might be included on
several electoral lists with or without his permission. Any "eyewitness" or later researcher was thereby too often given free rein
to come to whatever conclusion he wished about another's affiliation.[21]

When the Central Committee of the Twenty Arrondissements kept badgering the Government of National Defense with
demands for the election of a Paris Commune, the pronouncements of the more radical and well-known members of the Committee exposed communal doctrine more precisely than would
even be done by the Commune itself. Later investigators, therefore, probably knew more about what the Commune was supposed to be than about what it actually was. The origin and
membership of the Central Committee of the National Guard,
on the other hand, is far less clear than that of the earlier Committee, except for the fact that better-known men came to join it
later and to dominate it. The initiative belonged to men who
were hardly known beyond their own electoral districts, patriotic
National Guardsmen evidently distressed by the signing of the
armistice, largely proletarian, the great majority certainly not
revolutionary. But since the first major act of this Central Committee, upon finding itself in power on March 18, was to call for
communal elections on March 26, it seemed to follow that the
members were proposing a Revolutionary Commune. Most likely
they were uncomfortable with the political responsibility they
assumed on March 18 and sought the earliest and most obvious
way to shift that responsibility to people of greater political experience and social position.[22]

At this late date it seems impossible to draw up a complete
and accurate list of initial members on the Central Committee of
the National Guard. Various accounts of committee meetings

21. Bourgin, *op. cit.*, pp. 11–13.
22. Charles Rihs, *La Commune de Paris, sa structure et ses doctrines* (*1871*),
Geneva: E. Droz, 1955, p. 21.

differ about both names and numbers on the committee. Part of the confusion derives from the fact that a number of meetings took place before the formal constitution of the committee on March 15 and involved men who never became formal members; and, of course, as in the case of the earlier Central Committee, the membership changed quickly, particularly after the election of the Commune. The original membership list, published later by the French government,[23] was reproduced from the committee minutes in the hand of G. Arnold, an architect who commanded the 64th Battalion. The carelessness he revealed in spelling members' names may also account for some evident omissions on the list.

Despite such flaws, it seems safe to draw several rough conclusions about the membership: seven arrondissements—the more bourgeois or well-to-do arrondissements (1, 2, 7, 8, 9, 16, 17)—had no elected representatives on the Central Committee. Approximately half of the initial membership (nineteen) later won election to the Commune. Of those nineteen, fourteen had clear political affiliation—seven being Jacobins, four being Blanquists, and three having had association with International; and all nineteen represented arrondissements comprising the eastern half of Paris. No occupational or class unity can be found among the nineteen. As nearly as we can tell six were artisans, six were workers, three were businessmen, two were employees, and two were professionals, at least at that moment.[24] For such a breakdown does not take into account the changes in occupation that occurred in a number of these men's lives, nor does it tell us personal facts about them: how many of them were embittered and revengeful; how many were mere placeseekers, ambitious to rise and thus bandwagoners. The only pattern which emerges is the one suggested earlier: Those who instigated the movement were obscure patriots in the National Guard. By March 10, when the National Assembly revealed its intention not to move into Paris, significant members of the International like Louis-Jean Pindy had begun to participate in Committee discussion. And

23. *Enquête parlementaire sur l'insurrection du 18 mars*, III, 39.
24. Winock and Azéma, *op. cit.*, pp. 48–49, 182–183.

five days later, when the Committee was formally established, better-known Jacobins and Blanquists were on the scene.[25]

Even so, these better-known, doctrinaire radicals were unable to dominate the Central Committee when it assumed the governance of Paris on March 18. The Blanquists on the Committee—Emile-Victor Duval, Emile Eudes, H. Mortier, and Gabriel Ranvier—proposed an immediate armed assault upon Versailles; but the majority insisted upon municipal elections first. The majority were willing, meanwhile, to provide public administration until the elected government could assume office. The appointments to public office that the Central Committee made on March 19 revealed the political innocence of the majority, for in virtually every case the new officials were more extremist than the Committee that appointed them, and the implication of such appointments seems to have been unrecognized.[26] Eudes was given the Ministry of War; Duval and Raoul Rigault took over the Prefecture of Police, Blanquists all. L.–E. Varlin, a collectivist member of the International, and businessman François Jourde were named to oversee finances. Edouard Moreau was given the National Printing Works while the Post Office went to Combaz, who had been a Garibaldian *franc-tireur*.

The pacific bent of the majority was also evident in votes to grant amnesty to all political and press offenders, to raise the state of siege, and to restore civil jurisdiction in place of military courts in Paris. Electoral procedures for the coming municipal election also had to be settled, and the Central Committee opted for proportional representation rather than representation by district, one delegate for each 20,000 people. The effect of this was to give the more industrial arrondissements a preponderance of the seats. Voter registration was the same as that for the plebiscite confirming the Liberal Empire in 1870, and seats were allotted accordingly. (In fact, the population had changed somewhat since then, as about 60,000 had died during the siege, and between 60,000 and 100,000 more had abandoned the capital immediately after the capitulation. Still others uncounted were migrating to Versailles as the danger of civil war loomed large.)

25. Bourgin, *op. cit.*, p. 35.
26. Jellinek, *op. cit.*, p. 132.

Clearly the Central Committee expected that other municipalities would copy the Parisian example and move to establish communal governments. In a few cities to the south, the north being German-occupied, communes were easily proclaimed because of the momentary weakness of the National Assembly. As none of them were strongly constituted or led, they were soon suppressed —in Lyon, Marseille, Toulouse, Narbonne, St. Etienne, and Le Creusot—leaving the Paris Commune unique and alone.[27]

When the National Assembly reconvened in Versailles on March 20, the monarchist majority was already incensed by the events in Paris on the eighteenth, and even the moderate Republicans believed that the Central Committee's posture of independence must be resisted. One possible avenue of reconciliation remained as Thiers, in evacuating Paris on the eighteenth, had granted the arrondissement mayors authority to administer Paris. This gave the mayors the legal position to challenge the legitimacy of the Central Committee; and, as the mayors were Republican, presumably they could negotiate with the Central Committee with greater sympathy and in better faith than could a delegation representing the monarchist majority in the Assembly. Some of the mayors, Georges Clemenceau for instance, had also been elected deputies in the Assembly, enhancing their position as go-betweens.

The odds, however, were against successful mediation. Disastrous war and humiliating peace had ignited the search for scapegoats, not to speak of the fact that the recent months had served to focus eighty years of constitutional and religious disagreement. Parisians in particular had often seen the Second Empire as an uncongenial regime maintained by rural votes and did not mean to permit a reincarnation. Rural France continued to view urban workers as anomalies crammed with ideas unsuitable to real Frenchmen and saw no reason why such oddities should presume to dictate to the majority. The climate, in sum, suggested a showdown, not reasonable reconciliation. The mediators themselves, however legally or logically situated, were seriously handicapped from the outset by the fact that a sizable part of the Parisian delegation had resigned from the Assembly

27. Winock and Azéma, *op. cit.,* p. 56.

in Bordeaux, making it clear that they did not accept majority decisions. This helped reduce the influence of those Parisian deputies who remained, already suspect as representatives of the Left. Similarly, the majority in the Assembly and a majority of the arrondissement mayors were too prejudiced by mutual suspicions to possess the good will essential to finding a just solution.[28]

Louis Blanc and Henri-Louis Tolain, both deputies from Paris, nevertheless took the initiative in summoning a delegation of deputies and mayors to be mediators. It included the deputies Millière, Clemenceau, Cournet, and Lockroy; mayors Bonvalet and Mottu; deputy mayors Malon, Murat, Jaclard, and Melliet; as well as the two initiators. These twelve called on the Central Committee of the National Guard on March 19 to plead for conciliation, warning against any action likely to arouse the wrath of all France against Paris. The Committee answered that it meant to do no more than guarantee municipal liberties, but added that it had little faith that the Republicans remaining in the Assembly would be able to make themselves heard there.[29] And, as we know, the Central Committee did not pause in its preparations for municipal elections.

The Assembly was also unconciliatory. On March 21 Minister of the Interior Ernest Picard proposed the militant action of declaring the Department of Seine-et-Oise, of which Versailles was the *chef-lieu,* to be in a state of siege. His motion passed. Clemenceau then tried to counter the implication of the measure by asking the Assembly to pass its own law providing for municipal elections in Paris, thus to respond positively to Parisian concern to preserve municipal liberties and to demonstrate that the Assembly hoped to mend the rift peaceably. A.-J. Langlois, another radical Republican deputy from Paris, added that the Assembly ought to support the Clemenceau motion if for no other reason than to avoid the ultimate embarrassment of having to annul elections sponsored by the Central Committee. But the Right, supported by moderate Republicans like Jules Favre, would have none of it, insisting that Paris was already in a state of insurrection. Was it not the duty of the Assembly, as Favre put it, to take the most energetic measures against those who put the Republic above the mandate from universal suffrage! [30] Thiers finally made his position clear the following day. Recognizing that the Leftist deputies in the Assembly had lost their authority in Paris (and indeed the Central Committee had by then taken command of most arrondissement *mairies*), and that the men in control of the Hôtel de Ville were not going to be deflected by a project voted in the Assembly, he reviewed the events of March 18, concluding, "Paris has given us the right to prefer France to her." [31]

Probably the monarchist majority believed that Thiers would now direct the destruction of the Republic, beginning with the subjection of Paris; forgetting that on the previous day he had formally promised that the Republic would not fall as long as he was in power.[32] He meant a conservative Republic, of course, and that implied only the suppression of extremism and forcing the Parisians to accept the peace settlement. The Assembly did, on the twenty-third, modify the Law of Maturities to postpone its effectiveness for a month, recognizing that the law had been impolitic. Any hope that this gesture would promote a reconciliation was dashed after that day when the arrondissement mayors arrived in a body and asked to be heard in the interest of peace and unity, but wearing their tricolor sashes of office. Upon their appearance, the deputies on the Left blew up in a frantic demonstration for the Republic, the Right became infuriated, and the sitting had to be adjourned.[33] Moreover, a contemporary incident in Paris seemed to confirm that the end of negotiation had arrived. On March 21 a small number of Rightists demonstrated in favor of the Assembly, giving notice of a larger manifestation on the next day. About one thousand turned out to march from the Place de la Concorde to the Hôtel de Ville, but were obstructed and fired upon by National Guards. Ten were killed and the demonstrations came to an

30. Jellinek, *op. cit.*, p. 163.
31. Zola, *op. cit.*, I, 110–117.
32. Joughin, *op. cit.*, I, 50–51.
33. Zola, *op. cit.*, I, 119–124.

end. The shooting of political opponents had begun, and Paris had a dangerous number of angered counterrevolutionaries within the walls.[34]

The Central Committee of the National Guard, if dominant for the moment in Paris, was not the sole organized group on the scene. Still in existence was the old Central Committee of the Twenty Arrondissements, its roster including men of greater renown than a majority of those on the Central Committee of the National Guard. By March of 1871, however, Jacobins and Blanquists had ceased to dominate the earlier Committee, a majority then being Proudhonian. Having lost the initiative to the Central Committee of the National Guard, the older Committee put out a manifesto the day before the election urging the voters to turn out in strength in support of the Central Committee of the National Guard, thus further helping to confuse the two committees in the minds of the counterrevolutionaries. After the election of March 26, the Central Committee of the Twenty Arrondissements quickly lost its coherence and ceased to be one of the revolutionary agencies.[35]

The Parisian chapter of the International was also on the scene, having reorganized itself on March 15. Momentarily the International stayed clear of the Central Committee of the National Guard, unsure of its political composition; but within a week some affiliates of the International were joining Committee discussions and accepting election to the Committee. By the date of the municipal elections, we find six affiliates of the International on the Central Committee: the Jacobins Antoine Arnaud and Clovis Dupont, the Blanquist E.-V. Duval, and the Proudhonians A.-A. Assi, L.-J. Pindy, and L.-E. Varlin. All six would win election to the Commune.[36] This crossing of organizational lines by men of various parties and persuasions, in other words, reached a point of rich confusion before the founding of the Commune and does much to explain why the Commune never developed a coherent program and why outsiders

34. Winock and Azéma, *op. cit.*, pp. 60–61.
35. Dautry and Scheler, *op. cit.*, pp. 232–239.
36. Georges Bourgin, *La Commune*, Paris: Presses universitaires de France, 1953, pp. 41–42; and Rihs, *op. cit.*, pp. 49–53.

failed to understand communal politics.

Municipal elections for the ninety-seat communal council were held as scheduled on March 26. About 229,000 voters went to the polls, a figure that has been variously cited as both a victory and a defeat for the Commune, depending upon how the incomplete figures are construed. Voter registration for the plebiscite of 1870 had been 482,000, and as that registration still applied, it meant that only 47½ per cent of the presumed electorate voted on March 26. On the other hand, as the actual population had declined during the siege and after the armistice, the registration figure is misleading. In February of 1871, roughly 328,000 Parisians voted in the elections for the National Assembly, on the basis of which one might claim that nearly 70 per cent of the electorate turned out on March 26.[37] None of the figures tell us how many voters were abstaining nor what abstention signified; just as the act of voting certainly did not necessarily imply enthusiasm for a revolutionary government. During the autumn of 1870, demands for the election of a Parisian municipal government had repeatedly come from a variety of people. Some saw in the collapse of the Empire the opportunity to establish revolutionary government; others were simply impatient with the military policies of the Government of National Defense and believed that only a Commune could fashion a victory—as in 1793. Whatever their understanding of the issues on March 26, the voters returned a municipal council that was overwhelmingly revolutionary.[38]

How confused the issues had been becomes clear when one looks at the initial composition of the Commune: sixteen of the ninety seats were immediately vacant as their holders refused to serve. These *refusés* were moderate Republicans like Edmond Adam, Jules Méline, Jules Ferry, and Pierre Tirard; and they were joined in a few days by five more moderates who offered resignations, Arthur Ranc being the most notable. With one exception, these twenty-one delegates represented arrondissements in the western half of Paris. Two more seats fell vacant because they were not claimed: The aged Blanqui had been arrested in le

37. Winock and Azéma, *op. cit.*, pp. 62–64.
38. Rihs, *op. cit.*, pp. 40–41.

Lot on March 18, and the Italian partisan Menotti Garibaldi made no appearance. Finally, three delegates had been elected in several districts. Of the ninety seats, only sixty-four were occupied. A by-election would have to be held.[39]

Of the sixty-four who retained their seats, nineteen were either recent members of the Central Committee of the National Guard or had been appointed to office by that Committee. As is generally recognized today, the Commune lacked homogeneity, and some of its members defy classification. Nine Blanquists can be identified as well as twenty-five Jacobins. Twenty of the deputies had had some prior affiliation with the International, most of whom espoused some aspect of Proudhonian philosophy.[40] A noticeable number of firebrand journalists won seats, suggesting not so much party affiliation as a notoriety gained professionally.[41]

By-elections were held three weeks later—on April 16—and one is immediately struck by a great reduction in voter turnout. Only one-quarter of those who had voted three weeks before bothered to cast ballots, suggesting either new-found apathy or alarm. By then, as we shall see, actual fighting had broken out between the Commune and the Versaillese, and many Parisians had no doubt come to question the wisdom of defying the Assembly. This great reduction in voters meant that some candidates did not receive the minimum number of votes to make them eligible to take their seats (one-eighth the number of registered voters in a given district), and several of the vacated seats were not even contested in these supplementary elections. Thus, the ninety-seat Commune never exceeded eighty-one members, and the supplementary elections promoted the factionalism already in the Commune. Nine of the new members were Jacobins, two were Blanquists, while six more had been affiliates of the International.[42]

39. G. Bourgin and G. Henriot, *Procès-verbaux de la Commune de Paris,* Paris: Leroux, 1924, 28–30.
40. Winock, *op. cit.,* 182–183.
41. Joughin, *op. cit.,* I, 32.
42. Jules Clère, *Les Hommes de la Commune, Biographie complète de tous ses membres,* Paris: E. Dentu, 1871, *passim;* and Winock and Azéma, *op. cit.,* 182–183.

Attempts to find homogeneity in the Commune by classifications other than party affiliation have also failed to produce a pattern. No age group predominated, for instance, and the average age of members was thirty-eight. Social origins of the members are somewhat harder to pin down—not merely because it is difficult to distinguish between an artisan who was an employee and an artisan who had successfully established his own shop, but because many of the Communards changed their vocations more than once, and several of them legitimately fit more than one general classification. Only roughly, then, can one say that about thirty-three were worker-artisans, the majority of whom were artisanal rather than industrial workers; that about thirty might be called intellectuals, many of them journalists; that eleven were what we call white-collar workers; that five were businessmen, and two were professional soldiers.[43]

Many members of the Commune sincerely believed that they were simply continuing and promoting earlier French revolutions. Indeed, some of the journalists on the Commune began using the revolutionary calendar before it was officially adopted by the Commune itself.[44] Disunited in ideology the Communards certainly were, but almost to the last man they emerged from some segment of the French revolutionary tradition. Only two members of the Commune seem to have had any serious knowledge of German socialism—Edouard Vaillant and the Hungarian Leo Frankel—and might properly be called Marxian Communists. Some, following Marx, were to see the Commune as the pattern for the future; in fact, the Commune makes much more sense if regarded as the climax of older revolutionary traditions. Had the various socialists in the Commune been united, they could have constituted a majority. But both the most anti-revolutionary and the most revolutionary members of the Commune were from the socialist camp.

Perhaps the most easily defined group in 1871 were the Blanquists, if one accepts the proviso that party lines cannot be too rigidly drawn. Here the line of revolutionary succession had come from Hébert through Babeuf to Blanqui, the latter a revo-

43. Winock and Azéma, *loc. cit.*
44. Bourgin, *La Commune*, p. 37.

lutionary Socialist without a definite socialist program. That is, Blanqui was not a system-builder like most Socialists of his day and shunned discussions of mutualism, communism, and collectivism as simply new forms of scholasticism. He was an egalitarian, an atheist, with great compassion for the poor, and he found it inconceivable that socialism in any form could ever be established without the violent destruction of religion, the bourgeoisie, and the state. Thus the Blanquists meant to seize power and place it in the hands of a dictator who would guide the people toward the social justice or equality implied in communism. Had Blanqui or his party become dominant in Paris on March 18, no municipal elections would have been called. The Blanquists, in sum, who had perhaps 3,000 to 4,000 adherents in Paris in 1871, represented the revolutionary tradition in its simplist form. After the Commune those Blanquists who survived tended to gather in London where they came under Marxian influence and lost their identity as Blanquists.[45]

The Jacobins were less unified as a movement than the Blanquists and were political rather than social revolutionaries. Spiritual descendents of Robespierre, these neo-Jacobins had for several generations clung to the memories of '93 and the reign of terror. Favoring a dictatorship of a group rather than by one man, believing in the one and indivisible Republic, the Jacobins emphasized the sovereignty of the people and insisted on municipal elections after March 18. They detested both Blanquists and Proudhonists as socialists, and the Proudhonists especially as federalists.[46] After a half-century of resistance to established society, these Jacobins had become skilled, professional revolutionaries, but also quixotic and romantic, "seeking in demagogy, an inflammatory press and the barricades the true instruments of progress." [47] The goal of social justice might suffice for the Blanquists, but the Jacobins were haunted by the possibility of the perfectibility of man.

The Blanquists and Jacobins coalesced to make the revolu-

45. Rihs, *op. cit.*, pp. 47–48, 143–147.
46. *Ibid.*, pp. 151–152.
47. David Thomson, *Democracy in France Since 1870*, New York: Oxford University Press, 4th ed., 1964, p. 25.

tionary Commune possible, an uneasy alliance of Hébertists and Robespierrists; but a minority in the Commune opposed both the idea of a revolutionary commune and a dictatorship in principle. Socialists all, some seemed to be followers of Saint-Simon or Fourier or Louis Blanc; others in the Proudhonian school favored decentralization, and to them the commune was the natural unit of society. It is difficult to pigeonhole many of the socialists, as only a few of them followed faithfully the line of a leader or adhered unequivocally to a school, which helps to account for why, as individuals, they sometimes cooperated and sometimes dissented with others in presumably the same category. This socialist Minority in the Commune, tending to follow the leadership of the Proudhonians, was not tied to the memories of '93 or to a reign of terror through a revolutionary commune, but espoused new political forms that would presumably produce the social republic.[48] At no time did they dominate the Commune; and in its later days the formation of a Committee of Public Safety to exercise a dictatorship provoked an open schism between Majority and Minority.

The new municipal government convened for the first time on March 28 at the Hôtel de Ville. Its first decrees were simple reforms that all parties could agree upon and which reflected no social or political program: official salaries were limited to 6,000 francs, loyalty oaths were abolished, and pluralism made illegal. Payment of rents and debts was postponed, not abolished, while the former conscription system was scrapped in favor of the nation-in-arms principle. This meant no armed force in Paris except the National Guard, of which every able-bodied male was regarded a member. The National Guard had never been celebrated for its discipline, and most of the little it had vanished after the armistice. But, remembering that a disciplined army had been vanquished by Prussia, many Communards believed that civilian *élan* sufficed to scatter regulars should the Versaillese dare to attack Paris.[49]

On March 29 the Commune divided up functions and responsibilities by forming ten commissions, each one replacing a

48. Rihs, *op. cit.,* pp. 172–175, 211–212.
49. Plamenatz, *op. cit.,* pp. 147–151.

former ministry: Executive; Military (presumably replacing the Central Committee of the National Guard) ; Supplies; Finances; Justice; General Security; Labor; Industry and Trade; Public Services; and Public Instruction. At the outset, Jacobins dominated these commissions, losing ground only as the military situation worsened in April.[50] The Central Committee of the National Guard, meanwhile, announcing that day that it was retiring from the scene having fulfilled its interim role, began meeting twice daily from March 30. These midwives of the Revolution could not bear to give up its supervision. Not only did their continual proclamations make the task of the Commune more difficult, but they soon abandoned all pretense of limiting their concern to military affairs.[51] As the communal officials came to be increasingly preoccupied with military matters, the members of the Central Committee came to represent the claims of the proletariat and revolutionary socialism more than did the Commune itself.[52]

Had Paris launched an attack upon Versailles immediately after March 18 as the Blanquists wished, the National Assembly would most likely have found itself in an untenable position. The armistice terms had limited French regulars north of the Loire to 30,000 men, and most of them were not in the vicinity of Versailles. On March 28 Bismarck agreed to allow the force to be augmented to 80,000 men; and, with prisoners returning from Germany, Thiers's forces actually reached 130,000 men—with Bismarck's tacit consent. Thiers prevailed upon Marshal Mac-Mahon to accept their command. The Parisian National Guard battalions, in contrast, were withering away. The paper strength was about 160,000 but these were irregulars not continually on duty; and by the time the fighting began troops on the ready probably numbered not more than 30,000. Officers abounded as one might expect in a system where self-nominations were in style, but professionalism was both absent and unlamented. The first "general" to command was the Jacobin Jules Bergeret, a former infantry sergeant who had also been a typographical

50. Bourgin, *La Commune,* p. 39.
51. *Ibid.,* pp. 42–43.
52. Bourgin, *"La Commune de Paris et le Comité Central* (1871) ," p. 63.

worker and a bookstore accountant. He was a latecomer to the Central Committee of the National Guard, had been elected to the Commune from the XXe Arrondissement, and was then named to the Executive Commission.[53]

Fighting opened on April 2 when Versaillese artillery shelled the northwestern suburb of Courbevoie, then occupying it. Communard forces abandoned the district, but five prisoners were taken and shot by the Versaillese. Each side had now shot political opponents, setting the stage for the ultimate massacre. The Executive Commission of the Commune denounced the event as a royalist conspiracy: "The royalist conspirators have ATTACKED. Despite the moderation of our attitude, they have ATTACKED. No longer able to count on the French Army, they have attacked with Pontifical Zouaves and Imperial police." [54] Most of the revolutionaries, of course, had long ceased to be friends of the Church; and, having publicly identified the Church and the clergy as allies of Versailles, the Commune responded to the loss of Courbevoie with a decree separating Church and state, suppressing the budget for the Church, and confiscating religious property.[55] Actually, the Commune did little to implement the confiscation decree, and religious services were not forbidden. On the other hand, the Commune did nothing to stop the looting of churches and convents that followed the decree.[56]

The second communal response to the loss of Courbevoie was a counteroffensive against Versailles, launched on April 3, the columns led by Generals Bergeret, Eudes, Duval, and Flourens. No Trochu was on hand to preach of military realities, and the poor enthusiasts who went forth to do battle under this magnificently amateur leadership were simply led to slaughter. By the fifth the survivors were back in Paris, but they did not include Duval and Flourens who were captured and shot along

53. Chastenet, *op. cit.*, I, 91–92.
54. Arthur Adamov, *La Commune de Paris, 18 mars–28 mai 1871*, Paris: Editions Sociales, 1959, p. 30.
55. Jean Bruhat, Jean Dautry, and Emile Tersen, *La Commune de 1871*, Paris: Editions Sociales, 1960, p. 215.
56. Georges Bourgin, *Histoire de la Commune*, Paris: Cornely, 1907, p. 114.

with all regular army troops caught fighting for the Commune.[57] To this the Commune responded with the Law of Hostages on the fifth, which provided for the arrest and trial of those thought to be pro-Versailles. They were to be held as hostages, three of them to be executed for every Communard prisoner shot by the Versaillese. This law brought to the forefront the Blanquist Raoul Rigault, Procureur of the Commune, who, at twenty-five, was the youngest member of the Commune. An atheist, an anti-religious fanatic, Rigault primarily directed his prosecutional efforts against priests. He was not a lawyer by training, but had a passion for police work, showing a fascination for police spies even under the Empire.[58]

Indeed, when one has surveyed the actions of the Commune, ignoring for the moment its doctrinal pronouncements, one might well conclude that the only realm in which the Commune was truly revolutionary was that of religion. No attempt was made to seize the Bank of France, both the Commune and the Central Committee of the National Guard drawing on the ten million francs credit the city of Paris had in the Bank. This kept the credit of the Commune good and made unnecessary the return to assignats that was popularly feared.[59] Somewhat later in April, after the bombardment of Neuilly, vacant apartments were requisitioned by the Commune to accommodate the inhabitants of bombed areas. But the owners' furnishings were stored and protected under seal. Even the matter of debt collection, that had so aroused the Parisians against the Assembly, was resolved moderately by decree on April 16. Debtors were given three years, as of July 15, 1871, to complete their payments, to be made in three installments without interest.[60] Whatever the unorthodox financial aspects of that decree, it was a sane and compassionate remedy for debtors caught by the wartime collapse. A truly revolutionary solution would surely have been more drastic.

It has been argued that the Commune had to be primarily

57. Joughin, *op. cit.*, I, 34–35.
58. Clère, *op. cit.*, p. 166.
59. D. W. Brogan. *France Under the Republic (1870–1939)*, New York: Harper, 1940, pp. 66–67.
60. Bourgin, *Histoire de la Commune*, pp. 120–121.

concerned with military affairs and with preserving the Republic, so that its immediate attention could not be given to meeting the social and economic grievances of the population. Such grievances were still aired in many popular clubs, many of which now convened in churches; and such popular claims could be called socialist without applying more specific labels such as Utopian, Proudhonist, Marxist, or Blanquist. Such clubs were ready for more extreme measures than the Commune seemed inclined to take.[61] It took until April 19 for the Commune to produce an official program, a reflection of the widely disparate philosophies present in the Commune, and the announcement came only after many compromises. The committee that drew up the manifesto included the Jacobin Delescluze and the Proudhonians Theisz and Vallès. Delescluze was officially given credit for the document, but quite clearly Theisz and Vallès prevailed; and Jacobins and Blanquists voted for a declaration in which the views of the socialist Minority were dominant:

"Paris once again," the French people were reminded, "works and suffers for all of France, the groundwork for whose intellectual, moral, administrative, and economic regeneration, greatness, and prosperity lies in [Parisian] struggles and sacrifices. What is wanted? 1) Acceptance and consolidation of the Republic, the only political form compatible with the rights of the people and with the normal and free development of society. 2) The absolute autonomy of the Commune extended to every locality in France, guaranteeing each [locality] the entirety of its rights and each Frenchman full exercise of his faculties and aptitudes, as man, citizen, and worker. 3) The autonomy of the Commune shall have as its limits only the equal right of autonomy of every other commune adhering to the contract, and the association of said communes will guarantee French unity."

The declaration went on to spell out the "inherent rights" of each commune, then returned to the political relation of Paris to the rest of France:

"Unity, such as it has been imposed upon us up to this time

61. Eugene W. Schulkind, "The Activity of Popular Organizations during the Paris Commune of 1871," *French Historical Studies*, I, #4, (Fall 1960), 398, 407, 414.

by empire, monarchy, and parliamentarianism, is only despotic, unintelligent, arbitrary, or onerous centralization. Political unity, as Paris wishes it to be, is voluntary association at local initiative, free and spontaneous conjuncture of all individual energies toward a common goal, the well-being, freedom, and security of all. The communal Revolution, begun by popular initiative on March 18, inaugurates a new era of experimental, positive, scientific politics. It means the end of the old clerical and governmental world, of militarism, of bureaucracy, of exploitation, of speculation in stocks, of monopolies, of privilege, to which the proletariat owes its bondage and the fatherland its misfortunes and disasters." [62]

Meanwhile, if the Commune could not undertake immediate social and economic reforms, it did find time to deal with priests and to exercise a puritanical censorship. Suspected gambling dens were raided, as were cafés which high-class prostitutes were known to frequent, the solicitors and solicited all arrested as befitted an egalitarian government. The two most notable figures held under the Law of Hostages were Darboy, Archbishop of Paris, who had actually been arrested before the passage of the law in the hope that he could be traded to Versailles for Blanqui; and President Bonjean of the Cour de Cassation, a former senator of the Empire. Before the end of April more than a hundred priests were taken by Rigault among the many held as hostages.[63]

In the Assembly at Versailles, the question of municipal liberties had also arisen in April. Thanks to the Great Revolution, the Republicans had captured the centralizing movement, and the Monarchists had necessarily become decentralizers. Adolphe Thiers, a centralizer, was made into a Republican, albeit a conservative one, in order to preserve the unitary state. He could no more support the Monarchists' desire to enhance local authority than the communalism of the Parisians. The imperial government had appointed all mayors; the Government of National Defense permitted municipal councils to appoint the mayors; and Thiers now proposed to allow only communes with

62. Rihs, *op. cit.*, pp. 126–136.
63. Chastenet, *op. cit.*, I, 93.

fewer than 6,000 people to elect mayors locally. An amendment was presented by the Right to give all municipal councils the right to elect their mayors, regardless of size, and the amendment passed to the annoyance of Thiers. He threatened resignation, forcing a compromise on the issue, for the Assembly still needed him to complete the arrangements born of the military defeat. An agreement was reached making a population of 20,000 the critical figure. Towns and arrondissements below that number might elect their own mayors; over that number, the government reserved the right.[64] Léon Say, the Republican economist, then moved to permit Paris to elect its own municipal council —though not on the basis of proportional representation so as to prevent its domination by the more crowded and radical arrondissements. He would give each arrondissement four members on the municipal council. Say hoped that this concession to Paris might help to end the schism, and his amendment was adopted overwhelmingly. This Municipal Elections Law, as amended, passed on April 14, 1871, but was a far cry from Parisian intentions of that moment.[65]

The difficulties that the Commune had that April in preparing an official program were only a part of the problem of achieving unity. Local committees of National Guardsmen were dissolved on April 6 to try to end divisiveness, but members of the Central Committee continued to agitate in their various arrondissements, even obstructing the implementation of communal decrees. Certain individuals, moreover, manufactured trouble wherever they trod. No doubt all politics has its opportunists, its cranks and eccentrics; but revolutionary moments offer unusual opportunities, not merely for those who are calculating place-seekers, but for those with axes to grind and those possessed by formulas for instant paradise. A few examples should suffice. Félix Pyat, classified a Jacobin, was one of the evil geniuses of the Commune. A journalist, he was not really a party man, but a hater with the means to vent his wrath.[66] Opposed to every

64. Reclus, *op. cit.*, pp. 67–68.
65. Zola, *op. cit.*, I, 171–175.
66. *Enquête parlementaire sur l'insurrection du 18 mars,* Déposition de Edmond Adam, II, 158; and Bourgin, *Histoire de la Commune*, p. 100

regime he had lived under, Pyat was nourished by a fixation on the Terror of '93. Elected to the Commune from the Tenth Arrondissement, he continued to publish his *le Vengeur,* campaigning to destroy his competition by casting doubts about the revolutionary reliability of rival journalists. Along with his two continual associates, the Jacobins Théodore Régère and Raoul Urbain, Pyat was a leading proponent of terror and an architect of mistrust.

The Jacobin Pierre Vésinier was another vicious personality whose grotesque hunchback was the least of his deformities. Like Pyat, he had been a major figure in the insurrection of October 31 and continued to publish his *Paris-Libre* under the Commune, though simultaneously editor-in-chief of the *Journal officiel,* calumniating anyone suspected of being moderate. For if Vésinier had one consistent quality, it was his systematic opposition to moderation.[67] Even Henri Rochefort, hardly a man of sweet reason, published warnings about the danger from fanatics and eccentrics, and he had Vésinier, Pyat, and Rigault in mind, men from whom he had to flee though sympathizing with their cause.

Jules Babick, chemist and perfumer, had a unique brand of eccentricity. Of no particular political faction, he voted with the moderates; but his primary occupation was mysticism. He was a disciple of a contemporary syncretic cult called fusionism and spent most of his time visiting the graves of well-known people, haranguing the dead and uttering mystical formulas. His Communal colleague, Jules Allix, spoke to the living, all the while fixing them steadily with an eyepiece; but spoke so continuously, mouthing such deplorable insipidities, that the Commune in desperation had him arrested on May 10 as a bizarre windbag, embarrassing to the Commune and virtually paralyzing government in his constituency, the Eighth Arrondissement. The list of peculiarities does not end with Jules Allix. Suffice it to say that a satisfactory theory about revolutions must account for those who emerge from the woodwork and thrive.

Two days after the publication of the communal program, Charles Delescluze, the leading Jacobin, proposed a major reor-

67. Clère, *op. cit.,* pp. 206–208; and Williams, *op. cit.,* pp. 112–113.

ganization of the Commune. It amounted to reconstituting the Executive Commission and designating each member of it as a delegate to one other administrative commission, thus increasing the authority and the efficiency of the executive power. The moderate businessman François Jourde, author of the measure on debts and rents, remained as Delegate for Finances; Gustave-Paul Cluseret, a professional soldier of fortune with socialist leanings, became Delegate for War; the Jacobin Auguste Viard became Delegate for Supplies; the Jacobin journalist, Paschal Grousset, an associate of Rochefort and a well-known *boulevardier*, took over Foreign Relations; Eugène Protot, a Blanquist lawyer who had made a career defending radicals, became Delegate for Justice; the Socialist Edouard Vaillant became Delegate for Public Instruction; Jules Andrieu, former accountant and bureaucrat who had been affiliated with the International, took over Public Services; while the Blanquist Raoul Rigault contined his prosecutional duties by becoming Delegate for General Security.[68]

This arrangement, dating from April 21, did not last many days. As the military situation became obviously more threatening, it sharpened the political divisions in the Commune and inflamed mutual distrust. The inexplicable abandonment of the fort at Issy on the twenty-seventh, on the southwestern perimeter of Parisian defenses, raised a suspicion of treason; and units of National Guard demonstrated in protest at the Hôtel de Ville. General Cluseret managed to have it reoccupied before the Versaillese could take advantage of the breach, but could not save himself from arrest. He was replaced by Louis Rossel, the first true professional soldier employed by the Commune, an engineering officer who had failed in an attempt to supplant Bazaine at Metz with someone more energetic. A man embittered against the regular army, he was still too professional to tolerate the interference of amateurs.[69]

The reformed Executive Commission was the second casualty of the Issy panic, as this hint of military disaster sharpened memories of 1793 and hopes that a Committee of Public Safety

68. Bourgin, *La Commune*, p. 40.
69. Brogan, *France Under the Republic*, pp. 67–68.

could produce a military miracle. The more revolutionary members of the Commune favored such a committee while the Minority—Socialists and Internationalists—feared that a Committee of Public Safety would simply be a dictatorship that would destroy the young democracy. Only forty-five members voted on May 1 to replace the Executive Commission by a Committee of Public Safety, twenty-three voting against and the rest abstaining; while only thirty-seven members voted for the five names to make up the new executive body: three Jacobins, Antoine Arnaud, Charles Géradin, and Félix Pyat; the Blanquist Gabriel Ranvier; and the opportunist lawyer Léo Meillet. This development made the Minority into an open Opposition, putting the Minority in personal danger and leading the new executives to seek greater collaboration of the Central Committee of the National Guard, which had been getting increasingly radical by the week. If the government thus reinforced the radical tone of the Commune, it also contributed to a woeful amount of civilian interference into General Rossel's conduct of the defense, as the members of the Central Committee were certainly political and military novices.[70]

One might even argue that the Commune really ceased to exist after May 1. So complete was its abdication of power to the Committee of Public Safety that the Majority members ceased attending the communal sessions regularly. At the session of May 15, for example, only Minority members were present.[71] By May 1, also, the Versaillese began shelling the perimetal arrondissements, notably the Seventeenth and Eighteenth, and suspicions and recriminations within the city multiplied accordingly. The Issy fort fell to the Versaillese on the eighth, this time in reality, after which the Central Committee pressured the Committee of Public Safety to designate Edouard Moreau (a member of the Central Committee) as civilian superintendent to the Delegate for War. In disgust, Rossel resigned as Delegate for War, demanding to be arrested as his predecessor Cluseret had been.[72]

70. Plamenatz, *op. cit.*, p. 153.
71. Bourgin, *Histoire de la Commune*, pp. 91–94.
72. Bourgin, "La Commune de Paris et le Comité Central," p. 64; and Bruhat, Dautry, and Tersen, *op. cit.*, pp. 240–241.

Following this crisis on May 9, the Committee of Public Safety was reorganized, Arnaud and Ranvier remaining, the Jacobins Charles Delescluze and Ferdinand Gambon and the Blanquist Emile Eudes joining. The chief military command was now given to the Polish refugee soldier Jaroslaw Dombrowski, but he was soon a suspect, probably compromised by Thiers's unsuccessful attempt to bribe him. Delescluze then left the Committee of Public Safety, replaced by the Jacobin Edouard Billiorary, to become the last Delegate for War.[73]

With the fort of Vanves lost to the Versaillese on May 13, Paris found herself immediately threatened by assault, and what remained of government in Paris seems to have become overwhelmed by panic or fury. By communal decree the "demolitions" began. First went the chapel commemorating the death of Louis XVI, then Thiers's house in the Place St.–Georges. Three days later, on the sixteenth, the destruction of the Vendôme column took place as part of a political ceremony, for the column had been built in the style of the Empire and had a statue of Napoleon I atop. And on May 19 a threat to begin the execution of hostages was published, though not at once implemented.

That very week the National Assembly was faced with the final settlement of the Franco-Prussian War. The terms, earlier accepted by the Assembly in Bordeaux, had since been put into definitive form; and the formal convention was signed in Frankfurt on May 10. Two days later Jules Favre presented it to the parliamentary treaty committee in Versailles, where once again bitter breastbeating ensued, General Chanzy in particular opposed to the harshness of the treaty. Thiers insisted that the terms were the best that could have been negotiated at the time and that, certainly, because of the civil war, France was in no position to demand softer terms. The treaty was thereupon accepted by the Assembly, 433 votes to 98, taken back to Frankfurt by Favre, where ratifications were exchanged by the two governments on May 21.[74]

A doubly fatal date, for it also marked the beginning of the final week of the civil strife that has for very good reason been

73. Bourgin, *La Commune*, pp. 40–41.
74. Reclus, *op. cit.*, pp. 65–66.

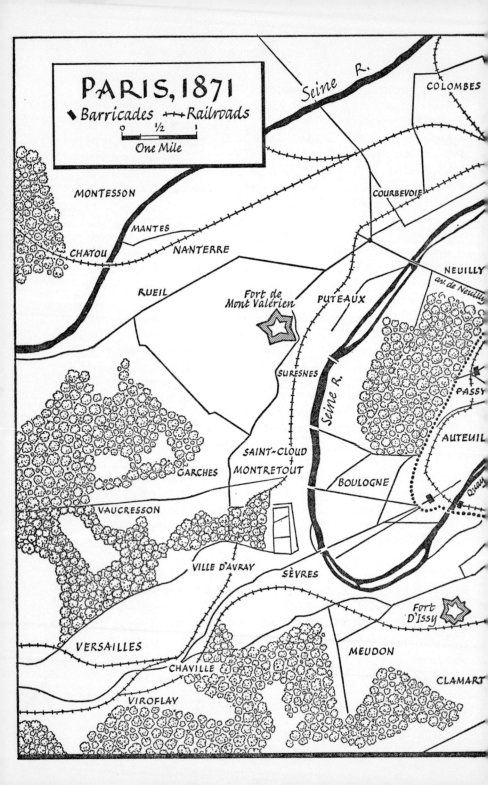

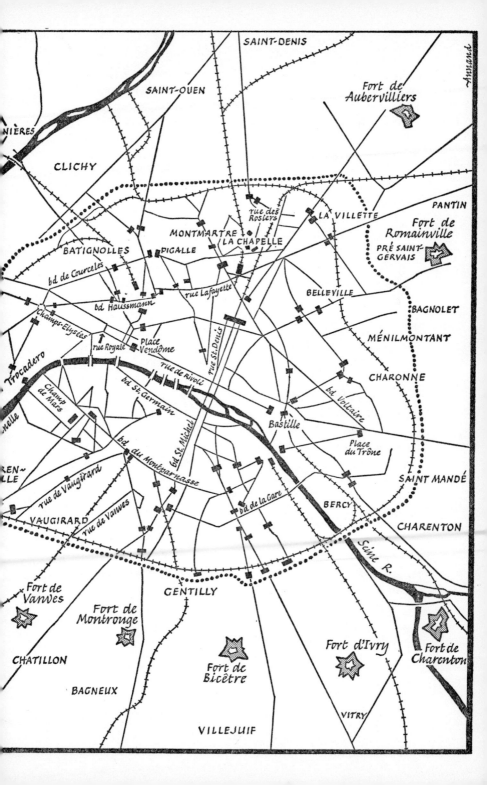

called the Bloody Week. Because suspicions of betrayal had so saturated the air, much has been made of the undeniable fact that a worker named Ducatel revealed to the Versaillese that the Porte de Saint-Cloud was undefended at the moment, enabling them to slip into Auteuil and Passy and to occupy most of the Sixteenth, Fifteenth, and Eighth Arrondissements before the end of the day—Sunday, May 21.[75] But who can seriously believe that Paris could have held out much longer given the numerous obstacles to victory! The great disparity in armed forces and supplies was increasing daily in favor of Versailles, and National Guard battalions showed a dangerous tendency to want to defend only their home arrondissements, helping to account for why such an important sector as the Porte de Saint-Cloud had been left undefended. Large numbers of Parisians were disaffected, anxiously awaiting liberation by the National Assembly, so that there was no possibility of a united front against Versailles. Parisian military leadership was a true mirror of the ineptitude and confusion in Parisian government where charge and countercharge occupied Communal members. Rigault was known to favor liquidating the Minority, several of whom had already been jailed, now called "latter-day Girondins" as a group by Paschal Grousset to keep the revolutionary issues clear.[76] They survived only because Delescluze and Pyat thought their execution would deepen the chaos.

Rigault still had his hostages and regarded them not as indivuals guilty of specific crimes but as mere representatives of a religious and a social order he meant to destroy, a view considerably more extreme than that of most Communards. He was accordingly unconcerned for the usual judicial guarantees and procedures, not to speak of the fact that the hostages represented a guilt to him beyond the need for proof. A Jury of Accusation had been organized when the Law of Hostages was decreed, the jury to include eighty National Guardsmen, but no trials took place until May 19. This revolutionary tribunal had no judges, only the jury and Rigault as prosecutor. Many members of the Commune, whether Majority or Minority, were uneasy about such

75. Bruhat, Dautry, and Tersen, *op. cit.,* p. 242.
76. Jellinek, *op. cit.,* p. 290.

proceedings but, before they could act to limit Rigault's judicial license, they learned of the entry of the Versaillese through the Porte de Saint-Cloud and abandoned the Hôtel de Ville. The Commune as a government had come to an end.

At the Ministry of War, Delescluze put together a proclamation to the people of Paris and to the National Guard that appeared on the morning of the twenty-second: "Enough of militarism, no more staff officers bespangled and gilded along every seam! Make way for the people, for fighters, for bare arms! The hour for revolutionary warfare has struck. The people know nothing of intricate maneuvers; but when they have a gun in hand, paving-stones underfoot, they have no fear of all the strategists of the monarchical school. To arms! Citizens, to arms! It is now a matter, as you know, of either winning or falling into the merciless hands of the reactionaries and clericals of Versailles, of those wretches who have deliberately handed France over to the Prussians, and who are making us pay the ransom for their treachery!" [77] A classic expression of the old Jacobin revolutionary ideal, Delescluze's appeal was an invitation to destroy what little military discipline remained. No effective resistance was even possible west of the Rue Royale on the Right Bank and the Boulevard St.–Michel on the Left Bank, and the fighting became a chaos of ambush, assassination, and arson.

Explanations for the crescendo of violence of the Bloody Week have generally seen reason on the side of the Communards and savagery on the side of the Versaillese, rather than seeing the violence on both sides as a total defeat for reason. This partiality can be easily accounted for: The Communards were obvious underdogs; poorly armed but resolute human beings confronting an impersonal, battle-hardened military machine; noble patriots who would not accept a humiliating peace with Prussia; Republicans and reformers who would not permit the restoration of an anachronistic regime; representing the claims of humanity against bourgeois niggardliness and crassness. Because there was more than an ounce of truth in each of those descriptions, and because Paris itself was the setting for the savage drama, the

77. Bruhat, Dautry, and Tersen, *op. cit.*, p. 244.

Versaillese were seen as outsiders assaulting the citadel of rectitude.

But they, too, had legitimate grievances to account for why, in the last moments of the civil war, they disobeyed orders forbidding unnecessary violence. Largely rural in background, the Versaillese troopers had an instinctive hatred of Paris: resentment against the traditional political preeminence of Paris; resentment of snubs both imagined and real; regarding urban workers as abnormalities in French society, as people who organized riots at home in time of war and whose lack of patriotism was merely proved by the destruction of a monument to French glory, as people who took sole credit for suffering in the late war without awareness of the agonies of rural France, enabling them to accuse rural France of indifference to the outcome of the war and of a callous sellout to Prussia. After entry into Paris the Versaillese were soon confronted by the deliberate fires which added so much confusion and horror to the scene beginning on May 23, and they were fired on from houses and barricades, a type of warfare that usually leads to reprisals and massacre. And both sides had been fed on atrocity stories ever since the murder of the two generals on March 18.

Some of the blazes were inadvertently set by artillery fire, such as that which ignited the documents in the Ministry of Finance. But Jules Bergeret ordered the firing of the Tuileries,[78] Paul Brunel turned the Rue Royal into a wall of flame after his retreat from the Ministry of the Marine, and Rigault hoped to make the Cité the last center of resistance, the Palais de Justice and Notre Dame to be the final buildings put to fire.[79] But he was caught by the Versaillese near the Luxembourg, his body left to be insulted by the women of the district. Théophile Ferré, another Blanquist, took over the Procureur's duties, and he issued the orders to begin the shooting of hostages, for the Versaillese had been killing freely as they advanced toward the hard-core revolutionary arrondissements. The Archbishop of Paris fell murdered as his two predecessors had been—in 1848 and in 1857.[80] By then the Prefecture of Police, the Palais de Justice,

78. Bourgin, *La Commune,* p. 101.
79. Brogan, *France Under the Republic,* pp. 69–70.
80. Jellinek, *op. cit.,* p. 349.

and the Hôtel de Ville were all aflame.

On May 25, with the Communards restricted to the northern and eastern arrondissements, the United States Minister E. B. Washburne urged Delescluze to end the futile resistance by seeking Prussian mediation. The sick and despairing Delescluze agreed to try, but he was turned back at the Porte de Vincennes by his own National Guards, so fearful had they become of betrayal. The senseless fighting had to continue, and Delescluze found death by exposing himself to enemy fire at a barricade. Fort de Vincennes was the last Communard stronghold and fighting there ceased on Sunday, May 28, actual surrender coming the following day. On the evening of the twenty-eighth, Marshal MacMahon issued his victory bulletin: "The Army of France has come to save you. Paris is liberated. Fighting has ended today: order, work, and security are going to reappear." [81]

For some, perhaps, but not for all. The number of casualties during the Bloody Week has never been precise, somewhere between 17,000 and 20,000 killed, many of whom had been given no quarter but simply butchered. Nearly 36,000 more were taken prisoner and crammed into the Satory camp at Versailles to await trial. (The Versaillese admitted their own losses to be 877 killed.) A surprising number of men elected to the Commune managed to escape, taking refuge abroad: Jules Andrieu, Antoine Arnaud, Arthur Arnould, Jules Babick, Jules Bergeret, Charles Beslay, Paul Brunel, Emile Eudes, Leo Frankel, Ferdinand Gambon, Jules Johannard, Benoît Malon, Léo Meillet, Eugène Protot, Félix Pyat, and Edouard Vaillant were among them. Some of the notable officers of the Commune, like Delescluze, Rigault, and Dombrowski, had perished during the fighting; but quite clearly the brunt of Versaillese vengeance fell not upon the great but upon the small. Otherwise, life resumed its regularities. "For the past few days," noted Edmond de Goncourt on June 6, "the crowd has reappeared on the deserted asphalt of the Boulevard des Italiens. This evening, for the first time, one begins to have difficulty carving a path amidst the sauntering of the men and the prostitution of the women." [82]

81. Bruhat, Dautry, and Tersen, *op. cit.*, p. 267.
82. Goncourt, *Journal,* Paris: Charpentier, 1903, IV, 332–333.

The horrors of the Commune, however, had not really ended. Twenty-two courts-martial were established by the army to try the prisoners and to hear charges made against people not yet detained. Bad as this administration of justice undoubtedly was, it could have been far worse given the climate of vengeance. For in the three weeks following the entry of the Versaillese into Paris, the authorities received 379,823 letters of denunciation from outraged, but anonymous, citizens, from which one may judge what the volume of oral denunciations must have been. Of the nearly 36,000 taken prisoner, nearly 24,000 were acquitted for lack of evidence; but, as there were further arrests, the record shows that between 1871 and 1875, when the trials ended, 46,835 cases had been heard. From that total there were roughly 13,000 convictions, the penalties ranging from death to banishment, jail, forced labor, and deportation to New Caledonia. Most of the members of the Commune had to be tried in contumacy, as only twenty-three members were ever captured. A commission on pardons softened a number of the sentences; of the 110 condemned to death (including those condemned in contumacy), only twenty-six were actually executed.[83]

The Commune had been many things and had encompassed many ideas and all the passions. And so it would remain in history and myth. Above all else, however, the Commune amounted to a demand for decentralization of authority, to a demand to replace the nation-state with a federal state where small self-governing groups or units would become the dominant feature. In crushing this movement in 1871, Adolphe Thiers not only became a Republican by insisting on the one and indivisible state, but a Republican more consistent than the Jacobins who championed that ideal but found themselves fighting for Parisian autonomy in the Commune. Thus Thiers deserves to be included with those contemporaries who are more usually noted as the champions of the strong nation-state: Cavour, Bismarck, Lincoln, and even his old enemy Napoleon III.[84]

83. Maurice Garçon, *Histoire de la Justice sous la IIIe République*, Paris: Arthème Fayard, 1957, I, 73–98.
84. David Thomson, *Ibid.*, pp. 26–27.

SIX *The Royalist Republic,*

1871-1875

We are no more than sheepdogs. We guard the flock, but we do not drive it. —*Comte de Chambord*

THE REACTIONARY movement in 1871 was not a response to the Commune of Paris, but was evident as early as the elections to the National Assembly in February of that year. The reaction merely deepened after the violent suppression of the Commune in May. Certainly the Monarchists were entitled to expect an imminent restoration after the electoral results of February. Yet, as we have seen, their political rifts led to the temporary establishment of a Republic, producing a political climate of great uncertainty. One thing was sure by summer: The national antagonism to the Communards meant that, whatever the ultimate form of the government would be, it would be conservative in spirit. In February the popular demand had been for peace; by June a popular demand for order had been added. The Right, of course, had always stood for order and authority, so that the significant change in attitude was apparent in the libertarian Left that had been compromised by the failures of the Government of National Defense and by the violences of the Commune. Thus, a majority of the Republicans in the 1870s proved to be more conservative than they had been under the Liberal Empire, even less interested in social reform than before.[1]

Similarly, the trade-union movement and the various brands of socialism were discredited by the events of 1871, for many of the Communards had been socialist. Most of them had *not* taken up arms to establish socialism, and private property had not been confiscated in Paris. Nevertheless, the propertied classes saw the Commune as a Red conspiracy against property and society and remained indifferent to, or ignorant of, the actual facts of the civil war. Trade unions had expanded significantly in the late Second Empire—especially after 1868 when the government agreed to tolerate them, if not to legalize them. (The labor reforms of 1864 permitted temporary coalitions only, not permanent unions.) By 1870 there were sixty-seven unions in Paris alone, perhaps twenty-five in both Lyon and Marseille, and a few in the smaller cities of France. The legal reprisals following the suppression of the Commune, however, shattered the unions, their leaders being either in flight or in prison. Because the National Assembly preserved martial law until 1876 in the revolutionary centers, most of which were industrial areas, and because anyone suspected of little more than sympathy for the Communards risked prosecution by the military courts,[2] the labor movement throughout the country remained discreetly quiescent until after 1876. A few of the prewar unions did begin to revive by 1872 in Paris alone, but were shunned by a great majority of the workers. Perhaps many of them recalled the failure of the strikes of 1869–1870, but many also recoiled from the extremism of 1871. By the end of the decade hardly 25,000 workers were organized,[3] and many workers remembered the Second Empire as a regime more congenial to labor.[4]

Even the civil courts were used by the new regime to bolster

1. John Plamenatz, *The Revolutionary Movement in France, 1815–1871*, London: Longmans, 1952, pp. 156–157.

2. Jean Joughin, *The Paris Commune in French Politics*, Baltimore: Johns Hopkins, 1955, I, 74–77.

3. Maxwell R. Kelso, "The Inception of the Modern French Labor Movement (1871–79): A Reappraisal," *Journal of Modern History*, VIII, #2 (June 1936), 174–177.

4. David I. Kulstein, "The Attitude of French Workers Towards the Second Empire," *French Historical Studies*, II, #3 (Spring 1962), 374–5.

the young Republic against opposition, many verdicts after 1871 obviously being politically inspired. Since this new regime justified itself as necessary, not merely to restore order after civil strife, but to restore "moral order" (of which more later), the regime exposed itself to satire in any case in which absolute justice was not demonstrable; which, in the nature of things, turned out to be much of the time. The radical Left especially made merry with the phrase, since it was easy to associate the "moral order" with the reestablishment of ecclesiastical interests and thereby suggest that Thiers and his crowd were not real Republicans. To establish this "moral order," societies more or less secret were mercilessly prosecuted, and the press was watched nearly as closely as the societies. At first even the old caution-money regulation was revived, and a myriad of interdictions and petty nuisances were available to harass any newspaper suspected of opposition or subversion.[5]

In other words, the post-Commune climate was punitive, and on June 17, 1871, the Assembly adopted legislation that revealed little disposition to forgive. One measure created a parliamentary commission to inquire at length into the origins of what was now officially called the Insurrection of March 18. A second measure on that date established a fifteen-man parliamentary committee on pardons and defined the powers to pardon and to amnesty. The right to pardon was given to the executive, who could exercise it freely except in cases involving the Commune. In such cases, the power had to be exercised jointly with the new parliamentary committee. An amnesty could be declared by the Assembly alone, a power superior to the right to pardon. For an amnesty wipes the record clean, and it applies not to individual cases but to whole categories. What the conservative Assembly assured in 1871 was that individual cases might be reviewed, but that an amnesty could be postponed indefinitely.[6]

By-elections to fill vacant seats in the National Assembly were scheduled for July 2, 1871. In the February election party issues had necessarily given way to the question of peace or war.

5. Maurice Garçon, *Histoire de la Justice sous la IIIe République,* Paris: Arthème Fayard, 1957, I, 137–142.
6. Joughin, *op. cit.,* I, 54–59, 88–91.

The rural areas, desiring peace, had voted for local notables who represented peace, most of them conservative gentry or aristocrats who were often Monarchists. By July, however, party issues had become clearer. Not only were Monarchists in a clear majority in the Assembly, but Legitimist and Orleanist pretenders were in the wings awaiting restoration, as the law exiling former royal families had been abrogated on June 8 despite Thiers's opposition. A number of the Monarchist deputies were even advocating French intervention in Italy to restore to Pius IX the temporal power he had lost the previous year. Thus, if the February electoral results could be duplicated in July, a monarcho-clerical regime would be a distinct possibility.

But the rural voters now showed their true colors. Rural freeholders were the largest social group in the country, and they were primarily concerned to preserve their property rights. Especially after 1848 they had become suspicious of city radicals, who presumably plotted to confiscate peasant land and money. At the same time the peasantry had not lost its far more ancient hatred of aristocracy and clergy under the old monarchy. And to many of these peasants a restoration meant the Old Regime with the reestablishment of feudal dues and tithes.[7] Except in the Vendée, Anjou, Mayenne, and Bretagne, royalism was essentially dead amongst the rural masses, something that Thiers seems to have known better than the Monarchist majority in the Assembly did.[8] The electoral results of July 2 confirmed Thiers in his belief: Only a dozen Monarchists were returned as against nearly one hundred Republicans. The erosion of the great monarchical preponderance in the Assembly had begun, a drift that would in time force the more realistic Monarchists to accept the inevitability of a Republic and lead them to work for as royalist a Republic as possible. But, for the moment, the Monarchist factions seemed to be on the verge of a compromise that would permit the immediate restoration of the Legitimist Comte de Chambord with the support of the Orleanists.

7. J. Néré, "The French Republic," *The New Cambridge Modern History*, Vol. XI, *Material Progress and World-Wide Problems*, Cambridge: Cambridge University Press, 1962, p. 302.
8. Daniel Halévy, *La Fin des notables*, Paris: Grasset, 1930, p. 21.

Had the Comte de Chambord made an appearance in Bordeaux at the time the National Assembly first convened there in February, he most likely would have been acclaimed as Henri V by the royalist majority since the Orleanist candidate, the Comte de Paris, was clearly his heir. Chambord, however, was no man of action and far too imbued with the righteousness and the legitimacy of his cause to take any step that might smack of opportunism. He would neither seize a government then seeking an executive nor appeal to a representative assembly elected by the people. He preferred to wait for divine interference, an act of God that would place him on the throne, a posture that evoked the memory of Charles X and the last Bourbon encounter with modern France. Many of the Monarchists, it is true, had not favored an immediate restoration, not wanting to burden the monarchy with the odium of the approaching peace treaty or with the financial exactions that would follow it. Thiers seemed not only to be the best qualified executive for the moment, but a safe one since he was thought to be an Orleanist.[9]

Postponement, on the other hand, was particularly risky for the Legitimists as they constituted a distinct minority within the royalist camp. Moreover, if a compromise with modernity should become necessary, the Orleanists, as the liberal branch of the royal family, would have the advantage. Then came the by-election of July 2 to suggest that the country was not royalist, much less Legitimist. It was safe for the Monarchists to tarry no longer, and it appeared that the two royal factions were at last prepared to cooperate, Chambord to ascend the throne, accepting the Comte de Paris as his heir. Suddenly, on July 5, the Pretender dismayed the royalist flock with a pronouncement published in *l'Union:* "Henri V cannot abandon the white flag of Henri IV. I received it as a sacred trust from the old king, my grandfather [Charles X], dying in exile; for me it has always been inseparable from the fatherland from which I was absent; it draped my cradle, and I hope that it will shade my grave." [10]

9. Frank H. Brabant, *The Beginnings of the Third Republic in France: a History of the National Assembly* (February–September 1871) , London: Macmillan, 1940, pp. 87–89.
10. Halévy, *op. cit.,* p. 28.

He would not, in other words, serve under the tricolor, the flag of the Revolution, as Republicans, Bonapartists, and Orleanists had done; and it would have made little difference to him to have known that the white flag went back, not to Henri IV, but to the Bourbon Restoration of 1814. The Legitimists begged him in vain to accept the standard dear to most of the French as a compromise necessary to gain the throne, but the white flag was in fact symbolic of a variety of deeper issues, the first of which was that of sovereignty. He meant to be King of France, not King of the French.[11] However appalled the Legitimists may have been by Chambord's refusal to compromise, they were in fact very close to him in outlook and in fidelity to principle. Monarchy to them meant a Christian monarchy governing a society based on Christian principles. Numbering about one hundred deputies and known as the Chevau-légers after the street where their headquarters was situated, they held themselves to be beyond and above the well-to-do bourgeois, having a traditional responsibility to the lower orders of society and not a selfish concern for profits. And they did not forget that the House of Orleans, the bastion of bourgeois monarchy, had twice betrayed the elder branch of the family: in 1789 and in 1830.

In contrast, the religious position of the House of Orleans was much more dubious. Officially anticlerical during the July Monarchy, Orleanism had abandoned its anticlericalism after 1848, seeing the Church as a useful barrier to radicalism. As Gallicanism was essentially a dead issue by 1850, the Orleanists moved into alliance with Liberal Catholicism and thus preserved some tie with their traditional liberalism. At that moment, however, ultramontanism had triumphed in Rome and most French Catholics, including the Legitimists, had been swept into the ultramontane camp. It meant that the new religious orientation of Orleanism was something less than an *entente* with the official Church.[12] The Legitimists could take the more "purist" stand: they did not equivocate about Christianity; they did not come to

---

11. Samuel Osgood, *French Royalism under the Third and Fourth Republics,* The Hague: M. Nijhoff, 1960, pp. 3–12.
12. René Rémond, *La Droite en France de 1815 à nos jours,* Paris: Aubier, 1954, pp. 122–131.

terms with the economic liberalism of the middle class; they disdained the impersonal, callous attitudes of the industrializing society. Had they come to power in 1871, or even in 1873 when a second opportunity was presented, it is questionable how long their principles could have satisfied the requirements of the later nineteenth century. It is proposed, however, that their political eclipse after 1871 helped to postpone humane social legislation.[13]

After the by-election of July 2 one could discern seven political factions in the National Assembly, subdivisions of the major parties:

1) *Extreme Right:* The "Chevau-légers," Legitimists who refused to disavow Henri V after his impolitic manifesto, perhaps eighty in number led by Lucien Brun, a bourgeois from l'Ain.

2) *Moderate Right:* Roughly twenty Legitimists who were ready to accept the tricolor, but voted usually with the extreme Right; led by Audren de Kerdrel and Edouard Ernoul.

3) *Center Right:* The largest of the royal factions, numbering about two hundred, Orleanists who favored fusion of the royalist parties in support of the restoration of Henri V with the Comte de Paris as his heir. Its leaders included the Ducs d'Audiffret-Pasquier and de Broglie.

4) *Center Left:* A handful of Orleanists already prepared to accept a conservative Republic, Thiers's own group that included Casimir-Périer, Léon Say, Jules Dufaure, Baron Rivet, and Henri Wallon.

5) *Left Republican:* The former Left in the *Corps législatif* —"the four Jules"—Grévy, Favre, Ferry, and Simon notably.

6) *Republican Union:* The principal group of younger Republicans led by Gambetta (who had been returned on July 2) and including René Goblet, Henri Brisson, and Jules Méline.

7) *Extreme Left:* About fifteen democrats, mostly socialist, of whom Louis Blanc was the best known.[14]

Thiers had been given the executive power the previous February as the ideal compromise candidate because he was on

13. Osgood, *op. cit.,* pp. 13, 32–34.
14. Maurice Reclus, *L'Avènement de la 3ème République, 1871–1875,* Paris: Hachette, 1930, pp. 102–104.

good terms with both Royalists and moderate Republicans. If *the* man of the moment, he was also a man of the past and, like Louis-Napoleon, a man of the French Revolution. Thiers, in his youth, had taken the Carbonari oath; he had been a revolutionary leader in 1830; and evidently he expected to govern after 1830 while the King merely reigned. His ambitions were then frustrated, as again after 1848 when he became the chief rival of Louis-Napoleon for power, both men believing that they should be chosen Chief of State by the people. During the Second Empire, Thiers nurtured a bitter hatred of his rival, hating him as a radical and demagogue. For Thiers was more authoritarian, more conservative than the Emperor. During the same period, it is probable that Thiers became a Republican, a tacit recognition of the political posture he must assume if he were ever to achieve power.[15] His personal ambitions aside, Thiers had always been consistent in his espousal of the centralized unitary state. Thus he resisted the Commune's challenge to central power, simultaneously blocking monarchical efforts in the Assembly to enhance local authority.

No doubt it would have been impolitic, with such a large royalist majority in the Assembly, for Thiers to reveal himself as a Republican that both ambition and principle had led him to become—but his actions tipped his hand. The abrogation of the law of exile for members of former royal families was passed 484 to 163 on June 8 despite his objection,[16] and earlier he had forced the Right to modify its attempt to increase municipal autonomy. Similarly, in debates over the Law on General Councils (August 10, 1871), regulating the functioning of the departmental councils, Thiers was again for central authority, the Majority decentralist.[17] What is more, the Republican victory in that summer's by-election and the disarray in royalist ranks led him to believe that time was on his side.

Indeed, one of Thiers's associates, Baron Rivet, moved on August 12 to give Thiers the more precise title of President of the French Republic for a term of three years, a bald attempt to

---

15. Halévy, *op. cit.*, pp. 30–37.
16. Rémond, *op. cit.*, p. 122.
17. Reclus, *op. cit.*, p. 85.

force the Majority to recognize the existence of the Republic and to free the executive from direct responsibility to the Assembly. Unable to press for the immediate restoration of a king, the Majority was willing to permit the change in title, but only if it was stated that the President exercised his powers "under the authority of the National Assembly." [18] This compromise, passed on August 31, seemed to strengthen Thiers and to be a clearer admission of the existence of a Republic, but in fact the Rivet Law changed Thiers's responsibilities and powers hardly at all. The Republic might now be official, but it was still provisional in the minds of the Majority. Accordingly, those Republicans to the left of Thiers began to press, in the autumn of 1871, for dissolution of the Assembly and new national elections as the only way for public opinion (presumably Republican) to make itself definitive.[19]

In their campaign these Republicans used effectively a religious issue created by the new "captivity" of the Pope in Rome. He had appealed to the Catholic powers to assist him in the recovery of his temporal power, and to that effect the French episcopate had petitioned the Assembly. Thiers, as always, was opposed to any interference in Italian affairs and asked for a vote of confidence on the matter, adding that of course he would protect religious interests in France and the spiritual independence of the Papacy. He got the vote of confidence only after the Majority amended the confidence motion with an order to send the Bishops' petition to the Minister for Foreign Affairs for his consideration. That minister, the Republican Jules Favre, immediately resigned his position in protest, and Thiers had to replace him with Charles de Rémusat, a personal associate. The incident enabled the Gambetta crowd to accuse the Majority of being willing to risk war in Italy, thus sacrificing the national interest on behalf of the Church.[20]

The question of a general political amnesty also became an

18. *Ibid.*, p. 87.
19. David Thomson, *Democracy in France Since 1870*, 4th ed., New York: Oxford, 1964, pp. 78-79.
20. François Goguel, *La Politique des Parties sous la IIIᵉ République*, Paris: du Seuil, 1958, p. 37.

issue in the fall of 1871 when, on September 13, Henri Brisson
introduced a motion to grant amnesty to all those condemned for
political offenses during the past year. His motion was signed by
forty-eight members from the Left, including Gambetta. Aside
from the obvious fact that the question of amnesty was compromised by the bitter memories of the recent fratricide, Thiers had
added further heat to the matter by introducing a bill on August
7 making membership in the International illegal, a bill which
implied a close association between the Commune and the International. These bills were referred to committee where the Majority successfully prevented an amnesty bill from reaching the
floor of the Assembly. Thiers's bill, on the other hand, became
law on March 14, 1872, condemning the International and thus
contributing to partisan interpretations of what the Commune
had been.[21]

Throughout these months of political uncertainty, Thiers
was heavily engaged in meeting the financial obligations of the
Treaty of Frankfurt. The original war indemnity charged to
France by Germany was five billion gold francs, a figure subsequently reduced by three hundred twenty-five million francs in
recognition of the value of the railway concession lost in Alsace
and Lorraine by the *Compagnie des Chemins de Fer de l'Est*.
Article VII of the Treaty specified a payment schedule: 1) five
hundred million within one month after the reestablishment of
the Assembly's authority in Paris; 2) one billion between that
date and the end of 1871; 3) another five hundred million by
May 1, 1872; 4) the remaining three billion by May 2, 1874. Not
only did the Germans demand strict observance of the schedule,
but French financial prudence required it. For the French were
required by the Treaty of Frankfurt to provide lodging, rations,
and forage for the German occupation forces in northern France,
the numbers of which were to be reduced proportionately as the
French made their indemnity payments. In fact, the indemnity
charged by Germany proved to be only a fraction of the bill
ultimately paid by the French government: that indemnity plus
the occupation costs, plus compensations paid to various railway
companies, municipalities, and departments, approached fifteen

21. Joughin, *op. cit.*, I, 68–70, 79–81.

billion gold francs,[22] an unprecedented sum in its day. That it could be paid testified to the prosperity that was a legacy of the Second Empire; that it was paid confirmed the probity of the Thiers government.

His government made its initial payment with funds borrowed from the Bank of France and from British and German banks, meanwhile preparing for the first of two issues of government bonds to cover the indebtedness. The first sale of government bonds, bearing 5 per cent interest, took place on June 27, 1871, and the response was an astounding vote of confidence in the new regime. The loan, limited to two billion francs, was oversubscribed about two and a half times. Thus Thiers was able to pay the 1871 installment on October 2 and to secure the German evacuation of six departments several months ahead of schedule; and he had the money ready for the May 1, 1872 installment.[23]

When it came to finding new taxes to retire the bonds, Thiers revealed his fiscal conservatism. In June of 1871, when the government exposed the probable total cost of the war and was preparing for the first bond issue, Henri Germain, a founder of the Crédit Lyonnais, held that an income tax would be necessary to meet the financial crisis. Thiers would have none of it, saying that he not only opposed an income tax in principle, but that nothing must be done to frighten off the potential investors in government bonds. Between July 8 and September 16, six new tax laws were passed by the Assembly, measures acceptable to Thiers because they did not alter the tax structure in the slightest. They simply augmented the tax rates—sometimes as much as 100 per cent—for customs, licenses, postage, stamp duties, and registration duties.

Perhaps it was unreasonable to expect the seventy-four-year-old President to be a reformer or an innovator. It is more surprising to discover that the firmest support for his fiscal conservatism came from the Republicans rather than from the Right.[24] Politi-

22. Reclus, *op. cit.*, pp. 118–119.
23. *Ibid.*, pp. 122–124.
24. Guy Chapman, *The Third Republic of France, the First Phase, 1871–1894*, London: Macmillan, 1962, pp. 21–25.

cal and economic lines, in other words, did not necessarily coin-
cide during the infancy of the Republic, a fact which greatly
complicated parliamentary life and made the executive's position
the more precarious. Each major political faction in the Assembly contained men of widely diverse economic views. Thiers, for
instance, was a protectionist, yet knew that the Republicans, on
whom he depended, were divided on the issue of free trade. Two
of the outstanding advocates of free trade in the Assembly,
Casimir-Périer and Féray, were from Thiers's own faction, the
Center Left; and they were joined by the Left Republican Jules
Simon in preferring some sort of income tax to a restoration of
import duties. As for economic groups within the country, manufacturers continued to be protectionist as they had been under
the Second Empire, arguing that the lower prices brought by free
trade also had the effect of lowering the wages that manufacturers could afford to pay. Farmers were very influential in the
Assembly and had not become the protectionists they would be
later in the century. They believed naturally that real estate could
not bear a significant increase in tax burden, something with
which Thiers concurred; but they believed that the heaviest burden ought to fall on personal wealth and assumed that an income tax was inevitable.[25]

Thiers's first Minister of Finance was Pouyer-Quertier, a
Norman spinning-mill owner, who had been a conservative
Bonapartist and an opponent of Napoleon III's free trade policy.
As such, he went along with Thiers's protectionism and his preference for a multiplicity of new indirect taxes, to the distress of a
great many deputies. The crisis in fiscal policy finally came to a
head early in 1872 when the budget for that year came up for
debate. Approximately 80 per cent of the government's income
had been coming from indirect taxation. Pouyer-Quertier's proposals for 1872 called for all additional revenues to come from
increased indirect taxation. The legislative committee on the
budget, however, proposed the adoption of an income tax instead, but this was beaten on the floor of the Assembly. Thiers
countered with a proposal for new duties on imported raw materials—to the annoyance of the manufacturers. In the confusion,

25. Robert Schnerb, "La politique fiscale de Thiers," *Revue historique*, 201–
202 (April–June 1949), pp. 202–205.

the income tax advocate, Féray of the Center Left, moved to send Thiers's proposal back to the budget committee, and the motion (January 19, 1872) passed, 367 to 297. Thiers at once threatened to resign, forcing his fiscal opponents to give way; for they had no satisfactory replacement for him and felt the primary need to retain him at least until the German indemnity was settled. In consequence, the tax reform movement collapsed. Backed by the Left, Thiers preserved the system most desired by the middle class and was able, on February 2, to terminate the commercial treaties with Britain and Belgium.[26] With some justice he could argue, as he later would, that he was more genuinely conservative than the Right.

This posture no doubt contributed to investor confidence in the future of France, but the Germans greeted the signs of French recovery with some uneasiness, especially in view of proposed French military reforms—of which more later. Bismarck had presumed that the financial exactions of the Treaty of Frankfurt would incapacitate the French for many years, or even that they might be unable to pay the indemnity and thus permit an indefinite German occupation in the North.[27] By 1872 such a notion was no longer tenable, and Bismarck responded by showing a new spirit of friendship for the Thiers regime. He now calculated that Thiers was the man most likely to discourage irredentism in France, Bismarck fearing the traditional militarism of the Right as much as the recent militarism of the Gambettists. And he thought that a republic stood less chance than a monarchy of finding a warm ally among the monarchical states of Europe. Bismarck also knew that the German Ambassador in Paris, Harry von Arnim, had improperly been conniving with French Royalists for the restoration of Henri V, a bizarre contrivance that included Arnim's ambition to unseat and replace Bismarck in Berlin. Finally, Bismarck in no way wished to encourage the revival of French clericalism, which might find an alliance in Germany among his political enemies.[28] Thus it was that Bismarck signed a special convention with Thiers on June

26. *Ibid.*, 208–212; and Chapman, *op. cit.*, pp. 26–27.
27. A. J. P. Taylor, *The Struggle for Mastery in Europe 1848–1918*, Oxford: Clarendon Press, 1954, p. 217.
28. Chapman, *op. cit.*, pp. 30–32.

29, 1872, presumably to ease the financial burden for the French by prolonging the date for the final indemnity payment from May 2, 1874 to May 1, 1875.

A month later the French issued the second series of bonds at 5 per cent to cover the remaining three billion francs indebtedness. Fourteen times the needed subscriptions poured in, meaning that the French could have raised nearly forty-three billion francs instead of the needed three billion, much of it from foreign investors. By March of 1873, half of the remaining debt was paid; and, on the fifteenth of that month, Thiers signed his last convention with the Germans, providing for the final payment to be made the following September and for an end to the occupation. In so doing, he saved the French many months of occupation costs.[29] However meritorious, Thiers's very success threatened his tenure in office. The royalist Majority, having grown apprehensive about Thiers's political ambitions, were anxious to bring him down—but not until he had solved the odious problems emanating from the recent war.

The political tone of the Majority in the Assembly by 1872 was revealed in the formal report of the Daru Committee, which published on December 22, 1871, its inquiry into the insurrection of the previous March, ending its report with a lengthy recommendation for curing the evils it held responsible for the Commune. Society must be protected, the prescription began, from further attacks by the International and any other association that conspires against the social order. On the other hand, as repressive legislation will not revive class harmony, the Committee recommended that the Assembly authorize the systematic study of social and economic problems in order that they might be constructively attacked. The Committee saw the new army as a place for social classes to mingle and to share duties and dangers, thus as an instrument to remove prejudices, and announced themselves as favoring universal military service. At the same time they approved the recent abolition of the National Guard because of its electoral feature, noting that the army ought to be a place to learn respect for authority.

The report then veered to the matter of universal suffrage,

29. Reclus, *op. cit.,* pp. 126–129.

repeating the axiom about the need to enlighten public opinion and urging the extension of primary education. Religious and moral instruction was held to be a necessary part of education; indeed, the Committee insisted that religious faith is the foundation for "true" education. They wondered if women and children might be represented better politically, not by giving them the vote, but by giving the head of the household votes according to the number of his dependents, simultaneously increasing his domestic influence and authority as a conservative force. Residence requirements for the vote, they concluded, should be lengthened to emphasize responsibility and tradition.

Freedom of the press was necessarily seen as a virtue by the Committee with the proviso that such freedom must not be misused as the International had presumably been misusing it. Similarly, public meetings and clubs ought not to be tolerated if they become arenas for conspiracy. Which led the Committee to remark that, if it was all very well to strengthen local governmental authority, the Majority ought to remember that the conspiracy against order had not vanished with the defeat of the Commune; and central power, with its primary responsibility for public order, must be kept strong. Yet the Committee really was decentralist in its suspicion of Paris and wanted to deny Paris her unique position in higher education by extending such education to the provinces, reiterating that all education must be both liberal and Christian, and not "pagan materialism."

The report ended with a condemnation of socialism, but also with a recognition that the aspirations of the lower classes to be spared the various forms of poverty, both material and moral, must be heard. Just as the peasant "became a proprietor because he was thrifty, worked hard, and led a virtuous and Christian life," so must it be possible for urban workers to rise into the middle class. The state, they implied, must provide for moral improvement, the keystone to economic advancement.[30] The new order, in other words, must be the moral order.

The voters failed to respond to this appeal for uplift with its implication of a clerical revival. A parliamentary by-election

30. *Enquête parlementaire sur l'insurrection du 18 mars*, Versailles: Cerf, 1872, I, 254–264.

took place in three departments on June 9, 1872, producing a Republican success as had occurred the previous summer. A delegation of anxious Royalists called on Thiers a few days later to express alarm about Republican progress, but found the President content with the Republic as then established and willing to promise only his continuing loyalty to conservatism. In consequence, the sole Legitimist in the cabinet, Baron de Larcy, gave up his portfolio in protest, and Albert Duc de Broglie resigned as Ambassador to Britain to become more active in royalist politics.[31]

When it came to remodeling the army, however, both Left and Right favored enlarging the military establishment, if not always for the same reasons; and Thiers found himself out of step with virtually all factions. As in his former years, he favored the small, relatively professional army, believing that short-term service led to military incompetence. No doubt these views were reinforced in 1871 by his desire to get the German indemnity paid off and the Germans off French soil, and he knew them to be uneasy about any sign of French military recovery. Since those desiring the enlarged military establishment did look forward to the day of revenge, they criticized Thiers for holding "German" views. The Left, in wanting universal military obligation, the *levée en masse,* was also consistent with its democratic views. The Right had also concluded that the army was the place to heal class rifts. The army chiefs themselves, after 1870, recognized the need for *trained* reserves, since a future war would require the use of reserves, however irritating this might be to their professional instincts.[32]

Thiers initially held out for a seven-year term of reserve training for a limited number of reservists to supplement the regulars. The military and most of the deputies preferred universal compulsory service for either three or four years, but ultimately had to compromise on the issue in 1872 to keep Thiers from resigning prematurely. Thus the law of July 27, 1892 was curiously complicated and inequitable, the product of a variety

31. Reclus, *op. cit.,* pp. 170–171.
32. Chapman, *op. cit.,* pp. 29–32.

of compromises.[33] In principle, at least, every male owed military service under the reform and could be called up between the ages of twenty and forty for a term of five years of active service. In fact, only half the annual contingent—determined by lot—remained in the barracks for the five years, the other half sent home on indefinite leave after one year. The law permitted men of considerable education and means to volunteer in advance of their conscription if they agreed to provide their own personal clothing and equipment. These men contracted to serve for a year, presumably to be trained as reserve officers, going on indefinite leave after the year.

After the five-year period of "active" service, all men were transferred to the active army reserves for the next four years, then to the Home Guards (*la territoriale*) for five years, and finally to the reserve for the Home Guards for six years. In sum, an obligation of twenty years. As reservists and Home Guards, they joined their home regiments for twenty-eight days each year to maintain ties with the men with whom they would serve in case of war. All men called up for service found to be without primary education were subjected to it through the army, and no one had the right to vote while on active service. Thiers accepted this law as the best he could get, but also worked thereafter to hamstring it by granting exemptions from service and working to reduce military appropriations. It became routine to exempt from service teachers, clergy, and men who were the sole support of a family.[34] For the public as a whole, however, the new military law implied a universality of responsibility that had been unacceptable as recently as 1868, and a return to austerity after the presumed frivolities of the Second Empire.[35]

Gambetta, meanwhile, who had been pressing for a dissolution of the Assembly and new elections since the fall of 1871, stepped up his campaign in the summer of 1872 as prospects for a

33. Henri Contamine, *La Revanche, 1871–1914*, Paris: Barger-Levrault, 1957, p. 30.
34. Jacques Chastenet, *Histoire de la Troisième République, L'Enfance de la Troisième*, Paris: Hachette, 1952, p. 133.
35. Paul-Marie de la Gorce, *The French Army, A Military-Political History*, New York: George Braziller, 1963, pp. 7–8.

Republican victory loomed larger. And, as we have seen, Thiers would give the Royalists no assistance when they sought to check the drift to Republicanism. He showed his hand openly for the first time when the Assembly reconvened on November 13, 1872, after the annual recess, by speaking out for the permanent establishment of a Republic as the form that "divides us the least." An infuriated Majority accused him of violating the Pact of Bordeaux, to which he replied that monarchy had become impossible since three dynasties could not sit on a single throne. He reiterated his desire for the Republic to be conservative. Still unwilling to turn him out before final arrangements with Germany were negotiated, the Majority now sought to reduce his authority first by changing the Assembly rules to deny him further part in parliamentary debate, second by raising the matter of ministerial responsibility.[36]

Thiers would have none of it and the issue was unresolved until a compromise was voted on March 13, 1873, a modification of the Rivet Law known as the *loi des Trente*. Thiers was allowed to speak in the Assembly if he asked permission one day in advance, but the new law deepened the separation between the executive and legislative powers and was aimed at making the President more of a figurehead. It created a new governmental post, Vice-President of the Council of Ministers, the chief function of which was to represent the President in Assembly debate.[37] As the final financial convention with Germany was signed two days later, compromises designed to placate Thiers were doomed. His work was really completed, and he had outlived his usefulness to the Majority.

The opportunity to dump him came a month later, growing out of a by-election in Paris on April 27, 1873. An ex-mayor of Lyon, Désiré Barodet, running as the candidate of the Gambettist Republicans, scored a substantial victory over Rémusat, the Minister of Foreign Affairs and a close associate of Thiers. Barodet had campaigned for a dissolution of the Assembly (in the expectation of Republican gains in any new election) and for an amnesty for ex-Communards. The Right at once sought to

36. Reclus, *op. cit.*, pp. 175–181.
37. Thomson, *op. cit.*, pp. 85–87.

show that Thiers's misguided faith in a Republic was responsible for this radical victory; and, when the Assembly reconvened on May 19, a resolution was presented signed by more than three hundred deputies: "The undersigned, convinced that the seriousness of the [present] situation requires a cabinet whose stability will reassure the country, asks to interpellate the ministry about . . . the necessity of having a resolutely conservative policy prevail in the government." Thiers's immediate response was to have a motion introduced calling for the creation of a two-house Parliament. The confrontation took place on May 23–24 and culminated with a motion expressing conservative dissatisfaction that passed, 368 to 339. Thiers resigned the presidency immediately. Unable to agree on a royal successor, the Majority decided to replace Thiers with Marshal MacMahon, expected to be a more pliant caretaker for the Royalists than Thiers had proved to be.[38] The change brought the Duc de Broglie, of the Center Right, into the vice-presidency of the Council of Ministers, a Royalist but asute enough to recognize that a restoration had probably become impossible. Like Thiers before him, he would work to ensure that the Republic would be truly conservative.

Though from a Legitimist family, MacMahon had served the July Monarchy and the Second Empire, and had commanded the assault on Paris in 1871. His title, Duc de Magenta, along with the marshal's baton, had been conferred by Napoleon III; but the old soldier, if conservative, seemed to be above party, simply a devoted patriot again doing his duty. "The government that we represent," he said on May 26, "must be and will be . . . resolutely conservative." Accordingly, the new regime used its repressive powers more actively than had been the case under Thiers, particularly against the Republican press. Press attacks against religion or the clergy, the foundations of the "moral order," were especially vulnerable to legal reprisal; and the prefects, who had powers to control peddling on public streets and ways, were instructed to keep material critical of the government off the streets. Newspapers suffering suspension sometimes sought to evade regulation by reappearing under a new name, but the

38. Joughin, *op. cit.*, I, 71–72; and Reclus, *op. cit.*, 183–192.

record suggests a more efficient repression than was ever known under the Empire.[39]

MacMahon's cabinet was entirely royalist, that is, Legitimist-Orleanist, but included one conservative Bonapartist, with Broglie the real leader of the government. Everything seemed to favor an orderly transition to monarchy: a royalist cabinet, a royalist Assembly, and the provisional constitution. Yet every member of the cabinet knew the difficulties ahead, arising not merely from the Pretender's intransigence or from the evident Republican sentiments among the masses, but from a growing suspicion in the world of business and finance that a restoration might trigger renewed social upheaval. Indeed, the only considerable royalist sentiment remaining in the country seems to have been Bonapartist despite the recent defeat, and the Royalists themselves wanted no part of such a restoration.[40] During the summer and fall of 1873, the two Pretenders and their followers struggled to reach a "fusion," but the flag and its implications continued to frustrate any agreement.

On October 9 Chambord arrived secretly in Versailles hoping to rally MacMahon's support. Not even Broglie knew of Chambord's presence. MacMahon, who made clear his loyalty to the tricolor under which he had served, and who believed that Chambord's restoration was impossible because of his insistence on the white flag, refused to receive the Pretender. Thus the Royalists were reduced to trying to preserve the provisional status of things indefinitely. Toward that end they proposed to modify the constitution to give President MacMahon a ten-year term, provoking such opposition from the Republicans that it was necessary to settle for a seven-year term on November 19.[41]

Passions about a possible restoration then faded, and public interest fixed on the Grand Trianon where Marshal Bazaine was being tried for treason. The formal inquiry had opened in May of 1873, but the court-martial sat from October 6 to November 10 with the Duc d'Aumale presiding in his capacity as ranking divisional commander. The case had a variety of aspects that transcended the question of treason, making it a matter of political

39. Garçon, *op. cit.*, I, 142–144.
40. Osgood, *op. cit.*, pp. 32–34.
41. Reclus, *op. cit.*, pp. 217–218.

controversy then and later. For one thing, the military system that had produced Bazaine had already been found wanting, condemned first by defeat and then implicitly by the military reforms of 1872. The Duc d'Aumale, a prince of the Orleans family, surrounded by generals better born and better educated than Bazaine, sat in judgment of a commoner who had reached the supreme rank. Aumale had been necessarily in retirement during the Second Empire, recalled to his rank and seniority only in 1872. Before him stood a man of the Second Empire, brave beyond any question but ignorant of good staff work, inexperienced in handling large military formations, never having shown a glimmer of strategic imagination. Quite clearly he had surrendered Metz before his resources were exhausted, but was it because he had become demoralized in his incompetence? Or was the surrender a clumsy maneuver designed to ruin the Government of National Defense to prepare the way for the restoration of Napoleon III, as some suspected?

Bazaine's legal defense was skillful. He explained his various ploys and decisions as designed to preserve his army in a neutral zone, so that it would be available to defend the social order which he believed was threatened, adding that after September 4 there was no legitimate authority in France to which he owed obedience, only a revolutionary regime. To which the Duc d'Aumale replied, *"Monsieur le maréchal, il y avait la France,"* [42] putting the matter in better perspective—especially since the loss of Metz proved fatal to a successful resistance to Prussia. The court condemned Bazaine to suffer death and military degradation, but privately asked President MacMahon to prevent the execution. Loyal to his former comrade and fellow marshal, the President not only reduced the sentence from death to twenty years of imprisonment, but cancelled the degradation. Interned at Fort Sainte-Marguerite, Bazaine escaped some nine months later, possibly with the aid of high-ranking accomplices, to live out his remaining twenty-four years of humiliation and poverty in Spain.[43]

If French military revival after 1872 was legitimate cause for

42. Denis W. Brogan, *French Personalities and Problems,* New York: Knopf, 1947, pp. 131–138.
43. Chastenet, *op. cit.,* pp. 169–170.

German alarm, and if the fall of Thiers in 1873 seemed to remove the principal bulwark against irredentism, it has to be
added that the new French government took great pains to assure
Bismarck that it meant to maintain order at home and to stave
off the question of revenge. The Foreign Service personnel remained virtually unchanged, giving the appearance of stability,
while the embassies and the ministries were in the hands of men
whose family names reeked of diplomatic experience and who
were welcome abroad as respectable and responsible. But names
like Decazes, La Rochefoucauld, Broglie, Rémusat, Choiseul,
and Gontaut-Biron also conjured up the image of a Bourbon-
Clerical restoration that, by 1873, Bismarck professed to fear,
identifying it with the "threat" from Catholicism in his own
country.

Bismarck did not seek a renewal of war against France, but
he was genuinely alarmed that his diplomacy might not contain
the French. With the *Dreikaiserbund* of that year he kept the
French isolated for at least the moment, and he should have been
somewhat relieved by the evident disappointment expressed by
the Legitimists over the failure to crown Chambord late in 1873.
In the subsequent months Broglie dropped cabinet ministers
known to be close to Chambord, replacing them with Orleanists,
and came under fire from the Legitimists for failure to pro-
nounce firmly and openly against the *Kulturkampf*. These
"ultras," in coalition with the Republicans, finally provoked a
crisis on May 24, 1874, bringing down the cabinet and forcing
MacMahon to form a new government, but also revealing the
deterioration of the royalist cause. Even so, a nervous Bismarck
began to consider means of promoting French expansion in
North Africa and the Near East to deflect French energies from
the Rhine.[44]

MacMahon's second cabinet was a hodgepodge headed by
General de Cissey, a friend of the Marshal, but really led by
Decazes the Foreign Minister. About all the cabinet could do was
to continue repressive policies in the slight hope that something
would halt the rising tide of Republicanism. The parliamentary

44. E. J. Pratt, "La diplomatie française de 1871 à 1875," *Revue historique*,
167–168 (May–August, #2, 1931), 61–72.

committee studying the amnesty question reported that same May and the vindictive tone of the report not only reflected the spirit of government repression, but revealed that many of the Republicans were now unwilling to jeopardize the good chances for establishing a Republic by appearing to be sympathetic to the Communards. The committee report was not even read on the Assembly floor, much less debated.[45] This confusion and uncertainty about the political future of France greatly hampered the deliberations of the parliamentary constitutional committee, confronted since 1873 with the problem of constructing a Republican constitution that would be agreeable to Royalists. Gradually it became clear to this Committee in 1874 that the way out lay in proposing a bicameral system, the upper house to be a conservative rein upon a lower house that would be elected by universal suffrage. Furthermore, the upper house—a senate—ought to be created before the election of a Chamber of Deputies to provide support for the MacMahon government during the transition to the new system.

On January 6, 1875, this proposal was defeated in the Assembly by a coalition of Republicans, Bonapartists, and *ultras* in a display of systematic opposition. MacMahon's second cabinet resigned in consequence, but had to remain in office because no alternative government could be formed. The Royalists were proving that they could not govern because of internal dissension, while the Republicans were trying to promote their own accession to office. As one of them, Edouard de Laboulaye, said to the Assembly on January 29, "You are refusing to establish a government republican in form. If you do not accept the [Republic], you will not be able to establish any government at all. If we do not constitute one, our mandate will expire; and it would be necessary to leave the decision to the nation."[46] To dissolve the Assembly, in other words, and call for new elections that would certainly return a Republican majority.

On the following day another Republican, Henri Wallon, brought forth a new proposition designed to accomplish what the Committee had failed to accomplish earlier in the month. He

45. Joughin, *op. cit.*, I, 73-74.
46. Reclus, *op. cit.*, pp. 234-237.

moved that the President of the Republic be elected by a majority vote of the Senate and Chamber of Deputies sitting together as the National Assembly; furthermore, that the President be given a seven-year term and be eligible for reelection. Bitter opposition was raised by the Bonapartists and the extreme Right, sensing that time was running out for them. But the motion carried by an eyelash, 353 to 352, thanks to a coalition of Republicans and liberal Royalists. The Republic was finally made—but by 1 vote.

The elections of 1876 under the new constitution produced the results that the compromisers had anticipated: The system of indirect election to the Senate worked to make that body spectacularly conservative. Royalists were in a clear majority and most of the Republicans elected were decidedly conservative, the radicals winning only fifteen seats. The principle of direct universal suffrage applied in the election of the Chamber of Deputies, and as a result the Republicans won 371 seats out of 514. During the campaign radical Republicans like Clemenceau, Barodet, and Louis Blanc argued for an immediate amnesty for the Communards; while more moderate Republicans like Gambetta turned their backs on the issue as inopportune. Not surprisingly, the radicals did better in Paris than elsewhere, but they won only 98 of the 371 Republican seats. With the Republic apparently safe, however, the moment had come when the two Republican factions would drift apart, the radicals to demand the social and economic reforms they had been unable to advance previously.[47]

The principle of universal suffrage was consistent, of course, with the traditional Republican principle of popular sovereignty, which had been historically associated with the Left. The founding fathers of the Third Republic, however, recognized the conservatism of public opinion after 1871 and finally understood that they could make popular sovereignty a bastion for the Right and ensure the end of the Revolution that had begun in 1789. About ten million people were enfranchised by the Constitution of 1875, more than half of whom lived by agriculture alone, many owning their own land. About three-quarters of a million

47. Joughin, *op. cit.,* I, 92–100; and Chapman, *op. cit.,* p. 73.

voters were in business or trade, but many of them lived in small towns and villages and had a rural outlook. With only about three million voters employed in industry, it is quite evident that France was a rural democracy with a great many voters still harboring the darkest suspicions about Paris and her politics.

The peculiar construction of the Senate served as a check upon democracy, it is true, partly because of indirect election through electoral colleges, but also because the constituent arrangement gave representational equality to all communes regardless of size. It meant that rural France was heavily overrepresented in the Senate, a fact bitterly resented by the Left. If rural interests were thus protected, the settlement of 1875 also provided political institutions that gave political preeminence to the middle class. The aristocratic revival in the nineteenth century, especially notable in 1871, was reversed in 1875, the nobility being defeated and supplanted in the key positions of state for the last time. One of the most notable constitutional features of the Third Republic was the existence of an administrative power in addition to the usual executive, legislative, and judicial powers: a bureaucracy of long-term professionals drawn largely from the middle class, who went on forever like Queen Victoria, ruling if not reigning, uninterrupted by the musical chairs of cabinet government, unruffled by changes in policy, sometimes developing policies not approved by the ministry of the moment. Quite a change, in sum, from the previous decade when the Emperor was accustomed to developing policies behind the backs of his ministers and forcing those policies upon a subservient bureaucracy. The parliamentary Republic, with its weakened executive power, may indeed be regarded as a greater triumph for the middle class than either 1789 or 1830 had been.[48]

What Thiers stood for, and what he had worked for, triumphed in 1875 despite his fall in 1873, and the regime then founded was to last far longer than any other known in France since 1789. The Republic was made by liberal Monarchists —Daniel Halévy would later call it *"la République des ducs"*—by men who accepted the liberal principles of 1789 and rejected the *ultras'* principle of legitimacy. Liberal rather than democratic,

48. Thomson, *op. cit.*, pp. 40–55.

they had clung to the idea of a monarch to avoid the "excesses" of a democratic republic and to provide the stability of legal succession to power. They were willing to accept a republic only when they saw the possibility of constructing one that would be as stable, durable, and conservative as a monarchy.[49] Long before the Commune, de Tocqueville showed how much of the Old Regime had been conserved by the Revolution; and, for all the new principles and forms by 1875, the heirs of the old monarchy were still required in order to build the structure of the New Regime.

49. Louis Girard, "Political Liberalism in France, 1840–1875," in E. M. Acomb and M. L. Brown, eds., *French Society and Culture Since the Old Regime,* New York: Holt, Rinehart & Winston, 1966, pp. 120–121.

SEVEN

The Intellectual Reaction

to Defeat and Violence

I am convinced that he died of what he used to call the swinishness
of the present age; he told me several times last winter that his life
had been shortened by the Commune, etc. . . . He had two hates:
hate of the Philistine in his youth—that fertilized his talent; and
hate of the hooligan in his maturity—this killed him. —*Flaubert
on the death of Théophile Gautier, October 28, 1872*

TO HAVE STUDIED the details of the defeat and the Commune
is not enough to understand their place in history. Distorted images of the Commune were refined into mythologies, and every historian knows that no amount of scientific or
historical inquiry ever suffices to banish completely prejudices
that have become enshrined as gospel truth. To say that the
Commune does not properly belong to socialist mythology on the
grounds that retribution fell on many people besides workers—or
because, as is usual in times of civil strife, the Commune provided a vast opportunity for the paying off of old scores—[1] does
not dispose of the matter. The distorted images of the Commune
led some men to suspect political and social democracy for the
remainder of their lives. While Labor and the Left saw the Commune as the third defeat of the French proletariat, the earlier
ones being in 1830 or 1848, and went on to reduce the complex

1. Guy Chapman, *The Third Republic of France, the First Phase, 1871–1894,*
London: Macmillan, 1962, p. 13.

events to a simple, precise ideology, making those events holy days on the socialist or communist calendars.[2] No doubt the peculiar events of 1871 lent themselves to class-struggle overtones, particularly as a wedge had been deepening between the workers and the state since the early 1830s; while the lengthy refusal of the new government after 1871 to grant an amnesty gave the appearance of implacable class hostility.[3]

To study the myths about the Commune would be to begin with the one that was current in 1871, the revolutionary or Jacobin myth, which saw the Commune simply as a stage in the Great Revolution of 1789 with neo-Jacobins and neo-Hébertists guided by what they thought would have been done in 1793 rather than by a well-developed doctrine. Similarly Thiers, author of a lengthy history of the Great Revolution,[4] believed that a National Assembly and a Commune could not exist side by side. Remembering 1792, he was obliged to show that he could master Paris on March 18, and he was no doubt right to abandon the city when the attempt to disarm it failed.[5] This revolutionary myth about the Commune soon gave way to a contest between the two other myths, each related to the other.

The first was the reactionary myth, which described the Commune as a premeditated "red" revolution, an instrument of atheists and communists in their attack upon property and morality, employing terror to gain their ends. Because the words *communard, communalist,* and *communist* were easily confused in everyday speech, language itself lent credence to the reactionary myth. So did the socialist myth about the Commune. Though the socialist myth denied that the Commune had resulted from conspiracy and emphasized the spontaneous, popular nature of the uprising, the socialist and reactionary myths were as one in seeing the Commune as a class struggle; beyond which the Marxists would see the Commune as the first example of the dictator-

2. Georges Bourgin, "Aperçu sur l'histoire de la Commune de 1871," *Revue historique,* 163–164 (May–August, 1930), 88–89.
3. Jean Joughin, *The Paris Commune in French Politics,* Baltimore: Johns Hopkins, 1955, I, 10–11.
4. L. A. Thiers, *Histoire de la Révolution française,* 10 vols., Paris, 1823–1827.
5. John Roberts, "The Myth of the Commune, 1871," *History Today,* VII (May 1957), 296–299.

ship of the proletariat.[6]

If there was a grain of truth in all the myths about the Commune, none of them provided an adequate analysis of the Commune. Yet they formed the bases for political faith and action down into recent times, the passions and poisons of 1871 spreading like outbreaks of plague, decreasing in virulence only with the passage of many decades. Much more than political life was affected: all intellectual life lived under the shadow of military defeat by the Germans, and of the subsequent civil violence and fratricide. The intelligentsia experienced a moral crisis which encompassed all the doubts about self and country, leading sometimes to confessions of guilt, sometimes to a hunt for scapegoats, and occasionally to formulas for reform.

The schism of '71 produced a further intellectual dislocation in altering the feeling between Paris and the provinces. Before 1870 Paris had certainly dominated France politically and culturally; but particularly in the Second Empire when Paris enjoyed notoriety as more than an intellectual center, the political Opposition managed to create the image of a crass regime governing a people caught up in frivolity and on the road to ruin. The image was enhanced not merely by the fact that ruin had come, but by the apparent irresponsibility of the Parisian masses and journalists in shrieking for war in 1870. Rural antagonism had to be directed against the Parisians themselves since the Empire had in fact been maintained by rural, not urban, votes. But it is nonsense to maintain that all intellectual life fled the city to flourish with Flaubert near Yvetot simply because the city also housed an Edmond About, a Jacques Offenbach, or an Emile de Girardin, men who successfully catered to popular taste.[7] Nonetheless, after the defeat a myth was born that worked to separate Paris from the provinces, really to isolate Paris whose writers ceased to have the national audience that a Hugo or a Lamartine had had. And before the end of the century many Parisian writers not only shunned the provinces but sneered at the democratic Third Republic which was rural France. The

6. *Ibid.*, pp. 291–293.
7. Michel Mohrt, *Les Intellectuels devant la défaite, 1870,* Paris: Corrêa, 1942, pp. 27–36.

Paris which sought an amnesty for the Communards was the city that became Boulangist and anti-Dreyfusard,[8] stances consistent only in their hostility to the Third Republic.

The various manifestations of the intellectual crisis after 1870 were all rooted in a preoccupation with Germanism, and that date amounts to a watershed in French thinking about Germany, what might be called the end of the Staëlian era. Before 1870 those intellectuals critical of the "bourgeoisification" of French taste and those critical of Catholicism and its influence upon government and learning had seen Germany as the temple of science and Protestantism, thus the nation to be emulated if France were to rid herself of ignorance and superstition.[9] Scientists like Claude Bernard, Adolphe Wurtz, and Louis Pasteur were painfully aware that their funds and research facilities were vastly inferior to what was available to their German and British counterparts. Educational reformers like Victor Duruy were equally aware that the attempt of Napoleon III's government to extend public instruction and to provide greater opportunity for higher education and research met the stingy complaints of bourgeois ministers of finance and the philosophical opposition of Catholic bishops who feared what may be summed up as the Voltairianism of lay teachers. But such reformers did not doubt the future of France. As Pasteur put it in 1867, "French physiology demands only that which can easily be given; genius has never been lacking." [10]

A coterie in France, however, had been forecasting ill for the French some years before 1870, men who were unreconciled to the political ideals of the French Revolution and who were prepared to believe any theory purporting to demonstrate the degeneration of the French "race" after 1789. Race theories have historically had a practical political purpose as in this instance when Comte Arthur de Gobineau published his *Essay on the Inequality of Races* in 1854, embodying some of Tacitus' ideas

8. J. Néré, "The French Republic," *The New Cambridge Modern History,* Vol. XI, Cambridge: Cambridge University Press, 1962, p. 322.
9. Claude Digeon, *La crise allemande de la pensée française (1870–1914),* Paris: Presses Universitaires de France, 1959, p. 535.
10. Roger L. Williams, *The World of Napoleon III,* New York: Free Press, 1965, p. 157.

about the Germans as well as ideas from other sources. Tacitus had meant his sketch of the Germans as a simple, unspoiled people to serve as a contrast to the corruption and artificiality of his own Rome. To a foreigner, all members of another nation tend to look alike and act alike at first; and Tacitus saw all Germans as yellow-haired and blue-eyed, suggesting that intermarriage with other nations had not taken place. The Germans also represented liberty for Tacitus, the virtuous warriors exercising a check upon their chiefs, a far cry from the tyranny of Roman emperors.

In the seventeenth century Comte Henri de Boulainvilliers had used the *Germania* to show that political freedom (for aristocrats, of course) came from the Germanic strain in French civilization, but that His Majesty's absolutism was the contribution of the Roman imperium. Gobineau, an aristocrat who fretted over the decline of his class in government, helped to keep the Boulainvilliers interpretation alive in the nineteenth century. By then the political purposes to be served had been altered by the French Revolution. The Abbé Sieyès, noting that the French nobility had based its rights on privileges won in the Frankish conquest and thereafter inherited by blood, went on to say that "We, the Gallo-Roman plebs, will now conquer the nobility by expelling or annihilating them." [11] But the conflict still presumably pitted Teuton against Latin.

Gobineau's purpose was to show that the Nordic strain, representing liberty and vitality, had been slowly absorbed by the Romanized strain in France and was leading to national degeneration. The inbreeding, in other words, was destroying the natural inequality of the "races"; and when inequalities of race disappeared, all other inequalities disappeared too. Hence the democracy of degenerate societies. Hegel, understanding Tacitus' purpose in *Germania,* had warned against exaggerating the virtue of primitivity, not to speak of the fact that German mythology suggested that there had been a good deal of intermarriage with dark-haired peoples by the time of Tacitus. Indeed, did not Tacitus' portrait of the Germans as remarkably heavy drinkers

11. Jacques Barzun, *Race: A Study in Superstition,* New York: Harper & Row, 2nd ed., 1965, pp. 17–20.

and gamblers illsuit them as models of heroic virtue! [12] But Gobineau in fact was not concerned to prove that Germans are superior to Frenchmen, and he clearly had little love for the German bourgeoisie.[13] He simply believed that the human races were becoming hopelessly inbred and were degenerating, because the aristocratic strain was lost in the fusion. Just before 1870 he predicted that France could have no more than thirty years of national life.

With the outbreak of the Franco-Prussian War, he thought the end for France would come even sooner and favored an immediate peace with Germany, no matter what the price. His sympathy for Germany was a sympathy for the German aristocracy which seemed more intact and unchallenged, its Saxon blood presumably unsullied; suggesting that his loyalty was more to class than to country. His ideas were not widely known in France, but were limited to friends like de Tocqueville, who had disapproved of them, and like Renan who borrowed them.[14] Renan, in fact, stole the limelight after 1870, though Gobineau continued to write. During the war he warmed over his racial theory in a volume called *Ce qui est arrivé la France en 1870* to account for the defeat, a book later published in Germany, describing the German victory as that of aristocracy over democracy. And, immediately after the armistice, he advocated political decentralization in France as the only way to avoid the domination of plebeian majorities, as the only way to prevent the spread of domestic rot.[15]

In Ernest Renan, however, we find an intellectual reaction to the defeat more congenial to the French since he remained a patriot. His essay, *La Réforme intellectuelle et morale*, first appeared on November 6, 1871. The essay was, in the first place, an expression of Renan's grief in seeing a lifelong dream destroyed: a dream of an Anglo-Franco-German political and intellectual alliance that would lead the world toward *civilisation libérale*,

12. Hubertus zu Loewenstein, *The Germans in History,* New York: Columbia University Press, 1945, pp. 15–16.
13. John Lukacs, ed. Tocqueville, *The European Revolution and Correspondence with Gobineau,* New York: Doubleday Anchor, 1959, pp. 179–187.
14. Mohrt, *op. cit.,* pp. 155–161.
15. *Ibid.,* pp. 161–169; and Barzun, *op. cit.,* p. 138.

the state he saw as the middle ground between the "blind naive-ties of democracy" and the "ridiculous" desire to return to the past. The extreme nature of the peace settlement meant, in his view, an irreparable chasm between France and Germany. More-over, as one of those French intellectuals who had seen all Ger-mans as descendants of Kant, Herder, and Goethe, he had been dumbfounded by the hostile behavior of German troops during the war, recalling to his mind the days of the Thirty Years War. He had somehow not supposed the Germans capable of "blind patriotism" and expected their leadership to be cultivated and cosmopolitan, devoted to the higher claims of humanity, not to the victory of a mere nation.[16]

Renan's review of the causes of the recent French disaster must be read with the reminder that he was considered a liberal in his day and had been hostile to the Second Empire as a cleri-cal regime. Noting the ignorance of the masses under the Old Regime, he attributed the maintenance of such ignorance not only to "feudal society" and the architects of royal power, but especially to the fact that Protestantism had been erased in France. For certainly the basis for Renan's enthusiasm for Ger-many was her claim to be the fatherland of the Reformation, the key to all other liberties. As for the French Revolution, he thought well of it in its early stages; and we may infer that the subjection of the Gallican Church was the aspect of the Revolu-tion that evoked his approval. But when the revolutionaries were carried away by the "false doctrines of Rousseau," they led the country into evil days. More precisely, "the day on which France decapitated her King, she committed suicide," for Renan came to believe that national unity and national traditions were bound inseparably with the Capetian dynasty.[17]

As for the Second Empire, the regime that had removed Renan from his chair at the Collège de France in 1863 for his public insistence that Jesus had not been divine, Renan summed up all the former Opposition's civilizational fears by saying that the government of Napoleon III had catered to the worst in-

16. Ernest Renan, "La Réforme intellectuelle et morale," *Oeuvres complètes,* Paris: Calmann-Lévy, 1947, I, 325–330.
17. *Ibid.,* pp. 337–338.

stincts of the nineteenth century—that is, to the bourgeois spirit, to materialism, always compromising with the clericals, and neglecting learning and the arts. No doubt the Emperor could be seriously criticized for the declaration of war in 1870, but Renan did not absolve the people from complicity: "The crime of France was identical to that of the rich man who chooses a bad manager for his fortune and gives him unlimited powers of attorney. Such a man deserves to be ruined." [18]

Renan's racism was particularly evident in his assertion that the war of 1870 had revealed the decadence of the French military spirit. Medieval France in his view had been built by a Germanic fighting aristocracy out of Gallo-Roman materials, while the gradual modernization of France amounted to the erosion of the Germanic strain, finally expelled by the French Revolution. With the Germanic strain went the military spirit, in place of which France got egalitarianism and became the most peaceful nation in the world. Renan's theory would not have survived an interview with Prussian soldiers who had fought against French infantry in 1870, but his theory was untroubled by such evidence. He further saw that the progress of socialism demonstrated the decline of Germanism, by which he meant that the military virtues of individualism and courage had been replaced by the search for peace and security and the opportunity to make money. By adding universal suffrage to the picture, he saw a further guarantee that mediocrity would triumph (back to the Second Empire again). "The source of socialism is egotism," he wrote, "the source of democracy is envy, and a society resting on such feeble bases can never have the capability of resisting powerful neighbors." [19]

In summing up, he claimed that "the victory of Germany has been the victory of the disciplined man over the undisciplined, of the man who is reverent, solicitous, attentive, and methodical over he who is not. It was the victory of science and reason, and at the same time a victory for the Old Regime, of that principle that denies the sovereignty of the people and the right of peoples to regulate their lot." The Commune had been

18. *Ibid.*, pp. 344-346.
19. *Ibid.*, pp. 347-362.

the capstone of the collapse, and he reckoned March 18, 1871 as the lowest day for French integrity in the past thousand years.[20]

Evidently Renan also believed that religion is an expression of race, for we find him proposing that Christianity must move farther away from Judaism in order that the spirit of the Indo-European race might become predominant at the heart of Christianity. All mysticism and nonsense, to use Castlereagh's words, but Renan's liberalism had always been full of contradictions, and those contradictions were finally brought to focus during the Franco-Prussian War.[21] Writing in 1897, the young Léon Blum insisted that Renan had never been a true liberal, notwithstanding his momentary anger at the clerical pressure that cost him his chair at the Collège de France in 1863. At that point, Renan had considered running for the *Corps législatif;* and Blum was willing to wager that, had Renan been elected, he would have ended up as Minister of Public Instruction in the Ollivier government in alliance with the Liberal Catholics. Sheer conjecture, of course, but Blum was quite right to assert that Renan's political judgment was not keen or his views consistent. What is more, his judgments and prophecies were even more erratic after 1871 than before, leading Blum to surmise that all writers of that period had two lives.[22] Just as Michelet saw Louis XIV's life as "before fistula" and "after fistula," so must we regard the spring of 1871 as a biographical watershed.

At the same time one must be careful to note that the crisis of 1871, if a watershed in men's ideas, often simply served to accentuate or distort views previously held. Hippolyte Taine is a case in point. Already a prominent intellectual before 1871, known for his materialism and determinism, his appointment to a chair at the École des Beaux-Arts in 1864 was popular with student radicals but raised a howl from the clericals. He held that all human reactions are determined by race, environment, and the moment; but notably by race, by which he meant innate or hereditary qualities, seeing them as the richest source of his-

20. *Ibid.*, p. 366.
21. Ernst Nolte, *Three Faces of Fascism*, New York: Holt, Rinehart & Winston, 1966, p. 43.
22. *L'Oeuvre de Léon Blum, 1891–1905*, Paris: Albin Michel, 1954, pp. 212–213.

torical events.[23] In 1871 he began work on what was to be his masterpiece, a lengthy examination of the roots of the 1870–1871 disaster under the heading *Les Origines de la France contemporaine.* The first volume on the Old Regime was published in 1875; three volumes on the Revolution of 1789 appeared between 1878 and 1884; and he published two more volumes on the post-revolutionary period before his death in 1893, the project incomplete.

His reaction against the Commune was everywhere apparent. Though a Republican and an anticlerical, he now showed a certain sympathy for the Old Regime. Perhaps as a political form it had outlived its usefulness, perhaps many of its characteristics and conventions were seriously artificial and lacking in vitality, but its social order had been graceful with the domestic barbarians confined. This ambiguity was resolved in the volumes on the Revolution. While not minimizing the legitimacy of popular grievances against the Old Regime, he primarily saw the Revolution as a popular attempt to redistribute property and saw the people collectively as a destructive beast. Thus old traditions and institutions were smashed to the ultimate detriment of society. In trying to eliminate social distinctions, in attacking the Church, Taine held the Revolution responsible for removing the traditional mediating forces between the individual and society, leading inevitably to an egalitarian attack upon private property and, therefore, upon individual liberty. Many of these claims had already been made by Le Play during the Second Empire, but Taine gave them the literary form necessary for wider acceptance.[24]

The views of Numa-Denis Fustel de Coulanges, historian of antiquity, were akin to those of Taine and Renan. But though Fustel was a racist to the extent that he saw the French aristocrats as descendants of Germanic conquerors whose blood was different from the conquered Gallo-Romans, he laid greater emphasis on the subsequent class hatred of bourgeois for aristocrat, seeing both the French Revolution and the Franco-Prussian War

23. Nolte, *op. cit.,* p. 45.
24. Paul Farmer, *France Reviews its Revolutionary Origins,* New York: Octagon Books, 1963, pp. 28–33.

as manifestations of that class hatred rather than as "race" wars.[25] Such an interpretation was acceptable to all those who believed that the Commune had been a class conflict, and useful to those who saw the bourgeois as the mongrel, the unheroic, the profiteer, the degenerate, and the cause of the national defeat.

From the intellectual turmoil after 1871 one must be careful to distinguish the racial determinists—first, from others who denied the superiority of the German "race" and found a variety of other explanations for the German military victory; and, second, from those who would soon produce a rationale for French superiority despite the military defeat. Moreover, "racial" thinking was not confined to France and debate on the matter not only influenced German racial theories, but was influenced in turn by German racists and by popular German attitudes toward France that became more apparent to the French during the war. It is well known that the Germans adopted Gobineau as their own, distorting his ideas to make him the authority on German racial purity and superiority, when he had merely sought to prove the superiority of racially pure aristocrats. *Die psychische Degeneration des französischen Volkes, ihr pathologischer Charakter, ihre Symptome und Ursachen. Ein irrenärtzlicher Beitrag zur Volkespathologie,* published by Dr. Karl Stark in Stuttgart in 1871 (and republished in Paris the same year as *La Dégénérescence physique de la nation française*), was presumably a scientific theory of French decadence.[26] But it reflected widespread popular conviction in Germany that the French were degenerate and immoral.

A curious ambiguity can be found in German attitudes toward the French that, in some respects, was quite comparable to the confusion engendered by the French in analyzing themselves. During the war, for instance, the thoroughness of German planning and discipline on campaign was in sharp contrast with the marauding drunkenness of French troops, a fact noticed by observers on both sides. The French had operated and behaved in a time-honored manner, whereas the Germans had a precision that

25. Nolte, *op. cit.,* p. 47.
26. Maurice Reclus, *L'Avènement de la 3ème République, 1871–1875,* Paris: Hachette, 1930, p. 142.

was entirely new to warfare. But, given the climate of opinion, the difference was simply seen as the contrast in behavior between Teuton and Latin. The Germans, indeed, were wont to see it as the contrast between the restraints of Lutheran piety and the laxity of Catholic morality or the loose living encouraged by revolutionary freethinking. Particularly during the siege of Paris, they exhibited "a gloating Protestant satisfaction at having the modern Babylon at their mercy," a satisfaction that some of the German commanders presumed would have been felt by the *Lanzknechten* of Charles V during the sack of Rome in 1527.[27] Quite clearly many of the Germans on the campaign believed that the French were hopelessly licentious and effete, deserving destruction; and they hoped that Paris would not surrender too soon so that the proper punishment could be exacted. They had come to believe that Germany had an historical role to play: the destroyer of rotten worlds. Tacitus' portrait of the Germans, in other words, revamped for the practical purposes of the nineteenth century; but still the picture of a virtuous, military, and chaste tribe on the outskirts of urban civilization. Yet, to their surprise, during the siege the Germans captured many messages from wives remaining in the city to husbands still fighting in the provincial armies, messages that revealed perfectly normal and virtuous sentiments and customs.[28] Not to speak of the fact that French infantrymen had won the respect of their adversaries during the fighting, suggesting anything but decadence. ("Lions led by asses," was a famous verdict.) Indeed, the pessimism and near-hysteria over the bogged-down campaign, at German headquarters in Versailles by January of 1871 revealed notable respect for the recuperative powers of the French.[29]

Aside from the ambiguity inherent in these reactions, the posture of noble savages safe from the iniquities of civilization had its liabilities. A later French generation, born too late to have experienced directly the agony of the debacle, would point to the Germans as the perpetual barbarian invaders of France

27. Michael Howard, *The Franco-Prussian War*, New York: Macmillan, 1962, pp. 353, 378–379.
28. Ludovic Halévy, *Notes et Souvenirs, 1871–72*, Paris: Calmann-Lévy, 1889, p. 272.
29. Howard, *op. cit.*, pp. 348–349.

and Italy and reassure themselves of the eternal importance of France, eldest daughter of the Church, the sword and shield of Western Civilization. This version of reality, however, was still "racial," implying the superiority of the French and dooming the Germans to barbarism as a birthright.[30]

The middle ground between the pro-German and the pro-French racists was occupied by men who sought explanations for the recent disaster without ascribing ethnic superiority to any national group, as well as by men who retained their faith in the ideals of the Revolution. Professors at the Sorbonne and at the Collège de France revived the claims that their counterparts under the Second Empire had been making, namely, that in the modern state national strength is dependent upon the importance placed on public education and research. The imperial government, if anxious to promote public instruction and to find more money for research, had equivocated in the face of clerical pressure; whereas the Prussians, since Jena, had been successful in using their schools to instill a sense of civic responsibility and discipline in the young. Thus the idea became current in France that the Prussian schoolmaster had been victorious over the French at Sedan, and that what was needed in France was serious educational reform.[31]

Presumably progressive and seemingly beyond reproach, such demands for educational reform were in fact often conservative in spirit. In the days of Victor Duruy educational reformers also wished to modernize and extend public instruction, but the spirit that guided them was liberal: the desire to liberate minds from superstition and prejudice, the desire to provide more technical and vocational secondary schools for those illsuited to the classical or preprofessional secondary schools. Whichever the curriculum, the reformers sought to preserve a balance between the educational rights of the individual and the educational requirements of society.[32] After 1871 one detects a new tone more appropriate to the First Empire than to the Third Republic—that the purpose of education is to make better citizens and patriots,

30. Barzun, *op. cit.*, pp. 140–145.
31. Reclus, *op. cit.*, pp. 143–145.
32. Williams, *op. cit.*, pp. 189–208.

to instill a sense of social and national responsibility. Certainly some academics resisted such attempts to abandon the goals of liberal education, but the conservative postwar educational claims were clearly congenial to those in public office after 1871.

In the time of the Second Empire, the Republicans had accused the French of self-indulgence and levity and associated those qualities with popular support for the imperial regime. That it was largely politics became clear in the continuing Republican principle of popular sovereignty and in the continual Republican demands that the people be given arms and training to become the military backbone of the nation. Had Gambetta not firmly believed in the nobility of the French character, he would not have been so convinced of an ultimate French victory in 1870; and, after the German victory, he attributed it to the superiority of German might, not to superiority in "race." [33] If one wishes to see the defense of the Republican tradition and the French Revolution after 1871, it can best be found in Gambetta's *la République française,* particularly in the editorials by Georges Avenel that were republished in 1875 as *Lundis révolutionnaires, 1871–1874: nouveaux éclaircissements sur la Révolution française à propos des travaux le plus récents et des faits politiques contemporaines.* Whereas Taine would see the Revolution as produced by the revolutionary spirit, by a small group of fanatics determined to put eighteenth-century ideals into practice, the Gambettists attributed the coming of the Revolution to a revolutionary situation that the old monarchy seemed powerless to manage. These Republicans were not indifferent to the ideas that the Revolution represented, to be sure, but they saw the Revolution created by circumstances rather than by a conspiracy. Had the old monarchy, in other words, been able to solve the problems of 1789, it would not have been turned out; had monarchical Europe been less hostile to the Revolution, there would have been no war in 1792.

The old device, Liberty, Equality, Fraternity, remained the motto of the Gambettists, but with the Commune in mind, they insisted that the device had never implied social equality and could not be held responsible for encouraging communism. In-

33. Barzun, *op. cit.,* p. 139.

deed, they attacked the claim that the Republicans had fostered class conflict by insisting that, in the revolutionary tradition, the Third Estate had been regarded not as a class but as the nation. Finally, they saw no justification for fearing that the Republic meant social upheaval. Had not the Republic of Thiers dealt firmly with the Commune, showing itself to be safely conservative? More radical Republicans, of course, were infuriated by this posture and would soon tag the Gambettists permanently as Opportunists.[34]

Many intellectuals saw a national moral crisis in the defeat and violence of 1871, some of them even experiencing a personal moral crisis from which they never recovered. The aged Jules Michelet, for example, who had written so enthusiastically of the French Revolution and so passionately about the greatness of France, was horrified by the violences of the Commune. To his dismay, "the people" had not even spared a statue of Voltaire at the National Library. In the months remaining before his death in early 1874, he brooded in misery about his earlier convictions, now doubting the progressive nature of revolutions, fearing that they produced only barbarism. Théophile Gautier was also sickened by what he had seen in both Versailles and Paris. Deeply depressed, he died in 1872, having cursed in his last book, *Tableaux de Siège,* those Parisians who had been willing to destroy in a day what it had taken centuries to build, along with those in the Assembly who had made Versailles the capital to deny Paris the crown that was legitimately hers.[35] "My sadness," Flaubert wrote to Ivan Turgenev in 1872, "is like that of the Roman patricians of the fourth century. I feel an invincible flood of barbarism rising out of the depths. I hope to be dead before it sweeps everything away, but the period of waiting is not very agreeable. . . . I have always tried to live in an ivory tower; but its walls are being battered by a tidal wave of filth that threatens to topple it. It is not a question of politics, but of the mental state of France. Have you read [Jules] Simon's circular letter, presenting a plan for the reform of public education? The

34. Farmer, *op. cit.,* pp. 38–41.
35. André Bellessort, *Les Intellectuels et l'avènement de la Troisième République,* Paris: Grasset, 1931, pp. 26, 32.

section dealing with physical training is longer than that devoted to French literature—a significant little symptom!"[36] He had eight more years of waiting, but saw nothing to improve his spirits. For a time he even toyed with the idea of leaving France as a place likely to become uninhabitable for people of taste. At his death in 1880 he left incomplete his marvelous compendium of platitudes suitable for bourgeois use as a final sneer at mediocrity.[37]

Louis Veuillot, the most notable Catholic journalist of that day, saw the investment of Paris and the entry of Italian troops into Rome as a product of a moral illness in both men and nations, but called that illness impiety. Becoming Voltairian in the eighteenth century had two principal results, according to Veuillot: first, it meant that the intellectuals in Paris had become *déracinés,* and that after 1789 Paris attempted to govern the country without concern for the most fundamental instincts and traditions of the nation; second, that Prussia was remodeled in the eighteenth century according to the Voltairian principles of enlightened despotism. As the French intellectuals preferred such a state to Catholic Austria, the way was paved for defeat in 1870. Thus both defeat and civil strife were attributed to loss of Catholic faith. Let France first experience a spiritual revival, and a national revival would be possible. Veuillot earlier had been essentially indifferent to form of government, only demanding that government give the Church and religion their "proper" sphere; and he had fallen out with both the Republic of '48 and the Empire for failure to be properly solicitous of clerical interests. By 1871, however, he had become convinced that a spiritual revival would depend upon the restoration of the legitimate king, ruling by the grace of God, and upon the revival of aristocratic leadership throughout the realm.[38]

While Veuillot was thus openly advocating the wholesale abandonment of the Revolution, Bishop Dupanloup of Orleans, already known to be a Liberal Catholic, sought more moderate

36. Francis Steegmuller, *Selected Letters of Gustave Flaubert,* London: Hamish Hamilton, 1954, p. 225.

37. *Dictionnaire des idées reçues.* The Aubier edition is the best; Paris: Noé, 1964.

38. Mohrt, *op. cit.,* pp. 149–154; and Bellessort, *op. cit.,* pp. 48–53.

ground after 1871. He would not condone revolutionary violence, but tried to separate that violence from those revolutionary ideals that he found "liberating" and in the spirit of the
Gospel. Dupanloup was resented by the Veuillot crowd for being
unwilling to condemn the Revolution *in toto,* even though
Dupanloup called himself a Legitimist and criticized the post–
1871 Republicans for their irreligion. Beginning in 1872, he ab-
sented himself from sessions of the French Academy as a protest
against the election of the positivist Littré.[39]

Liberal Catholics like Dupanloup were particularly vulnerable to attack from more conservative Catholics, because the
liberal position was in critical aspects comparable to that of
French Protestants, leaving the Liberal Catholics open to the
charge that they were flirting with heresy. French Protestants
were not numerous, it is true, and their publications were little
known beyond theological circles. One of them, Comte Agénor
de Gasparin, was a liberal of the Guizot stripe who admired
much about the French Revolution, especially its anti-Catholic
aspects. When conservative Catholics like Veuillot had arrived at
a point where they were willing to condemn liberalism in all its
roots and branches, it was only too easy to lump Protestants and
Liberal Catholics together as dangerous revolutionaries.

Denominational differences aside, most religious writers of
the period agreed that France had become a vast sink of moral
decay. Whereas Veuillot wrote of the necessity of recovering spiritual strength through a revival of Catholicism, Agénor de Gasparin argued for the rooting out of Catholicism and a return to
the native Calvinism of the sixteenth century. His last book, *La
France; nos fautes, nos périls, notre avenir,* properly belongs to
the literature of reaction in 1871; but his disenchantment with
modern society much antedated the defeat of 1870. The parliamentary corruption of the July Monarchy had been the first sign
to him that the regenerative ideals of the Revolution were being
betrayed, and he saw the events of 1848 and 1851 as further proof
that public morality, subjected to all manner of compromises,
might be irretrievably lost. Like Flaubert, he had come to feel
like an alien in his own country and, indeed, took himself across

39. Bellessort, *op. cit.,* p. 58.

the Swiss border to the Calvinist mecca where he died later in 1871.[40]

His puritanism made no noticeable headway in France after his death, nor did the spirit of Liberal Catholicism; but the religious spirit that pervaded French Catholicism for the final thirty years of the century was fundamentalist and penitential, reflecting the influence of a recent order (1844), the Augustinians of the Assumption. If one explained the recent disasters as punishment for having denied God, for having ignored His rights and transgressed His laws for seventy-five years; if one believed that the nation must do penance for the presumed frivolities of life under the Second Empire; then a penitential form of Christianity would seem most suitable. The defeat of papal temporal power was a further event about which to be repentant, particularly if one argued that the fall of the eldest daughter of the Church had led to the sack of Rome. Thus the new church of the Sacré-Coeur, commemorating the recent dead, was built on the most elevated point in the modern Babylon where the recent fires were symbolic of God's wrath, and French Catholicism entered an era of pilgrimages designed to save both France and Rome, an era that saw renewed faith in the mystical and the miraculous.[41]

The more one looks at the moralists' accounts of the defeat, the more one perceives a peculiar tendency to assume that the morality of earlier eras was necessarily higher than that of the moment. What is more, the defeat of 1870 really confirmed religious and political prejudices made known by the moralists during their years of opposition to the Second Empire. Having predicted disaster all along, the events of 1870–1871 provided the occasion for refining and extending the black prophecies and for adding prescriptions for moral regeneration. A former liberal Bonapartist, Esquirou de Parieu, a member of the Ollivier government in 1870, was bemused by the moralists' reaction to the defeat. Himself a man of integrity, he did not deny the usefulness of austerity on the part of those who govern; but he pleaded

40. Mohrt, *op. cit.*, pp. 174–183.
41. René Remond, *La Droite en France de 1815 à nos jours*, Paris: Aubier, 1954, pp. 132–136.

for a simple consistency when judging the past. If corruption and decadence had cost the French the war of 1870, did it mean that the victories in the Crimea and in Italy had been the fruits of virtue? He asked for an end to the elaborate explanations for the defeat, arguing that at the outset of the war Prussia had simply been better prepared and better led. The Germans, he claimed, had had three superiorities: their artillery, their trained manpower, and von Moltke.[42]

On one level at least, Parieu's assertion cannot be denied, as it is supported by the best military study of the war, that of Michael Howard. At the same time, since a military system reflects a social order, the failure of a military system must call the social order into question. Why had Prussia kept abreast of military and technical innovations during the previous half-century? Eager to improve her fire power, seeing the military significance of railroads and telegraph, willing to engage in the intensive prewar planning that the efficient use of rapid communications implied. Why, in contrast, did the French professionals prefer to rely on courage and dash, on improvisation, on *le système D*—to muddle through? [43]

No single answer will suffice, least of all the "racist" answer. Part of the answer lies in the fact that muddling through had succeeded from the Crimea to Mexico. No matter that the Emperor had been seriously disturbed by the inadequacies of administration and supply during campaigns, he could not prevail over the public or the professionals who believed the French army second to none. The French professionals, what is more, were not so much ignorant as they were contemptuous of developments beyond the Rhine. What could schoolmasterish officers and noncoms with all their technical learning do against *la furie française!* One might rightly insist that the contempt was a matter of ignorance—even Renan in one of his contradictory moments wrote, "What we lacked was not heart, but head" [44]—but the attitude reflected a hostility to technology, a determination to

42. M. L. P. Félix Esquirou de Parieu, *Considérations sur l'histoire du Second Empire*, Paris: Sauton, 1876, p. 44.
43. Howard, *op. cit.*, pp. 1–2, 16–18.
44. Renan, *op. cit.*, I, 391.

regard war as an art rather than as a science, and constituted a
rear-guard action against the encroachment of those aspects of
life we associate with a modern industrialized society. As such,
the attitude mirrored a national rather than a military state of
mind.

Reaction to defeat and to civil strife after 1871, in other
words, was especially extreme because it occurred in a society
deeply divided along various lines since 1789, and in a nation
vaguely aware that its international position was slipping and
that the French way of life was being successfully challenged by
neighbors presumably less humane in their espousal of mecha-
nization. During the Second Empire, as we have seen, the intellectuals had opposed the government's encouragement of industrialization and economic development, regarding the regime as
anti-art, anti-intellectual, bourgeois, crass, a threat to civilization. Yet many of the same intellectuals saw science as the key to
national salvation, perhaps reflecting their positivism or materialism, but also reflecting the French passion for science as something philosophical rather than something applied.[45] Science
had been for them a branch of literary culture, and they could
not see the modernizing state with its concern for society as a
whole (and not just for individuals) as anything but the sign of a
declining civilization.

There were other signs of relative stagnation in France in
the nineteenth century, however, the cause for which, the effect
of which, reveal something of the temper of the French. Various
conclusions have been drawn from the decline in population
growth that enabled both Britain and Germany to surpass
France in total population. Long the heart of European civilization, France had also been the most populous nation in Europe.
Germans and British multiplied more swiftly in the nineteenth
century, however, so that by 1860 there were more Germans than
French—more British than French by 1900. The disparity in
growth is even more impressive when one remembers that Britain
and Germany also experienced much more emigration than
France did in the nineteenth century. It has been proposed that

45. Henry E. Guerlac, "Science and French National Strength," in E. M. Earle,
Modern France, New York: Russell & Russell, 1964, p. 82.

this relative failure to increase was related to the revolutionary laws regulating land ownership and inheritance; and it has been rather clearly established that the French were among the first to use birth-control methods to limit the size of families—sometimes so that there would be only one heir. The argument then runs that the consequent lack of population pressure in the nineteenth century meant no particular drive to industrialize.[46]

There can be no doubt that this relative infertility was enormously significant, but its causes are probably more complex and more subtle than the above formula would suggest. For one thing, the laws were easily and often evaded. For another, primogeniture had never been a feature of French law, and its absence before 1793 had not inhibited the growth of the French population. Indeed, its absence in other continental countries in the nineteenth century did not have the effect claimed in France—at least not until much later in the century. Let us suggest, therefore, that twenty-five years of revolution and war, of profound shock and change, deracinated French society sufficiently to affect fertility for a number of generations; not because a substantial number of males were lost in battle, but because the disruptions, the uncertainties, and the cynicism—born of observing the betrayal of both old and new ideals—had long-term repercussions: doubts about the future of France in particular. Called in the early years of the century *"le mal de siècle,"* the condition did not gracefully fade away with the restoration of the old order in 1814. Because, in fact, the old order, except for its façade, could not be restored, and the new order had already revealed its vulnerability. The search for a *"juste milieu"* went on throughout the century, as is well known, and the political and religious facets of that search were no mere façade; for they reflected the search for new faith, new principles, new vitality.

The peculiarities of French economic development in the nineteenth century were a further aspect of this relative stagnation. Relating the failure to industrialize to the absence of population pressure, however, omits a substantial part of the picture. Because we see industrialization today as such a necessary response to population pressure, we too easily assume that

46. Chapman, *op. cit.,* p. 78.

failure to industrialize means lack of population pressure. Yet this industrial phenomenon occurred "naturally" as a part of a "normal" economic development only once in the past—in Britain—and not primarily in response to population pressure. The French had the scientific and technical culture sufficient for industrialization in the nineteenth century had the *will* been there. What is more, they had the capital for investment, but invested it abroad at a rate equaled by no other nationality in the century, equally exporting their industrial and organizational skills to other continental countries.[47]

Meanwhile, in France, the spirit of craftsmanship was engaged against the spirit of industrialism. "These workmen," wrote Charles Péguy, "had their honor and it was absolute. That the rail of a chair should be well made was a necessity: that was understood. It was not on account of the master that it must be well made or for connoisseurs or the master's clients. It was that the rail itself must be well made, in itself, for itself, in its very being." [48] And that attitude is what France has meant for those who have loved her, for whom she has been a second country, once the vanguard, now the rear guard of humanity in its struggle against barbarism.

The pessimism of 1871, in sum, was *le mal de siècle* immensely sharpened by military defeat and civil violence. The Revolution was over, and the bright vision of a heavenly city on earth peopled by paragons had faded into the inglorious spectacle of government by the well fed, no loftier in spirit than the dreams of the peasantry whose votes made such a regime secure. Baudelaire's prophecy, as yet unknown to the public, seemed to be coming true: "The world is about to come to an end. . . . I do not say that the world will be reduced to the expedients and grotesque disorder of the South American republics; or that perhaps we may even return to a state of savagery, and prowl, gun in hand, in search of food, through the grass-covered ruins of our civilization. No, for such adventures would imply the survival of a sort of vital energy, an echo of earlier ages. Typical victims of

47. Rondo Cameron, *France and the Economic Development of Europe 1800–1914*, 2nd ed., New York: Rand McNally, 1965, pp. 306–307.
48. Chapman, *op. cit.*, p. 144.

the inexorable moral laws, we shall perish by the thing by which we thought to live. Machinery will have so much Americanized us, progress will have so much atrophied our spiritual element, that nothing in the sanguinary, blasphemous or unnatural dreams of the Utopians can be compared to what will actually happen. . . . Those times are perhaps quite close at hand. Who knows whether they are not here already; whether it is not simply the coarsening of our natures that prevents us from perceiving the atmosphere that we already breathe?" [49]

And yet this humdrum Republic survived, stout enough to endure the most appalling scandals, sufficiently principled to strike down bigots and fanatics, and heroic enough to stand firm when invasion came again. The Revolution had done its work better than the pessimists of 1871 knew.

49. Charles Baudelaire, *The Essence of Laughter and other Essays, Journals, and Letters,* ed. Peter Quennell, New York: Meridian, 1956, pp. 173–175.

Bibliographical Essay

ABBREVIATIONS USED IN BIBLIOGRAPHICAL ESSAY

AHR   *American Historical Review*
EcHR   *Economic History Review*
FHS   *French Historical Studies*
JMH   *Journal of Modern History*
REN   *Revue des Études Napoléoniennes*
RH   *Revue Historique*
RHMC   *Revue d'Histoire Moderne et Contemporaine*

SINCE in the preceding chapters the intent has been to provide a synthesis and interpretation based upon recent research, the titles in this essay reflect that mission. On occasion, of course, older works have well stood the passage of time and still can be cited as fresh or useful. It ought to be clear at the outset, however, that a bibliographical essay can make no claim to be all-inclusive. At the same time, recent works containing specialized bibliographies are particularly noted here to extend indirectly the inclusiveness of this essay. The footnotes to each chapter, the citations being given in full, do in themselves constitute a bibliography; but an essay allows commentary on these sources, especially necessary considering the controversial nature of the period covered, plus the opportunity to note additional titles. The essay, like all Gaul, is divided into three parts: 1) the prerevolutionary period; 2) the revolutionary period; and 3) the period of reaction.

1. The Prerevolutionary Period

First among works on the Second Empire is Pierre de la Gorce, *Histoire du Second Empire*, 7 vols. (Paris, 1894–1905), monumental in its comprehension and elegant in spirit and execution. The final four volumes deal with the decline and fall of the Empire and, though the work is not indexed, the chapters are preceded by detailed tables of contents. The bias is Liberal Catholic, thus hostile to the Italian policy of Napoleon III, but favorable to the liberal drift in the '60s. Another distinguished general work, though on a lesser scale, provides a more Republican view of the Empire: Charles Seignobos, *Le déclin de l'Empire et l'établissement de la Troisième République 1859–1875*, which is Vol. VII of Ernest Lavisse, *Histoire de France contemporaine* (Paris, 1921).

Several bibliographical aids may be cited for this period: Robert Schnerb, "Napoleon III and the Second Empire," JMH, VIII, 3 (September 1936), 338–355, is now quite dated but still helpful. It can be well supplemented by Alan B. Spitzer, "The Good Napoleon III," FHS, II, 3 (Spring 1962), 308–329, a bibliographical article all the more useful in that it reflects the intellectuals' hostility to the Second Empire. Three bibliographical articles on economic history well supplement each other and introduce a vast literature: Henri Sée, "Recent Work in French Economic History," EcHR, I (1927), 137–153; Arthur Louis Dunham, "The Economic History of France, 1815–1870," JMH, XXI, 2 (June 1949), 121–129; and David S. Landes, "Recent Work in the Economic History of Modern France," FHS, I, 1 (1958), 73–94. A book not limited to France may also be cited: Edouard Dolléans and Michel Crozier, eds., *Mouvements ouvriers et socialistes: chronologie et bibliographie* (Paris, 1950).

As we know, the opposition to the Second Empire assumed a variety of forms. Shortly after the turn of the twentieth century, several books dealing with political opposition appeared that are still fundamental today: Georges J. Weill, *Histoire du Parti républicain en France de 1814–1870*, (Paris, 1900), is a detailed survey based upon wide reading, the citations being given in footnotes. The same can be said for his *Mouvement social en France, 1852–1910* (Paris, 1911). J. Tchnernoff's *Le Parti républicain au coup d'état et sous le Second Empire* (Paris, 1906) is more detailed than the Weill volumes, but less reliable. Intensely partisan, Tchnernoff was convinced that the Empire was too dependent upon conservative and Catholic support to have moved with any conviction toward a liberal regime; and he saw the declaration of war in 1870 as a deliberate attempt to restore the dictatorship. Yet his book has useful observations and electoral tables. A much newer book, but still very pro-Republican, is John Plamenatz, *The Revolutionary Movement in France, 1815–1871* (London, 1952), which has a notably intelligent introduction. Plamenatz believes that Napoleon III cared only for power, that he despised the people and was indifferent to their needs, views with which this writer disagrees; but Plamenatz also believes that the Liberal Empire had an excellent chance of survival had the war not intervened. Jacques Freymond, however, in "La France de 1870," *Études de Lettres*, XVIII, 57 (April 1944), 53–71, argues that the Empire was doomed despite the favorable results of the plebiscite in 1870, doomed by the very conditions that led to the Republican victory after 1871; a brief, perceptive article even if one disagrees with its conclusions.

Gordon Wright has given us several excellent archival studies illuminating political opposition to the Empire: "Public Opinion and Conscription in France, 1866–1870," JMH, XIV, 1 (1942), 22–45; and "The Distribution of French Parties in 1865: An Official Survey," JMH, XV, 4 (1943), 295–302. Howard C. Payne is the authority on the political police during the period. His views may be found summarized in several articles: "Theory and Practice of Political Police During the Second Empire in France," JMH, XXX, 1 (1958), 14–23; and "The Revolutionaries and the French Political Police in the 1850's," co-authored by Henry Grosshans, AHR, LXVIII, 4 (1963), 954–973. Or one may turn to his extensive book, based upon great research in Parisian and provincial archives, *The Police State of Louis Napoleon Bonaparte 1851–1860,* (Seattle, 1966), to see that the Second Empire was a far cry from the police state of the twentieth century. Similarly, David H. Pinkney, in studying the reconstruction of Paris, shows us the relation of public works to growing political opposition. See the culmination of his work in *Napoleon III and the Rebuilding of Paris* (Princeton, 1958), detailed, but readable and highly informative. Further information on the subject can be found in Louis Girard, *La Politique des travaux publics du Second Empire* (Paris, 1951).

Second Empire studies have also benefited from research on public opinion of French foreign policy. If not a major source of opposition to the regime, the failures in foreign policy during the '60s were fodder for the Opposition and, therefore, reflected it. The pioneer work was E. Malcolm Carroll, *French Public Opinion and Foreign Affairs, 1870–1914,* (New York, 1931), based largely on newspapers; but many of his conclusions have been altered by the more extensive research of Lynn M. Case, *French Opinion on the U.S. and Mexico, 1860–1867* (New York, 1936), and *French Opinion on War and Diplomacy During the Second Empire* (Philadelphia, 1954).

The religious squabbles of the Second Empire probably offer a better entry to the total picture of opposition to the regime than is generally recognized. To Georges Weill's earlier work on the Republican Party ought to be added his *Histoire de l'idée laïque en France au XIXᵉ siècle* (Paris, 1929), for materials on Republicans and religion, anticlericalism, French Protestantism, and Unitarianism. Jean Maurain's *La Politique ecclésiastique du Second Empire de 1852 à 1869* (Paris, 1930), is a massive, valuable monograph, but so detailed that it is almost an encyclopedia with an extensive bibliography. For a more general survey, see Adrien Dansette, *Histoire religieuse de la France contemporaine de la Révolution à la Troisième République* (Paris, 1948), a judicious work. A good discussion of Montalembert and the Liberal Catholic Opposition can be found in Joseph N. Moody, "French Liberal Catholics, 1840–1875," ed. by Evelyn M. Acomb and Marvin L. Brown, Jr., *French Society and Culture Since the Old Regime* (New York, 1966). Also see a published dissertation by J. B. Duroselle, *Les débuts de catholicisme social en France 1822–1870* (Paris, 1951).

Space does not permit inclusion of the extensive biographical literature on figures of the Opposition, though a few titles are here cited to illustrate profitable approaches for new research and study. Intellectual opposition to the Empire is well surveyed in Robert Reichart, "Anti-Bonapartist Elections to the Académie française During the Second Empire," JMH, XXXV, 1 (1963), 33–45. Philip Spencer's "Censorship of Literature under the Second Empire," *Cambridge Journal,* III (1949), 47–55, reflects the hostility of writers, both then and now, to the Empire, the author being an authority on Flaubert and the literature of that period. In André Billy, *Les écrivains de combat* (Paris, 1931), we find brief sketches of nineteenth-century polemicists along with samples of their prose; while Chapter 26 in Jacques Barzun, *Berlioz and the Romantic Century*, II (Boston, 1950), is a stimulating commentary on the spirit of that day entitled "Empire and Industry."

Jacques Vier has published *Daniel Stern. Lettres républicaines du Second Empire* (Paris, 1951), a title that is somewhat misleading. The correspondents are Republican all right, but the letters are of greater literary than political importance. More to the political point is Suzanne de La Porte, "Autour du 19 janvier. Tiers parti et opposition républicaine, fragments inédits de la correspondance d'Allain-Targé," RH, 179 (January–March, 1937), 135–145; and Mme. La Porte's edition of Henri Allain-Targé, *La République sous l'Empire, Lettres, 1864–1870* (Paris, 1939). Allain-Targé was an associate of Gambetta. Another recent work, Richard H. Powers, *Edgar Quinet, A Study in French Patriotism* (Dallas, 1957), is a brief, competent work with a good bibliography, revealing the politics of the Republicans. For a lucid and generous study of the elusive Proudhon, see George Woodcock, *Pierre-Joseph Proudhon* (London, 1956). A less charitable view can be found in Edward H. Carr, *Studies in Revolution* (London, 1950), Chapter 3 entitled "Proudhon: Robinson Crusoe of Socialism." Marcel Du Pasquier, *Edgar Quinet en Suisse, douze annés d'exil, 1858–1870* (Neuchâtel, 1959), supplements the Powers book on Quinet, while Pierre Guiral, *Prévost-Paradol 1829–1870): Pensée et action d'un libéral sous le Second Empire* (Paris, 1955), is an overly lengthy biography for the significance of the subject, but does reveal the tenor of moderate Republican politics.

Before enumerating some of the first-rate monographs to appear recently that illustrate social and economic conditions under the Second Empire, let us note several "classics": Frédéric Le Play was *the* sociologist of the Second Empire, a social reformer who had access to the Emperor, but a reactionary in his disapproval of much that the French Revolution had accomplished. Some of his work applied to Europe as a whole, but two publications concerned France: *La Réforme sociale en France,* 4 vols. (Paris, 1864); and *L'Organisation du Travail selon la coutume des ateliers et la loi du Décalogue* (Paris, 1871). The publishers A. and J. Picard have made available a *Recueil d'études sociales publié à la mémoire de Frédéric Le Play* (Paris, 1956). Most historians know of Emile Zola's documentary novels, published under the general title, *Les Rougon-Macquart, Histoire naturelle et sociale d'une famille sous le Second Empire,* 20 vols. (Paris, 1871–1893), a stupendous undertaking that did much to perpetuate a black reputation for the Second Empire —which was Zola's intention. A contemporary work, virtually unknown in the United States, Denis Poulot, *Question sociale. Le Sublime, ou le Travailleur comme il est en 1870* (Paris, 1872), had a better-balanced view of workers' lives than Zola did.

In citing more recent works on social and economic conditions in the prerevolutionary period, our aim is to note in particular those works that illustrate the revolutionary situation. A book remarkable for both its scope and balance is Georges Duveau, *La Vie ouvrière en France sous le Second Empire* (Paris, 1946). Edouard Dolléans then published a lengthy and useful review article of the Duveau volume, "Vie et pensée ouvrières entre 1848 et 1871," RH, 197–198 (July–September 1947), 62–78; followed ten years later by Fernand L'Huillier, *La Lutte ouvrière à la fin du Second Empire* (Paris, 1957). Rondo E Cameron has written extensively on French economic and financial conditions, and his articles illuminate both the relative economic stagnation of France in the nineteenth century and the redistribution of wealth going on during the Second Empire, both of which profoundly affected workers' lives. See his "The Crédit Mobilier and the Economic Development of Europe," *Journal of Political Economy,* LXI (December 1953), 461–488; his "French Finance and Italian Unity: The Cavourian Decade," AHR, LXII (April 1957), 552–569; and his "Economic Growth and Stagnation in France, 1815–1914," JMH, XXX (March 1958), 1–13. This last article has been much expanded in *France and the Economic Development of Europe 1800–1914,* 2nd ed., (Chicago, 1965). If one adds to these studies an essay on the labor movement during the Second Empire in Edouard Dolléans and Gérard Dehove, *Histoire du travail en France* (Paris, 1953–1955) ; and two articles by David I. Kulstein, "The Attitude of French Workers Towards the Second Empire," FHS, II, 3 (Spring 1962), 356–375, and "Economics Instruction for Workers During the Second Empire," FHS, I, 2 (1959), 225–234, we complete the roster of recent studies based on archival sources which go beyond the work of an earlier generation of scholars. That earlier work, however, remains influential, containing valuable insights about working conditions, the political activity of workers, and the imperial government's attempt to improve the workers' lot. See Hubert Lagardelle, *L'Evolution des syndicats ouvriers de France* (Paris, 1901) ; Albert Thomas, *Le Second Empire,* which is Vol. X of Jean Jaurès, *l'Histoire socialiste* (Paris, 1907) ; and E. Levasseur, *Histoire des classes ouvrières et de l'industrie en France de 1789 à 1870* (Paris, 1904), for older works sympathetic to the labor movement.

Other older works were more directed at the government's point of view and its legislative program to deal with the causes of labor unrest: P. L. Fournier, *Le Second Empire et la législation ouvrière* (Paris, 1911) ; Georges Bourgin, "La législation ouvrière du Second Empire," REN, IV (1913), 220–236, which contains a good bibliography; and Hendrik N. Boon, *Rêve et Réalité dans l'oeuvre économique et sociale de Napoléon III* (The Hague, 1936), which also has extensive bibliography. The extent to which the imperial public works program contributed to both labor and business opposition to the regime may be studied in the work of David H. Pinkney and Louis Girard, already cited.

Valuable contributions to the history of the Liberal Empire can be found in works cited above—Vol. VI of La Gorce, for instance—and in Weill and Freymond. The close relationship of the Liberal Catholics to the Liberal Empire is documented in Maurain's book while the dilemma of the Opposition, when faced with the imperial reforms, can be found in the volume by Guiral, in the works dealing with Allain-Targé, and in Léon Gambetta, *Lettres, 1868–1882,* ed. by Daniel Halévy and Emile Pillias (Paris, 1938). The position of a Catholic politician who was loyal to the Empire on all but the religious issues is well portrayed in Charles Chesnelong, *Les Derniers jours de l'empire et le gouvernement de M. Thiers, mémoires publiés par son petit-fils* (Paris, 1932). Theodore Zeldin has done the most distinguished recent work on the Liberal Empire: *The Political System of Napoleon III* (London, 1958), and *Emile Ollivier and the Liberal Empire of Napoleon III* (Oxford, 1963), books which he has supplemented by editing a two-volume edition of Emile Ollivier, *Journal 1846–1869* (Paris, 1961). This latter work is particularly useful for the Victor Noir affair of 1870, thanks to the Introduction, as is Eugénie de Grèce, *Pierre-Napoléon Bonaparte 1815–1881* (Paris, 1963).

While the coming of the Franco-Prussian War and the war itself are not the proper subjects of this bibliography, the progress of the revolutionary movement was obviously related to the way in which the war developed and how it was fought. The nature of the military establishment can be found in Arpad F. Kovacs, "French Military Institutions Before the Franco-Prussian War," AHR, LI, 1 (October 1945), 217–235, which contains the best discussion of the military reform movement after 1866 now available, though Pierre Lehautcourt (pseud.), "La Réorganisation de l'armée avant 1870," *Revue de Paris*, IV (August 1901), 525–552, remains valuable. For the Republican theory about a proper military establishment, see Richard D. Challener, *The French Theory of the Nation in Arms 1866–1939* (New York, 2nd ed., 1965), which contains a good bibliography.

A number of recent works on the origins of the war, while primarily concerned about foreign policy, shed light on the liberal regime of 1870, its precarious existence, and those parties seeking its demise. Richard Millman, *British Foreign Policy and the Coming of the Franco-Prussian War* (New York, 1966), is useful for its reconsideration of traditional distortions of French policy. Paul Bernstein, "The Economic Aspects of Napoleon III's Rhine Policy," FHS, I, 3 (Spring 1960), 335–347, contains important information but is equivocal in its conclusions. For a better-balanced view of Napoleon's Rhine policy, see Herbert Geuss, *Bismarck und Napoleon III: Ein Beitrag zur Geschichte der Preussisch-Französischen Beziehungen, 1851–1871* (Cologne,

1959) ; along with William E. Echard "Conference Diplomacy in the German Policy of Napoleon III, 1868–1869," FHS, IV (Spring 1966), 239–264, an important article revealing French desire to settle the German problem by negotiation. Note also a good study by Jacques Bardoux, *Les Origines du malheur européen—l'aide anglo-française à la domination prussienne, 1863–1875* (Paris, 1948).

For the last word on the Hohenzollern crisis and the French declaration of war, Georges Bonnin has edited the relevant documents in the German diplomatic archives, *Bismarck and the Hohenzollern Candidature for the Spanish Throne* (London, 1957), which documents Bismarck's role as precisely as is probably possible. For thorough and scholarly treatments, see W. E. Mosse, *The European Powers and the German Question, 1848–1871* (New York, 1958) ; and M. R. D. Foot, "The Origins of the Franco-Prussian War and the Remaking of Germany," *New Cambridge Modern History*, Vol. XI (Cambridge, 1960). The recent summary of previous interpretations by Lawrence D. Steefel, *Bismarck, the Hohenzollern Candidacy, and the Origins of the Franco-Prussian War of 1871* (Cambridge, Mass., 1962), is a masterpiece of objectivity, shying away from significant new interpretations. A poorly written book, but containing valuable information, is Willard A. Fletcher, *The Mission of Vincent Benedetti to Berlin 1864–1870* (The Hague, 1965), which reveals among other things the Ambassador's difficulties when caught between the personal diplomacy of Napoleon III and Bismarck's deviousness. William L. Langer in "Red Rag and Gallic Bull, the French Decision for War, 1870," *Europa und Übersee* (Hamburg, 1961), believes that the question of national honor was more significant than the Ems telegram in provoking the French government and people; and Douglas W. Houston, "Emile Ollivier and the Hohenzollern Candidacy," FHS, IV, 2 (Fall 1965), 125–149, focuses on the failures of the liberal regime during the crisis. One of the major strengths of Michael Howard's *The Franco-Prussian War: the German Invasion of France, 1870–1871* (New York, 1961), is the author's ability to relate military and political necessities, making it a particularly fine transitional study from the Second Empire to the Government of National

Defense. The bibliography in the Michael Howard book is excellent, bringing up-to-date the fine earlier work of Barthélemy-Edmond Palat, *Bibliographie générale de la guerre de 1870–1871* (Paris, 1896). Note that Palat wrote extensively on the war under the pseudonym Pierre Lehautcourt.

2. The Revolutionary Period

An unofficial, but very useful, chronicle of events after September 4, 1870, was kept by Amaury-Prosper Dréo, *Gouvernement de la Défense Nationale. Procès verbaux des séances du Conseil,* (Paris, 1905). Dréo kept this record for the use of his father-in-law, Garnier-Pagès, who was a member of the government. Dréo's notes were somewhat scanty, but remain very important since the executive body kept no official minutes. The parliamentary commission appointed in 1871 to inquire into the Government of National Defense used the Dréo notes and was criticized for doing so by General Trochu, *Pour la vérité et pour la justice* (Paris, 1873); not because Trochu questioned Dréo's facts, but because Dréo had worked unofficially and had produced a résumé rather than a verbatim record. Jules Favre left a more extensive record of the government's activity, *Gouvernement de la Défense Nationale du 30 juin 1870,* 3 vols. (Paris, 1871–1875), but bias is more evident than in the Dréo.

Let us note the more recent studies of the period: for brief but distinguished surveys, see the appropriate chapters in Dennis W. Brogan, *France Under the Republic, the Development of Modern France 1870–1939* (New York and London, 1940); and Jacques Chastenet, *Histoire de la Troisième République, L'Enfance de la troisième 1870–1879* (Paris, 1952). A general survey based on good reading and intended for the general reader is Jacques Desmarest, *La Défense Nationale, 1870–1871* (Paris, 1949). Henri Guillemin has produced three lively and well-documented volumes under the heading *Les Origines de la Commune: Cette curieuse guerre de 1870. Thiers, Trochu, Bazaine* (Paris, 1954); *L'Héroique Défense de Paris 1870–1871* (Paris, 1959); and *La Capitulation 1871* (Paris, 1960). Two other books on the siege are very much worth consulting: Georges Duveau, *Le Siège de Paris, septembre 1870–janvier 1871* (Paris, 1939);

and Melvin Kranzberg, *The Siege of Paris, 1870–1871* (Ithaca, 1950). The same cannot be said for two other recent books on the siege. Both are well written and directed at a large audience, which is legitimate; but neither benefit from much recent research, and significantly distorted interpretations are the result. Moreover, neither book reflects much compassion for those with the agonies and responsibilities for decisions. A greater wisdom is presumably the possession of critics out of power: Robert Baldick, *The Siege of Paris*, (New York, 1964); and Alistair Horne, *The Fall of Paris* (New York, 1965), the latter being the better of the two.

Studies of a more specialized nature include Hazel C. Benjamin, "Official Propaganda and the French Press During the Franco-Prussian War," JMH, IV, 2 (June 1932), 214–230, especially interesting in showing that official propaganda emphasized French superiority and invincibility, thus enhancing the ultimate popular disenchantment. For a good description of September 4 in Paris, see J. P. T. Bury, *Gambetta and the National Defense* (London, 1936), which also details Gambetta's drastic administrative measures and the consequent annoyance of routine officials in the War Ministry. Bury includes a good bibliography of the primary sources for this period. Gambetta's letters cited above, are thin for the period of the National Defense, for he was too busy to write much. Instead see Joseph Reinach, *Dépêches, circulaires, décrets, proclamations et discours de Léon Gambetta 1870–71*, 2 vols. (Paris, 1891). An excellent article that shows that the men of September 4 were not radicals in either politics or economics is E. L. Katzenbach, "Liberals at War: the Economic Policies of the Government of National Defense," AHR, LVI (July 1951), 803–823. For a study of the real radicals of that moment, see J. Dautry and L. Scheler, *Le Comité central républicain des vingt arrondissements de Paris* (Paris, 1960), the most detailed study on this Central Committee now available. In the Marxist tradition, Dautry and Scheler demonstrate that the initiators of the Committee were affiliates of the International, but were quickly superseded by Jacobins and Blanquists. The most recent biography of Trochu, Jean Brunet-Moret, *Le Général Trochu, 1815–1896* (Paris, 1955) is favorable to the General, as is the introduction by General Weygand, who has an understandable sympathy for scapegoat generals. The book was presumably written with the aid of family papers, but there are no footnotes or bibliography.

For the national elections during the armistice, note the article by R. A. Winnacker, "The French Election of 1871," *Papers of the Michigan Academy of Sciences, Arts, and Letters,* XXII (1936), 477–483, which demonstrates that the issue in the election was peace or war. Frank Herbert Brabant, *The Beginnings of the Third Republic in France: A History of the National Assembly (February–September 1871)* (London, 1940), remains the best survey of those turbulent months in the Assembly. The chapters on the Assembly and on the Commune in Adrien Dansette, *Les Origines de la Commune de 1871* (Paris, 1944), have been called "the most balanced view" to be presented by a Frenchman; but the survey is brief. A current Marxist survey, for those who read Russian, may be found in E. A. Jelubovskaya, [*The Decline of the Second Empire and the Founding of the Third Republic in France*] (Moscow, 1956). Thiers's role in 1871 has always been a subject of heated controversy; and in Herbert Tint, *The Decline of French Patriotism* (London, 1964), we are given in the first chapter rather too neat an explanation for Thiers's actions. J. Lucas-Dubreton, *Aspects de Monsieur Thiers* (Paris, 1948), is sympathetic to Thiers's middle-ground position and denies that Thiers allowed the Commune to mature in order to prove himself a Napoleon. This tone reflects the tradition of earlier books including Robert Dreyfus, *Monsieur Thiers contre l'Empire, la guerre, la Commune, 1869–1871* (Paris, 1928); Maurice Reclus, *L'Avènement de la 3ème République 1871–1875* (Paris, 1930); and Henri Malo, *Thiers* (Paris, 1932), said to be the best of the biographies.

Several early books on the Commune deserve mention for their durable significance. Lissagaray's *History of the Commune of 1871* is regarded as the classic by an eyewitness. Originally published in 1876, it was revised by Lissagaray for the 1886 edition, translated by Eleanor Marx Aveling, "seen and corrected" by the translator's father, Karl Marx. Written with deep prejudice, it remains a lively and insightful volume. Two days after the fall of the Commune, Karl Marx presented an address to the International entitled *The Civil War in France*. The 1940 edition produced by International Publishers is especially valuable for its inclusion of two prior addresses by Marx on the Franco-Prussian War. Marx was a marvelous polemicist, and the tone of this address can be revealed in several sentences: "But Paris armed was the revolution armed. A victory of Paris over the Prussian aggressor would have been a victory of the French workmen over the French capitalist and his state parasites. In this conflict between national duty and class interest, the Government of National Defense did not hesitate one moment to turn into a Government of National Defection." An immense work by Maxime Du Camp, *Les Convulsions de Paris*, 4 vols. (Paris, 1878–1880), is full of information but intensely anti-Commune, well illustrates the psychology of the Versaillese. After the turn of the century, Louis Dubreuilh published his *Histoire de la Commune* (Paris, 1908), as Vol. XI of Jaurès' *Histoire socialiste*. The socialist bias was natural, but Dubreuilh was one of the first to use the *procès-verbaux* of the Commune, then still in manuscript at the Musée Carnavalet. E. Lepelletier completed only three volumes of a projected eight in his *Histoire de la Commune de 1871* (Paris, 1911–1913), a well-documented work that is particularly useful for the Central Committee of the National Guard and for March 18; but he did not get past the first days of April 1871. The chapter on the Commune in Georges Weill, *Mouvement social en France, 1852–1910* (Paris, 1911) is still valuable.

Anyone working on the Commune owes an immense debt to Georges Bourgin, whose published works stimulated research for a half-century and who ultimately became the president of the l'Institut français d'Histoire sociale. His first short book was *Histoire de la Commune* (Paris, 1907). Then, with G. Henriot, he began editing the *Procès-verbaux de la Commune de Paris*; the first volume appeared in 1924, the second volume not until 1945. The first volume covers March and April of 1871, the second volume May. The accounts are not verbatim, but give the essence of the debates. And, of course, the work gives no hint of what was done or said in secret. (The *Journal officiel de la Commune* is less complete and less valuable than these two volumes.) Vol. II contains a useful summary of Commune members, brief vital statistics, a bibliographical reference for each member, and a statement about what happened to each member after the Commune. (We might note in passing that the *Procès-verbaux* of the Central Committe of the National Guard can be found in the *Enquête parlementaire sur l'Insurrection du 18 mars* (Versailles, 1872, III, 1–161). Bourgin then published several articles, "La Commune de Paris et le Comité Central (1871), RH, 149–150, 2 (September–December 1925), 1–66, the Central Committee in question being that of the National Guard, though the article is also valuable for its recapitulation of elections, committees, persons, and parties. The second article, "Aperçu sur l'histoire de la Commune de 1871," RH, 163–164, 2 (May–August 1930), 88–96, is a distinguished review of the interpretive problems that are the legacy of the Commune. Finally, *La Commune* (Paris, 1953) is the summary of a long career of research.

E. S. Mason, *The Paris Commune* (New York, 1930), is important for its use of Russian studies published in Moscow and for its anti-Marxist view. Frank Jellinek, on the other hand, provides the radical view of the '30s, *The Paris Commune of 1871* (Oxford, 1937), a very well-written book with excellent bibliography. A book concerned only for the ideologies during the Commune is Charles Rihs, *La Commune de Paris, sa structure et ses doctrines (1871)* (Geneva, 1955), an important, well-documented book with an extensive bibliography of works by the participants in the Commune. The most elaborate of recent studies has been edited by Jean Bruhat, Jean Dautry, and Emile Tersen, *La Commune de 1871* (Paris, 1960); avowedly pro-Communard and in the tradition of Lissagaray, this Marxist work was dedicated to showing how the people fought for progress and national independence against the "neo-Coblenzards." After an extensive bibliography, there follow useful appendices on newspapers, clubs, iconography, and biographical notes on the members of the Commune. The volume is wonderfully illustrated. A second book notable for illustrations is André Guérin, *1871 la Commune* (Paris, 1966). A recent article by Eugene W. Schulkind, "The Activity of Popular Organizations during the Paris Commune of

1871," FHS, I, 4 (Fall 1960), 394–415, is important for its discussion of the impact of popular clubs in Paris upon the communal movement and upon decisions of the Commune after its establishment. In the Marxian tradition, Schulkind sees the club movement as mainly proletarian, not specifically doctrinaire, and working for the improvement of social conditions.

Arthur Adamov has published a short anthology on the Commune, *La Commune de Paris* (Paris, 1959), selected statements about the Commune by Communards, by Versaillese, and by both the conciliators and the opportunists in the affair. Since many journalists were active in the Commune, A. Dupuy, *1870–1871, la guerre, la commune et la presse* (Paris, 1959), provides a brief history of the press and a particularly useful table of those journals published between January 1870 and July 1871, along with references as to where those journals may now be found. Raymond Postgate, *Revolution from 1789 to 1906* (New York, 1962), reprints a few documents from the Commune, as well as Marx's address to the International.

As for the men of the Commune, one may supplement the brief biographical sketches in the above-mentioned work by Bruhat, Dautry, and Tersen with the older Jules Clère, *Les Hommes de la Commune* (Paris, 1871), in which the anti-Commune bias is sometimes evident, but which is not extreme in tone. A good brief and illustrated survey is M. Winock and J.–P. Azéma, *Les Communards* (Paris, 1964), which has useful tables on the members of the Commune—as to their ages, political affiliations, and occupations. The book is pro-Communard, very anti-Thiers, and tends to boil down all the issues into a contest between patriots and those too crassly concerned for their property and for order. The long-time student of Babeuf, Blanqui, and the Commune, Maurice Dommanget, has published several relevant titles: *Blanqui* (Paris, 1924); *Les Idées politiques et sociales d'Auguste Blanqui* (Paris, 1957), a detailed, well-documented, important study; and finally his *Blanqui et l'opposition révolutionnaire à la fin du Second Empire* (Paris, 1960). Another reliable work is Alan B. Spitzer, *The Revolutionary Theories of Louis Auguste Blanqui* (New York, 1957). Perhaps the best way to get at what Jacobinism was in the Commune is to see the well-documented book of Marcel Dessal, *Charles Delescluze, un révolutionnaire jacobin 1809–1871* (Paris, 1952), the best biography of the man.

3. The Reactionary Period

Noting first the political reaction between 1871 and 1875, the general background may be found in the already cited works of Brogan, Chastenet, and Reclus. One of the more distinguished interpretations of the period 1870–1877 is Daniel Halévy, *La Fin des notables,* 2 vols. (Paris, 1930–1937), which expresses a nostalgia for the first decade of the Third Republic, seeing it as the foundation of the stability and the unity which would make so much difference in 1914. A bibliographical article, R. A. Winnacker, "The Third French Republic, 1870–1914," JMH, X, 3 (September 1938), 372–409, is very valuable for materials published before 1938. The work of F. H. Brabant, cited above, may be consulted for the origins of the Third Republic, and the first five chapters of David Thomson, *Democracy in France,* reissued in New York, 1964, are first-rate for the period. Guy Chapman has recently published the first volume of his *The Third Republic of France, The First Phase 1871–1894* (London, 1962), which is very stimulating and has a useful bibliography. The Marquis de Roux, a member of the Action française, produced his *Origines et fondation de la Troisième République* (Paris, 1933), which is based upon wide reading and reflects the opposition to the Republic.

The legal repressions and their effects after the Commune can be found first of all in Maurice Garçon, *Histoire de la justice sous la Troisième République,* 3 vols. (Paris, 1957), despite its lack of bibliography a useful reference work because of a good index. The amnesty issue is presented in precise detail in a fine study by Jean T. Joughin, *The Paris Commune in French Politics, 1871–1880,* 2 vols. (Baltimore, 1955); while the momentary paralysis of the labor movement is well outlined in Maxwell R. Kelso, "The Inception of the Modern French Labor Movement (1871–79); a Reappraisal," JMH, VIII, 2 (June 1936), 173–193. The interdictions suffered by the press can be found in both Irene Collins, *The Government and the Newspaper Press in*

France, 1814–1881 (London, 1959) and Raymond Manevy, *La Presse de la IIIè République* (Paris, 1955). For the case of Bazaine, see Philip Guedalla, *The Two Marshals: Bazaine, Pétain* (New York, 1943); and a somewhat more charitable view in D. W. Brogan, *French Personalities and Problems* (New York, 1947)—both volumes written with great verve.

For a survey of the political parties, note François Goguel, *La Politique des partis sous la IIIè République* (Paris, 1958); which may be supplemented with Jacques Gouault, *Comment la France est devenue républicaine, les élections générales et partielles à l'Assemblée nationale 1870–1875* (Paris, 1954). The first chapter of the Gouault, having to do with the plebiscite of 1870 and the problems of the Government of National Defense, is poorly informed but not the main topic of the book. In fact, the importance of the book is not so much its text as its electoral maps and annexes. Much statistical information can easily be found here, drawn from departmental archives, illustating in the main points long accepted by historians. The most recent study of the monarchical cause is the well-documented and judicious book by Samuel Osgood, *French Royalism under the Third and Fourth Republics* (The Hague, 1960). A more specialized study of royalism is that by Marvin L. Brown, Jr., *The Comte de Chambord, the Third Republic's Uncompromising King* (Durham, 1967). Chapter V in René Rémond, *La Droite en France de 1815 à nos jours* (Paris, 1954), covers the "moral order" between 1871 and 1879. A revised edition has been translated by James M. Laux as *The Right Wing in France from 1815 to De Gaulle* (Philadelphia, 1966). A work which reflects Legitimist idealism after 1871 is E. Beau de Lomenie, *Les Responsabilités des dynasties bourgeoises*, the first volume of which, *De Bonaparte à MacMahon* (Paris, 1943), is appropriate here.

Louis Girard has contributed an interesting article, "Political Liberalism in France, 1840–1875," to an anthology edited by E. M. Acomb and M. L. Brown, *French Society and Culture since the Old Regime* (New York, 1966). The article traces the drift of the Orleanists from royalism to conservative Republicanism as a matter of political logic. Several articles by Jean Bouvier, an historian with Marxist sympathies who has written a good deal about bourgeois finance, contribute to an understanding of conservative Republicanism: "Aux origines de la Troisième République. Les réflexes sociaux des milieu d'affaires," RH, 209–210, 4 (October–December 1953), 271–301, emphasizes the role of the urban and rural masses in forcing the republican form upon the bourgeois whom he believes were merely conservative; while in "Des Banquiers devant l'actualité politique en 1870–71," RHMC, V (April–June 1958), 137–151, Bouvier somewhat modifies his position by showing the world of finance to have been antiroyalist, fearful that a restoration would produce social disorder. A valuable survey of Thiers's fiscal career is provided in two installments by Robert Schnerb, "La Politique fiscale de Thiers," RH, 201–202 (1949), 186–212, 184–220. His footnotes amount to a good bibliography.

For the relation of Thiers's financial and foreign policies, see a well-documented paper by E. J. Pratt, "La Diplomatie française de 1871 à 1875," RH, 167–168, 2 (May–August 1931), 60–84; as well as Elie Halévy, "Franco-German Relations Since 1870," *History*, IX, 33 (April 1924), 18–29. Despite more recent publications, the discussion of postwar military reforms is fullest in J. Monteilhet, *Les Institutions militaires de la France (1814–1932)* (Paris, 1932). Henri Contamine's *La Revanche, 1871–1914* (Paris, 1957), is thin for the decade of the '70s.

A recent and as yet unpublished dissertation presented at Cornell in 1963, Sanford H. Elwitt, *The Radicals Enter French Politics 1870–1875*, is based on extensive archival research. It confirms the view that the radical opponents of Napoleon III really became his successors in developing the "underpinnings" of a democratic society. In the volume edited by Edward Mead Earle, *Modern France: Problems of the Third and Fourth Republics* (Princeton, 1951), note in particular the three articles by John B. Wolf, John Bowditch, and John B. Christopher on the decline of the French *élan vital*. In the same volume, David S. Landes, "French Business and the Businessman: a Social and Cultural Analysis," though primarily focused on France in the twentieth century, is useful for the previous century in suggesting the cultural bases for relative economic stagnation.

A book on the continuing revolutionary tradition, originally published in 1944 but reprinted in 1963, is Paul Farmer, *France Reviews its Revolutionary Origins: Social Politics and Historical Opinion in the Third Republic*. With a good bibliography, it is one approach to the intellectual reaction to 1870–1871. John Roberts, "The Myth of the Commune, 1871," *History Today*, VI, 5 (May 1957), 290–300, presents a brief, intelligent survey based on an excellent understanding of the Commune within the larger framework of French history. While Albert Thibaudet, *La République des professeurs* (Paris, 1927), meant to be an essay on the politics of the 1920s in the conservative intellectual and literary tradition, reflects the decline of Parisian influence after 1871, as does the previously cited work of J. Néré. John A. Scott, *Republican Ideas and the Liberal Tradition in France 1870–1914* (New York, 1951), is a learned, but tedious essay in intellectual history, most notable for its study of Charles Renouvier and of Emile Littré. The early pages of George Lichtheim, *Marxism in Modern France* (New York, 1966), well show the impact of the Commune on French socialism after 1870 and includes a good bibliography on socialism.

The most recent study of the intellectual consequences of the defeat of 1870 contains an extensive bibliography by chapter: Claude Digeon, *La Crise allemande de la pensée française, 1870–1914* (Paris, 1959). He takes into account both the reaction of different generations and the changing image of Germany in France between 1869 and 1914—from the temple of intelligence to the aggressive industrial and military empire. André Bellessort, *Les Intellectuels et l'avènement de la IIIe République, 1871–1875* (Paris, 1931), amounted to a latter-day indictment of the Republic; and Michel Mohrt, *Les Intellectuels devant la défaite, 1870* (Paris, 1942), surveys a variety of reactions to defeat, quite evidently written with the defeat of 1940 in mind. French racism is best surveyed in the new edition of Jacques Barzun, *Race: A Study in Superstition* (New York, 1965); and an illuminating, if very brief, sketch on Gobineau by John Lukacs is in the Anchor edition of Tocqueville, *The European Revolution and Correspondence with Gobineau* (New York, 1959). A very extensive study of Renan, particularly of the aging Renan and his influence, written from a moderate Catholic point of view, is

Louis Vié, *Renan, La Guerre de 70 et la 'Réforme' de la France* (Paris, 1949). Renan's controversial essay, "La Réforme intellectuelle et morale," may be found in his *Oeuvres complètes,* Vol. I (Paris, 1947).

Index

from Paris Commune, 131; members elected to office: in 1852, 15; in 1857, 15; in 1869, 55–56; in 1872, 167–68; in 1876, 176; moderates seize power in, 83–84; moderates organize Government of National Defense, 83–84; and National Assembly elections, 116–17; National Assembly tries to halt rising strength of, 174–75; opposition to reconstruction of Paris, 16–18; opposition to Second Empire, 45, 66–67, 69, 78; radicals preach revolt, 59–60; representation of in Thiers' cabinet, 118; supported by rural voters (1871), 156; support of Liberal Empire by, 61; threat of after conservative takeover, 79; urges dissolution of National Assembly, 169–70; urges Parisians be armed, 78; and Victor Noir assasination, 67–68; *see also* Central Committee of the National Guard; Central Committee of the Twenty Arrondissements; Government of National Defense

Republic of 1848, 4, 5, 46, 69, 194
République française, la, 192
Réveil, le, 26, 59
Revolution of 1789, 1, 3, 9, 10, 11, 13, 14, 32, 41, 58, 140, 160, 176, 177, 180, 182, 183, 185, 186, 188, 192, 195
Revue de Paris, 5
Revue des deux mondes, 6, 63
Richard, Maurice, 62
Rigault, Raoul, 126, 138, 140, 142, 143, 148, 150, 151
Rivet, Baron, 159, 160
Rivet Law, 161, 170
Robespierre, M. F. M. I., de, 13, 134, 135
Rochefort, Henri, *ix*, 25, 26, 27, 60, 83, 96, 101, 119, 122, 142; incites radicals to revolt over Noir murder, 67–68
Rossel, Louis Nathaniel, 143, 144
Rothschild, Baron James, 92
Rougon-Macquart, Les, 38
Rouher, Eugène, 4, 36, 54, 57, 59, 66
Rouland, Gustave, 48
Russia, 73, 96, 103

Sadowa, battle of, 41, 77
Sainte-Beuve, Charles-Augustin, 5
Saint-Cloud, Porte de, 148, 149
Saint-Simon, Claude Henri, Comte de, 15, 17, 28, 29, 30, 39, 45, 70, 135
Sand, George, 11, 64
Savoy, 99
Say, Léon, 141, 159
Schneider, Eugène, 43
Second Empire, 10, 12, 13, 25, 34, 47, 86, 88, 93, 90, 91, 92, 98, 102, 116, 118, 127, 140, 160, 163, 169, 171, 172, 173, 181, 185, 188, 191, 192, 194, 196, 198; as a police state, 46–47; attempt to form provisional government after Sedan defeat, 81–82; attitude of labor movement toward, 31–32; censorship of the press by, 3, 4–5; comparison to First Empire, 45; conservative financial interests in, 29, 30; constitution of, 18; criticized by intelligentsia, 6–7; dissolves the International in France, 23, 24; distribution of wealth in, 30, 41; economic development under, 27, 28–31, 38; educational legislation of, 52, 63; and elections of 1869, 55–57; exiles from 10–12; factionalism within administration, 54–55; and the Gallican Church, 14, 57–58; liberal reforms of, 25–26, 36, 51, 58–59; military system of, 41–42; muzzling of Parliament by, 3; opposition to, 2–4, 7–8, 9, 14; reaction to Prussian threat, 41–42; and reconstruction of Paris, 16–18, 40–41; revival of interest in, 44–45; support of in elections of 1870, 43; suppression of the legislative under, 47–49; traditional notions about, 44–46; *see also* Government of National Defense; Liberal Empire; Napoleon III
Second Republic, 25, 26
Sedan, French surrender at, 2, 80, 85, 87, 191
Segris, Emile-Alexis, 62
Senatus Consultum (1870), 69–70
Siècle, le, 15, 66
Sieyès, Abbé, 183